THE NEUROBIOLOGY OF CRIMIN

The Neurobiology of Criminal Behavior
Gene-Brain-Culture Interaction

ANTHONY WALSH and JONATHAN D. BOLEN
Boise State University, USA

Routledge
Taylor & Francis Group

LONDON AND NEW YORK

First published 2012 by Ashgate Publishing

Published 2016 by Routledge
2 Park Square, Milton Park, Abingdon, Oxon OX14 4RN
711 Third Avenue, New York, NY 10017, USA

First issued in paperback 2017

Routledge is an imprint of the Taylor & Francis Group, an informa business

British Library Cataloguing in Publication Data
Walsh, Anthony, 1941–
   The neurobiology of criminal behavior: gene-brain-culture interaction
   1. Criminal behavior. 2. Criminal behavior–Genetic aspects. 3. Criminal behavior–Physiological aspects. 4. Criminal behavior–Social aspects. 5. Neurobiology.
   I. Title II. Bolen, Jonathon B.
   364.2'4-dc23

Library of Congress Cataloging-in-Publication Data
Walsh, Anthony, 1941–
   The neurobiology of criminal behavior : gene-brain-culture interaction /
   by Anthony Walsh and Jonathon D. Bolen.
      p. cm.
   Includes bibliographical references and index.
   ISBN 978-1-4094-3841-0 (hardback : alk. paper)
   1. Criminal psychology. 2. Criminal behavior.
   3. Neurobiology. I. Bolen, Jonathon D. II. Title.
   HV6080.W235 2012
   364.3–dc23

                                                                            2011036965

ISBN 13: 978-1-138-11719-8 (pbk)
ISBN 13: 978-1-4094-3841-0 (hbk)

Contents

List of Figures and Tables

Figures

Tables

Foreword

The past decade has witnessed a subtle revolution in the study of crime. Criminology has moved, albeit slowly, from a widespread denial that biology plays any role in antisocial and criminal behavior to recognizing that, at a minimum, human beings are biological and social animals. Today, new research findings linking biology to behavior appear daily, challenging the outdated notion that human beings are merely passive recipients of socialization and culture, and sweeping away the powerful ideologies that led criminologists to a state of denial in the first place. Yet this new awareness remains precarious as old ideas and ideologies threaten to erase recent empirical and theoretical gains. Fortunately, Walsh and Bolen's book holds not only the promise to advance future criminological inquiry, but also stands as a testament to the power of science to vanquish conjecture, ideology, and dogmatism.

Much has been made about the capacity of the human brain to simultaneously perform a variety of complex actions. The thousands of miles of neural networks and their infinite complexity receive input from our senses, store this information, and recall the information when appropriate—all while coordinating all life-sustaining activities. But the brain is not merely an information processing machine. It is, after all, the brain that allows us to make decisions, to control our emotional instincts, to plan for our future, to contemplate the meaning of poetry and prose, and to feel joy at the sight of a newborn child. In short, it is the brain that makes us human, and it is the brain that has allowed, and maybe even encouraged, our humanity. The great neuroscientist Elkhonon Goldberg, for example, argues that human civilizations were able to form and to prosper because of the remarkable capacities found in the modern brain.

The brain has been subject to millions of years of evolution and selection. During most of our evolutionary history violence and warfare appear to have been common, as were sex roles that are still visible in hunter/gatherer societies today. Evolutionary processes favor adaptations that increase survival and reproductive chances over time. Under strong evolutionary pressures, the brains of men and women evolved in slightly different fashion. It is no accident, for example, that in every culture at every point in history men, and not women, have been the sex to engage in warfare, violence, and crime. And it is no accident that in every culture women have been primarily responsible for the care of offspring. Still, contemporary explanations for this indelible pattern range from the absurd to the patently false. Thankfully, Walsh and Bolen tackle this subject pointing out what has been lost in political discussions of the rights of women and men—that is, that men and women are fundamentally different.

An understanding of human evolution makes clear why individuals and the sexes vary, but it also makes clear that our evolution occurred in a system of mutual dependence. Men and women, for example, may be different but their differences are more often complementary than not. It is here, at the intersection between culture and biology that Walsh and Bolen strike out into new and controversial ground. With bravery not characteristic of many scholars, Walsh and Bolen tackle what we know about human intelligence, about human psychopathology, and about human addiction problems showing that the human brain is intimately linked to its immediate surroundings, and that these surroundings sometimes have the ability to influence brain functioning and chemistry—for better and for worse. Walsh and Bolen show us that understanding biology allows us to also understand exactly how and when the environment matters in the etiology of crime and other behavioral problems.

As respected scholars Walsh and Bolen should be listened to and their ideas given serious attention. Few criminologists could write such a book, and even fewer would. By bringing to light the role of the brain, the central nervous system, genes, and hormones in the etiology of crime Walsh and Bolen force us to think more seriously, more broadly, about the complex interplay between evolution, biology, and culture. This is no small task and should be recognized for what it is: an amazing scholarly contribution to the understanding of one of society's most pressing issues.

John Paul Wright, Ph.D.

Preface

This book is an attempt to convince fellow criminologists that they will reap a bounty of intellectual rewards by coming to grips with the neurobiology of criminal behavior. It is not a work of neurobiological reductionism, but one that examines what neuroscience has to offer from a biosocial perspective. The biosocial perspective maintains that all the behaviors, traits, and syndromes displayed by human beings are always the result of intricate gene–environment interplay captured in the circuitry of the brain. The neurosciences have made remarkable strides in the last quarter-century, particularly with regard to understanding the mechanisms of many of the concerns of criminologists such as drug addiction, attention deficit hyperactivity disorder (ADHD), low self-control, the gender-ratio in criminal offending, schizophrenia, psychopathy, and a number of others. We must understand these mechanisms, at least at a rudimentary level, if we are not to forfeit the study of criminal behavior to other disciplines. The challenge is formidable, but also exciting and potentially reinvigorating for those who open the latest edition of a criminological journal and sigh, "Not another test of self-control theory!" Such people will be enthralled to discover how the prefrontal cortex and the neurotransmitter serotonin are absolutely crucial to self-control, and will wonder why criminologists, with some notable exceptions, do not incorporate this knowledge into their theories.

To do this, of course, it is necessary to learn some genetics and neuroscience, not to mention a little evolutionary biology. Criminologists do not have to become experts in the deep mysteries of these disciplines, but they have to learn their rudiments to the extent that they can appreciate and apply the relevant concepts to criminological issues. We have all done this in learning the rudiments of statistics to conduct quantitative research without knowing the subject anywhere near the level of a mathematical statistician. Learning difficult new material is intellectually challenging and exciting, but the reluctance of some is understandable. However, as Thomas Kuhn (he of the paradigm shifts) intimates, those who fail to do so will find themselves irrelevant: "retooling is an extravagance reserved for the occasion that demands it," and the wise scientist knows when "the occasion for retooling has arrived" (1970:76).

Although paradigm switching is usually reserved for the young bucks in a discipline, eminent criminologists with long and distinguished careers such as Francis Cullen have also taken the plunge. Cullen is a true scientist who follows the data to where it leads, and is "persuaded that sociological criminology has exhausted itself as a guide for the future study on the origins of crime. It is a paradigm for the previous century, not the current one" (2009:xvi).

Cullen believes that the guiding paradigm for twenty-first-century criminology will be biosocial—"a broader and more powerful paradigm"—but he adds that biosocial criminologists must educate their sociological colleagues by "introducing biosocial science in ways that are accessible and understandable" (2009:xvii). From my very first publication in 1979 on the psychosocial precursors of hypertension (Walsh, 1979), I have been aware of the difficulty of conveying biological information to those having little background in the discipline, but believe that I have done a fair job both in my published work and in the classroom. It is in the spirit of Cullen's recommendation that this text is written. The information found within these pages seeks to assist our fellow criminologists in adapting to the changing tides of scientific advancement and to amalgamate the sociological tradition with the latest knowledge the neurosciences have to offer.

Chapter 1 introduces some basic information on brain structure and functioning, and alerts the reader to the fact that we are examining the neurobiology of criminal behavior from a biosocial perspective guided by Nikolas Tinbergen's famous Four Questions. We describe brain locations that are crucially important to understanding behavior, and emphasize brain plasticity (the process by which the brain "softwires" itself according to environmental experiences). We then introduce the concept of gene–culture co-evolution and the ways this process has affected brain evolution. We also briefly introduce the technology used in the neurosciences, such as positron emission tomography (PET), functional magnetic resonance imaging (fMRI), and diffusion tensor imaging (DTI), used to assess the structure, function, and integrity of the brain.

How the brain areas communicate with each other and with the outside world via its neurotransmitters and their receptor and transporter molecules is the focus of Chapter 2. We pay special attention to the neurotransmitters serotonin and dopamine because they are the chemicals underlying approach and avoidance behavior. Many of the problems associated with criminal behavior involve an imbalance between the behavioral activating and behavioral inhibiting functions of these two neurotransmitters. Our look at how culture matters in this chapter examines how different gene variants having to do with serotonin and dopamine lead to opposite outcomes in different cultural environments.

Chapter 3 takes a look at the effects of abuse and neglect on the developing brain. Abuse and neglect can start in the womb if the mother ingests teratogenic substances such as alcohol that affect the migration and hookup of newly minted neurons. Also discussed is the importance to brain development of the formation of affectionate bonds and breastfeeding. These are important experience-expected features of the evolutionary history of our species. We then discuss the effects of toxic stress on the brain and how those effects can increase the likelihood of criminal behavior. The epigenetics of nurturing is briefly touched on.

The major disorders of childhood associated with antisocial behavior—ADHD, conduct disorder, and oppositional defiant disorder—are addressed in Chapter 4. We examine the genetics and neurobiology of these disorders in the context of reinforcement sensitivity theory, first addressed in Chapter 2. We then look at the cross-cultural data to see how certain gene types may have been useful in some environments.

The topic of Chapter 5 is an attempt to explain the ubiquitous age–crime curve, which many traditional criminologists have opined cannot be done within the sociological criminology framework. We examine the neurohormonal events of puberty—the hormonal surge and the reshaping of the adolescent brain—and claim that these tumultuous events are adequate to explain the immaturity of much of adolescent behavior. We examine the cultural contributions to the age–crime curve in the context of Moffitt's dual pathway theory.

The scourge of alcoholism and drug addiction is the topic of Chapter 6. We examine the changes in neurotransmission and reception initiated by ingesting alcohol and cocaine, with special emphasis on how continued usage leads to the craving of addition via drug-induced permanent changes in the brain. We explore this in terms of epigenetics, the various processes by which environmental experiences affect DNA (deoxyribonucleic acid) transcription. Finally, cultural aspects of drinking and drug abuse are examined.

Chapter 7 discusses the relationship between intelligence (as measured by IQ tests) and criminal behavior. We examine the genetics of intelligence in terms of its large heritability and in terms of the inability of molecular genetics to zone in on specific genes accounting for variance in IQ. We also examine what the neurosciences have learned about the association of brain structure and functions with IQ. We then assess the environmental effects on intelligence guided primarily by the Flynn effect. Finally, we assess the roles of intelligence and conscientiousness in achieving occupational success.

Mental disorder (with a concentration on schizophrenia) is the topic of Chapter 8. We examine the genetics and neurobiology behind the symptoms of schizophrenia, concentrating on the "one-two hit" neurodevelopmental model. This model avers that schizophrenia is the result of a genetic vulnerability coupled with two neurodevelopmental "hits," occurring first prenatally and then at adolescence. We then look at schizotypy. People with this disorder have certain neurological and behavioral features that resemble schizophrenia, but without exhibiting the social deficits that prevent full-blown schizophrenics from functioning effectively in society.

Violence is the topic of Chapter 9, where we first ask if it is learned or unlearned. Violence has declined precipitously in modern postindustrial societies as they have evolved various social control mechanisms to blunt violent competition. We examine reactive violence in the context of the neurohormonal triple imbalance hypothesis, as well as taking a look at variants of the testosterone receptor gene and serotonin levels. We ask the evolutionary question "What is violence for?", and show that although humans tend to abhor and avoid violence, it easily emerges in evolutionarily relevant circumstances, such as the breakdown of social control mechanisms.

Chapter 10 is concerned with the "gender ratio problem"—the issue of why, always and everywhere, males commit far more crime than females. This is another question that many prominent criminologists maintain cannot be answered using only the conceptual tools of sociological criminology. Sex differences in all kinds of behavior begin with the sexing of the brain in utero, and without understanding that, we will never understand male–female differences in behavior. Females have higher levels of fear and empathy than males, and these two attributes are the natural enemies of crime. We look at Darwinian sexual selection processes to understand why natural selection would have selected for these differences.

The final chapter examines the psychopath, the quintessential criminal. We look at how psychopathy is measured, and the differences between it and sociopathy and antisocial personality disorder. We look at the possibility that psychopaths constitute a discrete taxon of our species, and the evolutionary argument that they do. We then explore the psychopath's lack of the social emotions and neuroimaging data, which reveal the disconnectedness of the rational and emotional areas of their brains. The sociopath is considered an individual who follows the same strategy as the psychopath, but it is not as clearly tied to the genotype. We look at the cultural factors said to produce sociopathy.

Anthony Walsh
Jonathan D. Bolen
January 2012

Acknowledgments

I would first of all like to thank commissioning editor Alison Kirk for her faith in this project from the beginning. Thanks also for the commitment of her very able assistant Sarah Horsley. This tireless duo kept up a most useful three-way dialog between author, publisher, and excellent reviewers. The proofreader, Huw Jones, spotted every errant comma, dangling participle, and missing reference and misspelled word in the manuscript, for which we are truly thankful, and our in-house editor Barbara Pretty made sure everything went quickly and smoothly thereafter. Anthony Walsh would also like to thank his first contact at Ashgate, the delightfully named Dymphna Evans. Thank you one and all.

We would also like to acknowledge the kind words and suggestions of the neurobiologists and criminologists who reviewed this project. We have endeavored to respond to those suggestions and believe we have adequately done so. Any errors or misinformation that may lie lurking somewhere in these pages, however, are entirely our responsibility. Thanks also to John Paul Wright who reviewed part of the work and who has written our foreword. Dr. Wright is a leading biosocial criminologist who has done much work in the area of the effects of lead on the brain.

Last but not least, Anthony Walsh would like to acknowledge the love and support of his most wonderful and drop-dead gorgeous wife, Grace Jean; aka "Grace the face." Grace's love and support has sustained me for so long that I cannot imagine life without her; she is to me nature's second sun, bringing forth a well of virtues wherever she shines. Jonathan Bolan wishes to acknowledge his wife, Angela, and his baby girl, Zoë. Angela, you are the anchor of my ship, the calm in my storm.

Chapter 1

The Basic Brain

The human brain—a walnut-shaped, grapefruit-sized, three-pound mass of gelatinous tissue—is the most immensely complicated, awe-inspiring and fascinating entity in the universe: "In the human head there are forces within forces within forces, as in no other cubic half-foot of the universe we know," wrote Nobel Laureate neuroscientist Roger Sperry (in Fincher, 1982:23). The brain is the magnum opus of the millions of years of human evolution, and is the place where genetic dispositions and environmental experiences are integrated and become one as the brain physically captures them in its circuitry. Within this blob of jelly, which consumes 20% of the body's energy while representing only 2% of body mass, lie our thoughts, memories, desires, emotions, intelligence, and creativity. Although we are a long way from fully understanding this "enchanted loom," we cannot ignore what is known, in particular aspects of it relevant to criminology. Robinson (2004:72) goes as far as to say that any theory of behavior "is logically incomplete if it does not discuss the role of the brain."

To travel the neurobiological road, criminologists need not be concerned with the minutia of brain anatomy and physiology any more than with the minutiae of mathematical derivations in statistics to conduct quantitative research. However, they should learn the basic language of neurobiology so that they understand the research it produces relevant to criminology, just as they learn the basic language of statistics to conduct research. We are not advancing a neurobiological-reductionist model of criminal behavior ("My neurons made me do it"), however. Neurobiological risk factors almost never represent a one-to-one causal relationship with behavior. Like any other risk factors, they are one aspect of a permutation and interaction of other risk and protective factors ranging from the molecular to the cultural. We intend to show that the brain is a marvelously plastic organ of adaptation that calibrates itself to environmental experiences. While this is a positive thing in general, it is also a negative thing for brains exposed to violent, abusive, and neglectful experiences and to noxious substances, as the brains of many seriously involved criminal offenders are. We intend to suggest how these negative exposures, in concert with congenital features of brain morphology and structure, diminish the control that affected individuals have over their behavior.

Holistic accounts of behavior cannot proceed with any kind of confidence without a solid foundation of fundamental knowledge, and that requires a large dose of reductionist science. Although holistic accounts are often more satisfying than reductionist ones because they supply *meaning* to our understanding of behavior, that meaning must rest on a solid foundation lest it collapse under the weight of error. Phenomena may find their *significance* in holistic regions, but they are *explained* by lower-level mechanisms. Science has made its greatest strides when it has picked apart wholes to examine the parts, and in doing so has gained a better understanding of the wholes they constitute. But we must never confuse the parts, however well understood, for the whole, and we must never overlook the parts in our haste to arrive at the whole. As Matt Ridley has opined: "Reductionism takes nothing from the whole; it adds new layers of wonder to the experience" (2003:163).[1]

Our approach conforms to Nobel Laureate Nikolas Tinbergen's (1963) famous Four Questions. Tinbergen maintained that it is necessary to inquire about the following four questions in order to understand the behavior of any animal, including *Homo sapiens*:

1. **Function**: What is the adaptive function of this behavior—how does this behavior contribute to reproductive success?
2. **Phylogeny**: What is the evolutionary history of the behavior—how did it come to have its current form?
3. **Development**: How do genes and environments interact in individuals to develop variation in this behavior?
4. **Causation**: What are the causal mechanisms that trigger this behavior?

For example, consider a situation in which altruism is elicited. The *Causation* question asks what the immediate mechanisms underlying altruism are. Altruism is motivated by an empathetic understanding of why someone needs help, and empathy is underlain by brain chemistry. Performing the altruistic act facilitates the release of chemicals that target the reward areas of the brain, thus the helper is reinforced internally as well as externally by the enhancement of his or her reputation in the eyes of others as kind and dependable.

The *Development* question asks why altruism varies from one person to another. There are strong genetic influences on altruism and empathy, but all traits and behaviors are either nourished or starved by one's developmental experiences across the life course.

The *Phylogeny* question asks how these traits/behaviors came to be in the course of evolution. Parental care and mother–child bonding surely serves as the template for later social bonding and for helping behavior that assists in forging those bonds.

The *Function* question asks what the adaptive features of helping behavior are—what are the fitness consequences of helping? Helping others ultimately helps oneself because it leads to reciprocal helping. Mutual help and support helps

---

1 We also repudiate reductionism when the term is meant to describe discipline reductionism in the social/behavioral sciences. Discipline reductionism occurs when complex phenomena are reduced to explanations from a single discipline or by a favored "cause" within that discipline. Examples include the Marxist penchant for reducing all social problems to capitalism, or feminists reducing all gender differences to socialization.

all those involved in a social group to avoid predators, to cooperate in hunting and gathering, and many other features of social life. Because these factors have obvious fitness consequences, there will be strong selection pressures involved.

No one carries out a research agenda animated by all of Tinbergen's questions, but it is understood that all levels have to be mutually consistent. That is, no biologist would hypothesize a relationship between a hormone and a neurotransmitter that contradicts the known chemistry of those substances, just as no chemist would advance a hypothesis that contradicts the elegant laws of physics. Likewise, no hypothesis about behavior at a higher level of analysis should contradict what is understood at a more fundamental level—the level that enjoys the greater "hardness" (consensus, certainty) of its theories, methods, and data.

Basic Neuroanatomy and Physiology

The nervous system is divided into the central nervous system (CNS), composed of the brain and the spinal cord, and the peripheral nervous system (PNS), which carries information to and from the CNS via the various sensory organs. The brain is endlessly fascinating and complex, and it is almost endlessly divisible. We will focus only on major areas that have been consistently implicated in all sorts of antisocial behavior. The brain is typically divided into four principal parts: the brain stem, diencephalon, cerebellum, and the cerebrum, but we favor the "triune" division into the reptilian, limbic, and neocortex system that reflects the brain's evolutionary history.

The most primitive part of the human brain is the reptilian system, so called because it is just about all the brain a reptile has. It consists of the brain stem and the cerebellum. The system controls the survival reflexes such as breathing and heart rate, as well as movement, sleep, and consciousness. Part of the brain stem contains a finger-sized network of cells called the reticular activating system (RAS). The RAS regulates cortical arousal and various levels of consciousness that underlie sensitivity to the environment. Variation in RAS functioning leads to augmenting or reducing the incoming sensory information from the environment.

Wrapped around the reptilian system like a protective claw is a set of structures known as the limbic system. It is in the limbic system that we experience pleasure and pain, affection, anger, and joy. These are the basic emotions upon which the so-called social emotions (shame, guilt, embarrassment, and so forth) are retrofitted. Among the many structures of the limbic system are the amygdala, hippocampus, and anterior cingulate gyrus (ACG), each of which is distributed bilaterally. The amygdala's primary function is the storage of memories associated with the full range of emotions, particularly fear. When the amygdala is aroused by a stimulus, it sends information to a part of the brain called the prefrontal cortex, which initiates a response geared to the stimulus. The hippocampus is specialized for storing and processing visual and spatial memories such as facts and events.[2] Connections between the amygdala and hippocampus help to focus the brain on what the organism has learned about responding to the kinds of emotional stimuli that have aroused it in the past ("Do I run, fight, talk, ignore?").

The curves of the cingulate gyri surround the wishbone-like structure of the limbic system and provide a connection between the limbic system and the cerebral cortex. The ACG has a number of functions, including mediating between conflicting response signals from the "rational" hippocampus and the "emotional" amygdala (Allman et al., 2001). It plays a role in self-control by helping the hippocampus to reign in negative emotions. People prone to aggression show attenuated activation of the ACG (Davidson, Putnam & Larson, 2000). The various parts of the ACG serve as processing stations for top-down and bottom-up stimuli arriving from various other areas, and assign appropriate control to them. According to Laurence Tancredi (2005:36), the ACG "provides for civilized discourse, conflict resolution, and fundamental human socialization."

The limbic system is thought to have evolved in conjunction with the evolutionary switch from a reptilian to a mammalian lifestyle, which included the addition of nursing and parental care, and audiovocal communication. It used to be thought that limbic system emotional activity was an evolutionary "throwback" to more primitive times, and that because it was non-rational, it required cerebral inhibition (McDermott, 2004). The evidence today now points overwhelmingly to the position that the emotions perform many functions vital to social and cultural evolution (Nicholson, 2002; Phelps, 2006). Emotions do require rational guidance (but not inhibition), just as cognitions require emotional guidance. There is an intimate relationship between rationality and emotion, as the huge number of projections between the amygdalae and the hippocampi, as well as the apparent "refereeing" function of the ACG, attest (Richter-Levin, 2004). As a basis for social interaction, emotions clearly preceded rationality in evolutionary time, with rationality being added later to the more important role of social emotions such as love, empathy, shame, disgust, and embarrassment. Descartes's famous apothegm "I think, therefore I am" would have been more accurately rendered as "I think and emote, therefore I am."

Situated at the foremost part of the brain stem and linked to the limbic system is the thalamus. The thalamus is a dual-lobed structure that receives signals from the RAS and serves as a relay station for all kinds of sensory information except smell, and organizes and sends the incoming messages to the appropriate brain areas for processing. Just beneath the thalamus is the hypothalamus, one of the

---

2   As with many of the brain areas we discuss, we unavoidably discuss them in grossly simplified and general terms. For instance, the hippocampus only stores memories temporarily before shunting them off elsewhere in the brain for consolidation. Where these memories go depends upon the content of the memory. Identifying a picture of an automobile, identifying its color, and naming the make of the car and its color will all activate different parts of the brain where motor, visual, and language memories are stored.

busiest parts of the brain. It is mainly concerned with maintaining homeostasis, the process of returning a biological mechanism to its normal set points after arousal. It also controls the endocrine glands via its control of the pituitary gland. Through its control of the pituitary and the autonomic nervous system (ANS) and the hypothalamic–pituitary–adrenal (HPA) axis, it helps to regulate stress and emotional expression by balancing arousal and quiescence.

The most recent evolutionary addition to the brain is the cerebrum, which forms the bulk of the human brain. The cerebrum is divided into two complementary hemispheres with their own specialized functions, and is connected at the bottom by the corpus callosum. The right hemisphere is specialized for perception and the expression of emotion, and the left hemisphere is specialized for language and analytical thinking (Parsons & Osherson, 2001), although the two hemispheres work in unison like two lumberjacks at each end of a saw. The right hemisphere is more specialized in processing visuospatial patterns and is more holistic, in that it grasps the fragmentary abstractions processed by the left hemisphere in a more integrated way. Figure 1.1 illustrates some of these important brain structures.

The surface of the cerebrum is covered by the cerebral cortex, an intricately folded layer of nerve cells about one-eighth inch thick. The cortex is the brain's "thinking cap" that receives information from the outside world, analyzes it, makes decisions about it, and sends messages via other brain structures to the right muscles and glands so that we may organize responses to it. It is our large cerebral

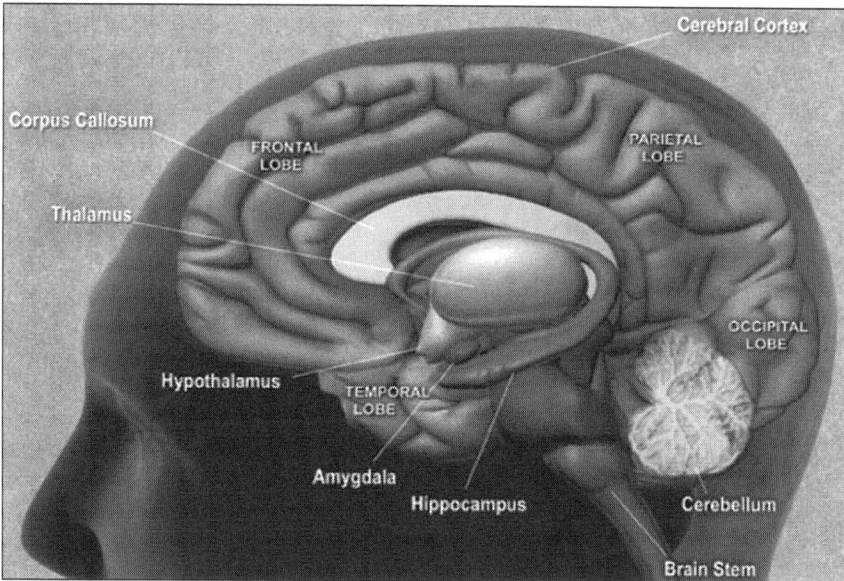

Figure 1.1 Some important brain areas pertinent to criminal behavior

Source: <http://www.nia.nih.gov/Alzheimers/Publications/UnravelingtheMystery/>

cortex that sets humanity apart from the rest of the animal kingdom, and which makes it possible for us to adapt to and survive in all manner of environments.

The folds of the cerebrum are known as sulci ("furrows"), and the deepest of these furrows divide the two hemispheres into four lobes which are named after the main skull bones that cover them: the frontal, parietal, occipital, and temporal lobes (see Figure 1.1). The occipital ("back") lobe is primarily devoted to vision, and need not concern us here. Structures in the parietal ("cavity") lobes provide us with our unified perceptions of the world by integrating information coming to us from our various senses by cross-matching sensory information with abstract symbols (language) representative of the sum of the sensory input surrounding it. Parietal lobe structures systematize, classify, and consolidate our knowledge and form it into abstract concepts—an ability which, as far as we know, is only possessed by human beings. Structures in the temporal ("temple") lobe are primarily involved in perception, memory, and hearing. While the parietal lobes integrate information, the temporal lobes' hippocampi are where these integrations are stored, retrieved, and associated with previous information. This associative process is obviously crucial for learning because we have to assign connotative properties to stimuli in accordance to their significance to us. If we did not associate incoming stimuli with the motivational and affective significance they have for us, behavior would never be modified because all stimuli would treated as more or less equivalent.

The most important of the lobes in terms of the behaviors of interest to criminologists are the frontal ("front") lobes, particularly the prefrontal cortex (PFC), "the most uniquely human of all brain structures" (Goldberg, 2001:2). The PFC is the terminal point for much of the emotional input from the limbic system, and the origin of our response to it. It is the most anterior portion of the frontal lobe, occupying approximately one-third of the human cerebral cortex, and is the last brain area to fully mature (Romine & Reynolds, 2005). The PFC is subdivided into a number of areas, the most important for our purposes being the orbitofrontal, ventromedial, and dorsolateral areas, and has extensive connections with other cortical regions, with deeper structures in the limbic system, and directly with the RAS, which indicates that it is on a high level of alertness. Because of its many connections with other brain structures, it is generally considered to play the major integrative and supervisory role in the brain, and is vital to the forming of moral judgments, mediating affect, and for social cognition (Romine & Reynolds, 2005; Sowell, Thompson & Toga, 2004).

Neurons

The brain contains at least a trillion cells, and about 100 billion of them are the communicating neurons that give rise to all those cerebral things—intelligence, emotion, creativity, memory—that define our humanity (Mithen & Parsons, 2008). The neuron is the basic unit of the brain, and each one is a fully integrated member of a network of other neurons with a particular set of kinship connections. Neurons are much like other cells in our bodies, containing a nucleus with DNA, ribosomes, mitochondria, and many of the other constituents of somatic cells, but their "specialness" lies in their patterns of connectivity. Although the number of neurons does not appreciably change after birth, the brain itself quadruples in size from neonate to adult. Much of this size increase is attributable to the increase in glial cells. Glial cells are much more numerous than neurons, and their special jobs are to provide neurons with physical support, maintain their homeostasis, and to form the myelin sheath around their axons.

Neurons are specialized for conducting information from one cell to another by transducing stimuli from the environment into electrochemical impulses and transmitting them via the appropriate networks (pathways) of other cells so that a response may be made. They accomplish this by way of axons that originate in the cell body, and dendrites, which are branched extensions of the cell. Axons are coated by a myelin sheath formed by special types of glial cells. Much like the insulation around electrical wiring, myelin functions to protect the axon from short-circuiting and to amplify nerve impulses. Myelinated axons transmit impulses about 100 times faster than unmyelinated axons, and are the brain's "white matter" as opposed to its "gray matter," which consists of cell bodies and unmyelinated axons. There is only one axon per cell, but the number of branching dendrites varies from neuron to neuron, and each dendrite may have thousands of tiny projections called dendritic spines. Axons serve as transmitters, sending signals to other neurons, and dendrites serve as receivers, picking up impulses from neighboring neurons which are then passed on to the next neuron in the chain.

Neurons pass their information along the axon in the form of electrical signals made possible by the exchange of charged atoms (ions) in and out of the axon's permeable membrane. The energy needed to perform the neuron's activities (as with the activities of all cells in the body) is provided by a chemical called adenosine triphosphate (ATP), which is synthesized from dietary proteins, fats, and sugars by mitochondria in the cell body. Impulses travel down axons like neon lights flicking on and off until they reach the axon terminal point known as synaptic knobs, or more simply, synapses. The message is changed from electrical to chemical form at the synapse, at which time neurotransmitters (see Figure 2.1) stored in vesicles open up and spill out into microscopic gaps between the presynaptic axon and the receptors of the postsynaptic cell. After the message is received by the postsynaptic neuron, it may again be converted to electric impulses to continue its journey to the next cell, depending upon the ratio of excitatory to inhibitory messages it receives. A neuron has the capacity to make many thousands of synaptic connections with other neurons, and the brain's 100 billion neurons "form over 100 trillion connections with each other—more than all of the Internet connections in the world!" (Weinberger, Elvevag & Giedd, 2005:5).

Brain Development and Plasticity

There are debates are about the relative contributions to brain development of processes intrinsic (in the genome) and extrinsic (environmental) to it, albeit not naïve "either-or" debates. Neuroscientists who favor innateness are called *selectionists* or *nativists*, and those who favor the power of extrinsic factors are called *constructivists* or *connectionists*. Both positions agree that the environment is hugely important in the development of the brain; the argument is not "*whether* the environment thoroughly influences brain development, but *how* it does" (Quartz & Segnowski, 1997:579). Both positions also agree that the typical social science "blank slate" view of the human mind is a neurological impossibility, and see neonates as arriving with a large number of built-in assumptions that frame the world for them, because it is a basic tenet of neuroscience that assumption-free learning is impossible (Mitchell, 2007).

Except for connections governing vital processes and reflexive behaviors, the human infant's brain at birth is not ready-wired to function independently in its environment almost immediately as are the more rigidly programmed brains of lower animals. Most non-human neonate mammals are developmentally at the stage that it will take human infants about one year to reach, at which time the infant's brain will be 60% of its adult weight (Mithen & Parsons, 2008).

Neuroscientists distinguish between two brain developmental processes that *physically* capture environmental events in the organism's lifetime: experience-expected and experience-dependent (Schon & Silven, 2007). Every human being inherits species-typical hardwired brain structures and functions produced by a common pool of genetic material; these are the experience-expected mechanisms that reflect the phylogenic history of the brain. Natural selection moves population traits towards genetic fixity (genetic variability is eliminated) the more important a feature becomes to survival. Although experience-expected mechanisms are hardwired, they require specific environmental experiences to trigger them. That is, there is an evolved neural readiness during "critical" or "sensitive" developmental periods to incorporate environmental information that is vital to an organism and which cannot be left to the vagaries of experiential learning. Natural selection has recognized that certain processes such as sight, speech, depth perception, affectionate bonds, mobility, various aversions, and sexual maturation are vital, and has provided for mechanisms (adaptations) designed to take advantage of experiences occurring naturally within the normal range of human environments. Pre-experiential brain organization (built-in assumptions) frames or orients our experiences so that we will respond consistently and stereotypically (Geary, 2005). Maturational (developmental) processes will always occur "as expected" in genetically normal individuals experiencing the normal range of human environments. If individuals experience gross departures from these so-called "species-expectable" environments, there may be many negative outcomes (Twardosz & Lutzker, 2010).

Experience-dependent mechanisms reflect the brain's ontogenic plasticity (Gunnar & Quevedo, 2007). Individuals will vary in brain functioning as their genes interact with the environments they encounter to construct those brains. That is, the wiring patterns of the brains of different individuals depend on the kinds of physical, social, and cultural environments they will encounter. As Depue and Collins (1999:507) wrote: "experience-dependent processes are central to understanding personality as a dynamic developmental construct that involves the collaboration of genetic and environmental influences across the lifespan." Although brain plasticity is greatest in infancy and early childhood, it is maintained to a lesser degree across the lifespan as we shape and reshape the brain in ways that could never have been genetically pre-programmed. The distinction between experience-dependent and expected-development is best illustrated by language. The *capacity* for language is entirely genetic (a hardwired experience-expected species-wide capacity), but what language(s) a person speaks is entirely cultural (softwired in experience-dependent culturally specific fashion). The experience-expected nature of language explains why children learn language almost effortlessly, as if by osmosis, while evolutionarily novel things such as algebra are learned with some difficultly.

The process of wiring the brain is known as *synaptogenesis*, a process that occurs both according to a genetic program and the influence of the environment. During the first few months of an infant's life, dendrites proliferate and specialized glial cells wrap around axons to begin the process of myelination, making for speedier transmission of electrical impulses. Dendrite growth and axon myelination continues throughout life, but proceeds at an explosive rate during infancy and toddlerhood. The experience-expected "lower" brain regions (spinal column and limbic regions) are the first to be myelinated, and some "higher" brain regions, especially the PFC, are not fully myelinated until early adulthood (Sowell, Thompson & Toga, 2004).

The birth of a set of synapses is less important than whether they will survive the competition for synaptic space. The most active period of synaptogenesis is infancy and toddlerhood, although about half of these connections will eventually be eliminated. The brain creates and eliminates synapses throughout life, but creation exceeds elimination in the first two years, after which production and elimination are roughly balanced until adolescence, when elimination exceeds production (Giedd, 2004).

This process of selective production and elimination has been termed *neural Darwinism* by Nobel Prize winner Gerald Edelman (1992), who posits a selection process among competing brain modules (populations of neurons). Neuronal connections are selected for retention or elimination according to how functionally viable (adaptive) they prove to be in the person's environment in the same way that environmental challenges select from a population's reservoir of genetic variation in evolutionary time. The brain's neuronal populations thus evolve in somatic time like species evolve in geological time by the selective elimination or retention of genes. The elimination of neurons (not just their connections) is carried out by a process of programmed cell death built into our DNA to get rid of inefficient, damaged, or redundant cells called *apoptosis* (Blomgren, Leist & Groe, 2007). This process is vital for the normal growth of the brain, and results (or should result) in a "lean, mean learning machine" prepared to react adaptively and flexibly to the challenges that its host organism will meet over its lifetime.

Neural network retention is a use-dependent process in which the connections that are sustained are those that exchange information frequently and strongly (Penn, 2001). Experiences with strong emotional content are accompanied by strong electro-chemical impulses, and become more sensitive and responsive to similar stimuli in the future (Shi et al., 2004). Frequently activated neurons are thus primed to fire at lower stimulus thresholds once neurological tracks have been laid down. This process is summed up in the neuroscientists' saying: "The neurons that fire together, wire together; those that don't, won't" (Penn, 2001:339). Figure 1.2 illustrates the explosive growth of the brain from birth to age one. The cell bodies increase in size, dendrite branching becomes more elaborate, and axons become myelinated.

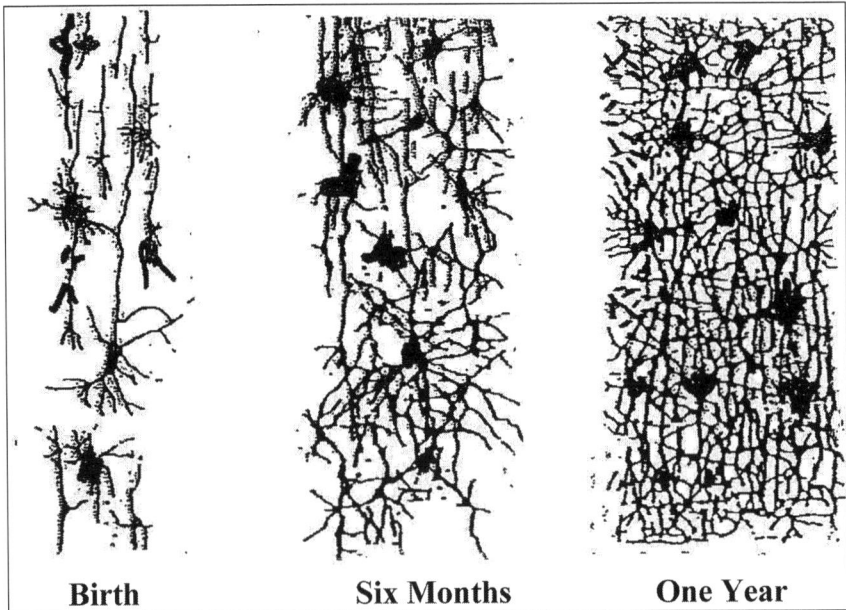

| Birth | Six Months | One Year |

Figure 1.2   The growth of neuronal networks from birth to age one

Culture Matters

The brain is often likened to a buzzing interactive computer network, with organic compounds substituting for silicon chips. The computer is a marvelous tool, but disconnected from its inputs and outputs and from its electrical energy, it becomes useless. The human brain disconnected from its environment would likewise be just a gelatinous mass of tissue. Genes are marvelous entities that carry an immense amount of information, but they are few relative to the much larger number of neurons and the staggering number of connections neurons make. Although 50–60% of human genes are involved in brain development, there are nowhere near enough to cope with the task of cultivating the neuronal jungle to the benefit of the being to whom it belongs. Of course, the brain cannot function without genetic input, but the environment plays a major role in specifying the billions of relationships that will eventually exist among the brain cells of the adult human being (Mitchell, 2007). It is thus safe to say that the neurological evidence is unequivocal on two major points about brain development: (1) the brain is always a "work in progress," and (2) its development is "use-dependent."

The brain is thus a plastic organ of adaptation. Plasticity refers to the dynamic, ever-vigilant brain's ability to calibrate itself to the demands of the environment it finds itself in. We cannot say it often enough: the brain physically captures aspects of the environment, both positive and negative, that have the most salience for the organism. Koukkou and Lehmann (2006:47) put it well when they wrote: "[E]xperience-dependent plasticity refers to the learning and memory mechanisms that extract personal meaning out of the interaction of individuals with their environment and that lead to the genesis of the neuronal networks that represent autobiographical memory."

Mithen and Parsons (2008) view the human brain as an artifact of culture. They are not naïve social constructionists saying that brains did not exist prior the evolution of culture. They are aware that most evolutionary adaptations, including brain adaptations, are the result of challenges to survival and reproductive success posed by ecology (finding food and mates, fighting off pathogens and predators, and a thousand other things) that all living organisms share. What they are saying is that culturally created environments have influenced both the anatomy and function of the human brain above and beyond the influences posed by the challenges of the physical environment. There are a number of studies of hominid crania dating as far back as 1.9 million years that show more robust increases in cranial capacity in areas with greater population density and in areas in which food procurement was most problematic, namely colder and most northerly areas of the globe (Ash & Gallup, 2007; Kanazawa, 2008). One study found that latitude was strongly related to cranial capacity (r = 0.61), but population density was more strongly related to it (r = 0.79). These authors (Bailey & Geary, 2009:77) concluded that the burden of evolutionary selection has moved from "climactic and ecological to social."

Genes and culture thus co-evolve because nature (genes) and nurture (culture) constitute an integrated reciprocal feedback system. Genes and culture are both information transmission devices, the former laying the foundation (the capacity) for the latter, and the latter then influencing the former (what genetic variants are useful in this culture at this time?). If a trait (say, empathy) or behavior (say, altruism) emerges that is culturally useful and desirable, those displaying it will be advantaged in terms of securing resources and mates. Individuals thus blessed will advance their fitness as the genes underlying the trait or behavior will be preserved and proliferate in the population gene pool. Laland, Odling-Smee, and Myles's (2010) review article cataloged a cascade of genetic variants that have been subjected to positive selection in response to human cultural activities.

The brain is a particularly expensive piece of machinery to be carrying around because of its voracious appetite for energy (it consumes 20% of the body's energy supply). Because the human brain is much larger than should be expected for animals of our size, the brain must have been vital to gene–culture co-evolution given its extravagant share of the body's precious energy. Studies of a large range of animal species show that group size is related to brain size, leading a number of evolutionary biologists and neuroscientists to propose that the intellectual demands of living in large groups drove the selection for what they call the "social brain" (Lindenfors, 2005). The social brain enables us to negotiate relationships, to understand the thoughts, feelings, and intentions of others, and to cooperate in securing resources and in defending the group (Dunbar & Shultz, 2007).

Understanding the thoughts, feelings, and intentions of others is commonly referred to as empathy. Gaining access to someone else's thoughts and feelings is governed by so-called "mirror neurons," explored in Chapter 10. Mirror neurons can be thought of as the physiological mechanism governing the psychologists' "theory of mind" or the sociologists' concept of "taking the role of the other." Both require that a person distinguish between the self and other, and that he or she can use his or her own mind to infer the feelings, thoughts, intentions, and desires of others. Brain imaging studies have shown that mirror neuron mechanisms are selectively recruited when attributing feelings to the self or to others in response to viewing a variety of emotional facial expressions (angry, fearful, sad, and so forth). Subjects with high empathy scale scores show stronger brain activation, particularly in the various frontal cortices, than lower-scoring subjects (Schulte-Rüther et al., 2007).

It was once thought that the process of gene–culture evolution was most salient during the Pleistocene epoch, when cultural change was slower than genetic changes driven by ecological challenges. It was also thought that culture evolution is too rapid for natural selection to track in historical times. However, using new genetic technology, John Hawks and colleagues (2007) have shown that the rate of genomic change has been an incredible 100 times greater over the last 40,000 years than it was during the 1.8 million-year-long Pleistocene. Like Bailey and Geary, discussed above, they attributed this to the greater challenges posed by living in larger and larger social groups: "[T]he rapid cultural evolution during the Late Pleistocene created vastly more opportunities for further genetic changes, not fewer, as new avenues emerged for communication, social interaction, and creativity" (Hawks et al., 2007:20,757). This should make sense to everyone with a nodding acquaintance with genetics and who realizes the mathematical truism that mutations (positive, negative, or neutral) will arise more frequently in large mating populations than in smaller ones. Although our most human characteristics (morphology, physiology, and basic nature) evolved during the Pleistocene, we do not operate with brains forged exclusively during that epoch. New genetic variations affecting the brain's structure and function have been discovered as it continues to evolve in response to new ecological and cultural conditions (Evans et al., 2005; Mekel-Bobrov et al., 2005).

The central message of this chapter is that genes have surrendered much of their control over human behavior to a more plastic, complex, and *adaptive* system of control called the human brain, and that the development of the brain depends greatly on environmental input. Put otherwise, we and the experiences we encounter will largely determine the patterns of our neuronal connections, and thus our ability to successfully navigate our lives.

A Brief Look at Technology Used to Study the Brain

Because we will be referring frequently to studies that use a variety of remarkable technologies to peer into the workings of the brain, it is necessary to briefly describe the most commonly used of these technologies. Criminologists Lilly, Cullen, and Ball (2007:291) note that the most dramatic developments in science come most often from new observational techniques such as those described here rather than new developments in theory (think of the huge "paradigm shifts" that accompanied two of the best-known of scientific tools—the telescope and the microscope). Lilly, Cullen, and Ball were talking primarily about brain imaging techniques, and suggested that these techniques should revolutionize criminology. We, of course, agree completely.

Electroencephalograph

The electroencephalograph (EEG) is the oldest neurological recording technique discussed in this book. The EEG records the aftermath of the electrical impulses of neurons' action potentials. The EEG is able to record the milliseconds of groups of neurons "firing," and the recording is separated into the categorical waves of delta, theta, alpha, beta, and gamma which are derived from the varying recorded electrical frequencies. This recording is typically done by a series of electrodes that are placed on the scalp of an individual.

The EEG allows researchers to monitor the functioning and cognition of the brain in real time. One example of how this is done is EEG experiments focusing on the P300 event-related potential (P3). The P3 is an electrophysiological brain response that is elicited by stimuli that are infrequent and novel and demand consideration. When subjects are presented with the novel stimuli, the record of P3 is believed to reflect the identification and processing of that stimuli as well as the repositioning of the stimulus into working memory. After repeat exposure to the once-novel stimulus, varying P3 response can be considered a reflection of one's ability to compare stimuli in working memory and adapt those memories on the fly. Varying levels of P3 have been suggested as evidencing various mental abilities, such as cognition and memory processing.

Positron Emission Tomography

Positron emission tomography (PET) is a neuroimaging technique that tracks the metabolic processes of the human body by identifying the radioactive decay of a radiopharmaceutical tracer called flurodeoxyglucose (a proxy for glucose), which is introduced to the body prior to the scan (Hartsthorn, 2000).

The decay of the introduced isotope is caused by positron[3] emission, and the resulting decay releases photons which are captured by PET. The tracer can be found in regions of the brain that are utilizing the largest amounts of glucose, the source of energy for the brain, which allows scientists to monitor the allocation of energy by particular areas of the brain. PET is a valuable tool for scientists, providing data on the metabolic function of the brain, and can create a vivid three-dimensional image of the brain illustrating what portions are dominant in thought processes and functions. PET is limited, however, in that requires the introduction of a radioactive isotope and does not have the precision needed to record the instantaneous "firing" of a group of neurons (Chiao & Ambady, 2007).

Functional Magnetic Resonance Imaging

Functional magnetic resonance imaging (fMRI) allows researchers to be witness to the brain while it thinks. fMRI functions by tracking the flow of blood in a subject's brain (hemodynamics), which allows scientist to understand what parts of the brain are being activated during a given mental process. Like PET, fMRI provides researchers with an anatomical image of neural activity that illustrates various regions used in processing. However, unlike PET scans, fMRI does not need multiple cases to average data responses; as such, fMRI can be used to study neural variations in individuals as well as groups (Chong, Sanders & Jones, 2000).

The use of fMRI can be found in studies covering a wide array of mental processes and neural disorders associated with criminality, such as psychopathy, schizophrenia, and emotional response. Although fMRI has given researchers invaluable insight as to how the brain works, it is not without its limitations. Chiao and Ambady (2007) note that both fMRI and PET rely on the tracking and recording of blood flow and metabolic distribution throughout the brain, and that this record is over seconds, and not the milliseconds associated with cognition. To track the millisecond firing of neurons, other neuro-recording techniques must be used.

---

3   A positron is a positively charged anti-electron, and is thus antimatter.

Transcranial Magnetic Stimulation

Both PET and fMRI data allow researchers to know what portions of the brain are correlated with a given mental process. They do not, however, prove that the portions of the brain used in these processes are necessary or designed for that process. Scientists wishing to investigate causality in the human brain can do so by utilizing transcranial magnetic stimulation (TMS). This technique introduces a magnetic field that conflicts with the electric field of the brain and is able interrupt, or suppress, brain activity in a specific region without the need for invasive procedures. By inducing neuron depolarization, neuroscientists can study brain functioning and connectivity between various regions. Repetitive TMS (rTMS) can produce long-lasting effects by changing the level of synaptic efficiency by artificially mimicking the process of neural Darwinism (mechanically increasing or decreasing the intensity of neuron excitation) (Fitzgerald, Fountain & Daskalakis (2006).

Diffusion Tensor Imaging

Diffusion tensor imaging (DTI) is a system based on magnetic resonance imaging (MRI) that allows neuroscientists to assess the integrity of connections between various brain systems at a micro-architectural level. It enables scientists to view the directionality (diffusion) of water molecules (the brain is in a highly salt-watery environment) along myelinated axon pathways. A tensor is a mathematical value that changes with changes of coordinates—in this case, changes in the positions of water molecules. Thus, DTI assesses "diffusion anisotropy," loosely translated as the flow of molecules in a single direction, as opposed to flowing in all directions as in isotropy. Anisotropic diffusion occurs along white matter tracts; isotropic diffusion occurs in gray matter and in compromised white matter (Mori & Zhang, 2006).

Voxel-based Morphometry

Voxel-based morphometry (VBM) is another MRI-based automated technique for the identification of structural brain changes across groups (not for assessing individual patients). A voxel (volumetric pixel) is the three-dimensional analog of the two-dimensional pixel (picture element). A picture can contain millions of pixels, the smallest assessable element of the picture, so close together that they appear connected. Likewise, a region of interest in the brain can contain millions or billions of voxels arranged in a structure that can be measured (morphometry). The automated tests perform statistical tests across all voxels in the region of interest to identify significant volume differences between groups (say, schizophrenics versus healthy controls) (Whitwell, 2009).

*   *   *

Each of these technologies and techniques (and there are others) is a powerful tool for the neurological researcher. However, each of them also presents difficulties and limitations when used as the only method to study a neurological process or phenomenon and cannot aptly identify the intricacy of the human mind. Integration of methods is essential to creating a vivid and robust appreciation of the brain's activities; as Chiao & Ambady (2007:241) remind us: "it is the convergence of findings from multiple techniques that enables us to make sound inferences about neural structures and their psychological function."

One unfortunate drawback of imaging studies in the past has been the limiting factor of cost on longitudinal studies and on sample sizes. However, with technology getting ever cheaper, there are a number of ambitious studies, both longitudinal and cross-sectional, being conducted today that are imaging anywhere from 400 to 2,000 subjects. Paus (2010) discusses four of these studies at length, including two longitudinal studies. All these studies are collecting mountains of environmental, behavioral, and cognitive data (for example, socioeconomic status, maternal smoking, drinking, breastfeeding, stressful life events, antisocial behavior, IQ, personality profiles, and many other factors). Three of these four studies are also collection DNA data. These efforts will push the social/behavioral sciences, including criminology, into more evidenced-based paradigms if their practitioners jettison their "trained incapacity" to appreciate reductionist (let us drop this term and substitute "fundamental explanatory") science. It is obvious from the wealth of data that the above studies are collecting that they are not looking at parts isolated from the whole.

Chapter 2
Neurochemistry, Gene–cultural Coevolution, and Criminal Behavior

Neurotransmitters and Receptors

The question for criminologists is no longer *whether* genes influence criminal behavior, but *how* they do. Meta-analyses of behavior genetic studies show a broad heritability of at least 50% for antisocial behavior (Ferguson, 2010; Guo, Roettger & Shih, 2007a; Moffitt, 2005; Rhee & Waldman, 2002). The question thus devolves to molecular genetics and becomes: "Which genes predispose individuals to criminal behavior?" Regardless of which genes are implicated, they have to be expressed in the brain before they can influence behavior. No less than 70% of our genes are expressed in the brain, where they produce and regulate the complex neurochemistry that helps to define our humanity (Chiao & Ambady, 2007).

Neurochemicals are the organic compounds that facilitate the brain processes that acquire, evaluate, and respond to the information the brain receives from the environment. These compounds include neurotransmitters, their receptors, transporters, and the enzymes that degrade them, all of which are biosynthesized in neurons. There is an alphabet soup of these and other brain molecules that do all sorts of wonderful things, but we only concern ourselves with the major players associated with antisocial behavior. We first look at neurotransmitters, the chemical messengers that transmit signals from neuron to neuron.

There are about sixty different neurotransmitters, but only a few have been implicated in criminal behavior. Some neurotransmitters are "excitatory" (they promote the continuation of a nerve impulse), whereas others are "inhibitory" (they prevent the continuation of an impulse). It is an oversimplification to describe neurotransmitters as such, but it is useful and conventional to do so. But a word of caution: the terms "excitatory" and "inhibitory" refer only to neurotransmitter activity; they do not refer to neurotransmitter effects on the behavior of the organism at the phenotypic level. Excitatory transmitters may have an inhibiting effect on an organism's behavior, and inhibitory transmitters may have an excitatory effect. For example, excitatory signals may suppress other signals, with the net result being an inhibitory or calming effect on the behavior of the organism. Conversely, inhibitory signals may have the net effect of suppressing signals from excitatory neurotransmitters that normally lead to calm, reasoned behavior, and may result in the organism expressing some form of agitated behavior such as aggression.

Information about all sorts of things from many thousands of dendrites is processed by the cell body of a receiving neuron. These signals are received, integrated, and summated when they enter the cell body (soma), where the decision is made whether the messages contained in this information should be forwarded or canceled. A neuron at rest (not signaling) is polarized—the inside of the neuron is electrically negative relative to the outside. Based on summated voltage inputs, the axon hillock, located at the axon end of the soma, "decides" whether an incoming signal will be forwarded. If the total strength of the excitatory signals exceeds the total strength of the inhibitory signals, the threshold limit of the axon hillock is breached and the signal will be fired down the axon. This is known as an action potential, and is caused by the inside of the cell becoming depolarized (it becomes electrically positive when ion channels on the neuron membrane open and positively charged sodium ions pour in). If the threshold is not breached, the cell remains polarized and the message is terminated (Garrett, 2009).

When an electrical impulse passes along the axon and arrives at the synaptic knob, it causes tiny sacs called vesicles to burst open and spill out one or more neurotransmitters. Neurotransmitters are the "translators" of the message as it switches the signal from electrical to chemical transmission. The neurotransmitters pour across the synaptic gap and lock onto receptor sites on a cell's postsynaptic membrane. Once the neurotransmitter has passed on its message, the excess is either transported back into the presynaptic vesicles or degraded by enzymes. The transmitter substances are the medium by which the message is transmitted, but they are not the message per se. What transmitters "do" depends on the region of the brain where they are being utilized, their interaction with other neurochemicals, and the internal and external environmental contexts forming the background of their functioning. They certainly do not "cause" criminal or any other kind of behavior; their only direct effect is on receptors.

Neurotransmitters are protein molecules that have a particular chemical shape that can only be locked onto by their chemical complements, known as receptors. The chemical transfer across the synaptic gap takes place in about two milliseconds and causes ion channels on the receptor membrane to either open or close. Depolarization occurs if these channels open, which results in the initiation of another action potential in the receiving neuron. Receptor functioning is important because more than one kind of transmitter can be present at a synapse and a target cell can respond to a transmitter differently depending on the specific receptor activated. There are many kinds of receptors: for instance, the two main neurotransmitters we look at in this chapter—serotonin and dopamine—have at least 13 and 5 different types, respectively (Garrett, 2009). These two neurotransmitters have long been major targets of exploration by scientists interested in behavior (for example, criminal conduct) and mental health (for example, schizophrenia). Figure 2.1 illustrates the general process of synaptic transmission.

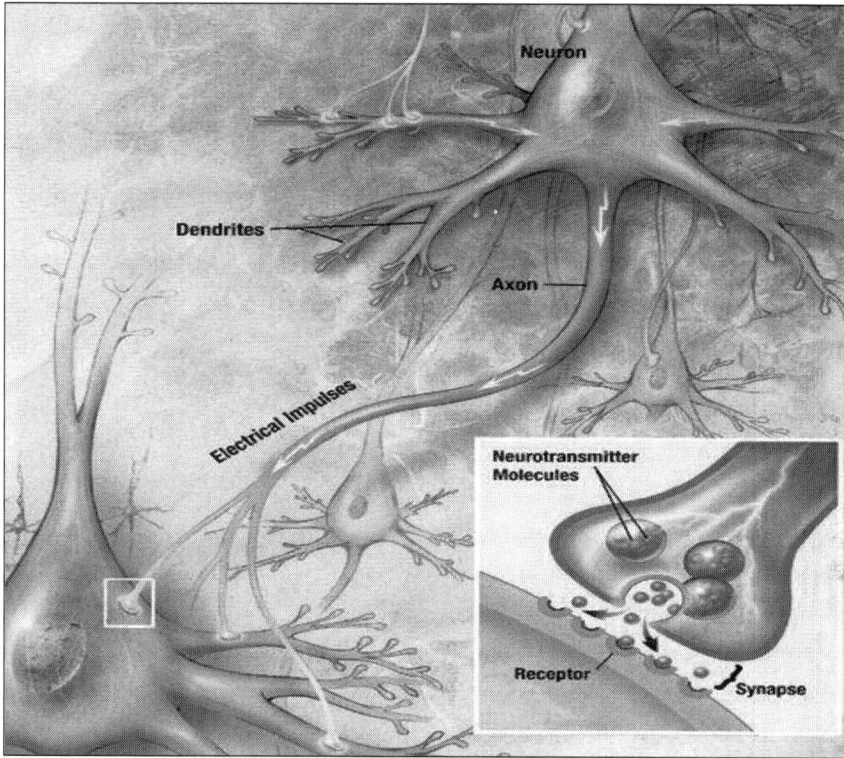

Figure 2.1   Neurons, axons, dendrites, and the synaptic process

Source:<http://www.nia.nih.gov/Alzheimers/Publications/UnravelingtheMystery/>

Reinforcement (or Reward) Dominance Theory

Before discussing the serotonergic and dopaminergic systems in detail, we introduce a theory with which we can ground our discussion in territory familiar to criminologists. Dopamine and serotonin are central to the major neurobiological theory focusing on emotional expression and behavioral control known as *Reinforcement Dominance Theory* (RDT) in biosocial criminology (Cauffman, Steinberg & Piquero, 2005). If social animals are to function normally in their social groups, they must possess the ability to respond to signals of reward and punishment with the socially appropriate approach and avoidance behavior. RDT posits three interacting systems of emotional/behavioral regulation located within separate brain circuits and relying on different neurotransmitters: the *behavioral activating (or approach) system* (BAS), the *behavioral inhibition system* (BIS), and the *fight-flight-freeze system* (FFFS). The BAS and BIS are part of the limbic system with extension projections into the lobes of the PFC, and the FFFS is part of the ANS. The BAS is sensitive to signals of reward from both conditioned (for example, alcohol, gambling) and unconditioned (for example, food, sex) appetitive stimuli. The BIS is sensitive to conditioned threats of punishment (for example, violations of social rules) and unconditioned ones (for example, heights, snarling creatures) (Corr, 2004). We defer discussion of the FFFS to Chapter 4.

The BAS is primarily associated with dopamine (DA) and with mesolimbic system structures such as the nucleus accumbens, a structure rich in neurons that produce and respond to dopamine (Day & Carelli, 2007). The BIS is associated with serotonin and with limbic system structures such as the hippocampus and the amygdala that feed their memory circuits into the PFC (Goldsmith & Davidson, 2004). Serotonin and dopamine are powerful regulators of behavioral and cognitive functions, thus any aspect of reduced or enhanced serotonergic or dopaminergic functioning results in emotional, behavioral, and cognitive dysregulation.

The BAS/BIS motivating/inhibiting system has been considered conceptually to be modern neuroscience's analog of the Freudian Id and Superego, with BAS–BIS balance being the Ego (Walsh, 2009a). The BAS can be likened to an accelerator motivating a person to seek rewarding stimuli; it obeys the pleasure principle, and is the biological raw material representing drives for acquiring life-sustaining necessities and life's pleasures. The BIS strives for the ideal, representing all the moral and social rules internalized by the person during socialization, and it can be likened to a brake that inhibits us from going too far in the pursuit of natural and acquired pleasures. Problems with the accelerator or brake may lead to a "craving brain" that can lead to many physical, social, moral, and legal difficulties, such as addiction to gambling, food, sex alcohol, and drugs. Because most of these rewards are natural (unconditioned), they evoke natural responses such as salivation, consumption, and sexual arousal (unconditioned responses); they thus constitute classical conditioning, as they become embedded in operant conditioning circumstances as they are actively sought out (Day & Carelli, 2007).

The Serotonergic System

Serotonin (5-hydroxytriptamine; 5-HT), is found in all organisms with a nervous system. It is an inhibitory (although it is sometimes excitatory) neurotransmitter that plays a major role in maintaining balance between other excitatory and inhibitory transmitters. Most serotonin (about 80%) operates in the gut, where it regulates intestinal movements, but central nervous system neurons containing 5-HT originate in the raph nuclei in the midbrain and project to multiple areas of the brain such as the brain stem, hippocampus, cerebellum, and PFC. Figure 2.2 shows the diverse targets of 5-HT (black lines), which is consistent with the wide variety of behavior syndromes associated with neural 5-HT. Dopamine projections (white lines) are more or less limited to the PFC and various areas of the limbic system. The disorders of major concern to criminologists associated with 5-HT are impulsivity, anxiety, and mood disorders, alcoholism, and psychotic disorders (Stoltenberg & Nag, 2007).

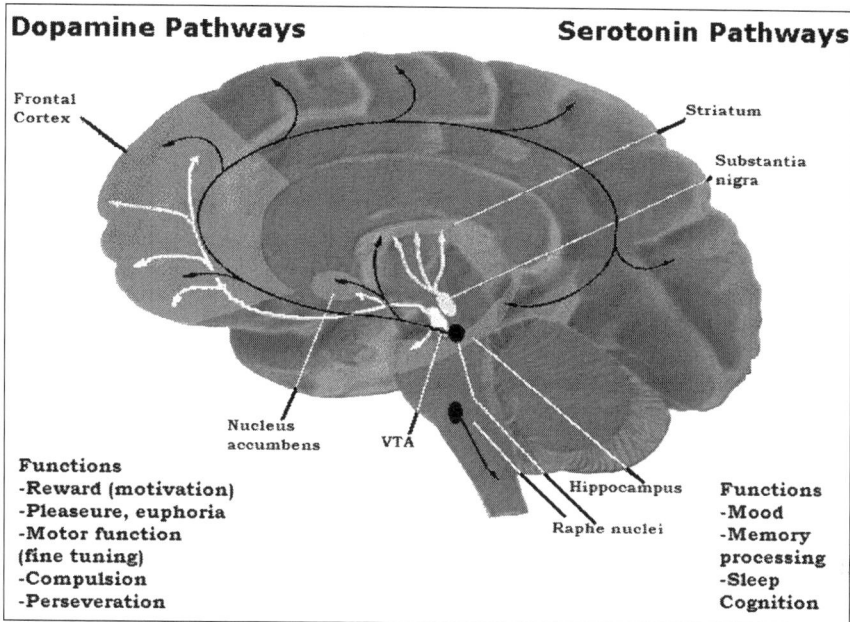

Figure 2.2   Major dopamine (white) and serotonin (black) pathways in the brain

Source: National Institutes of Health, United States Department of Health and Human Services

After a postsynaptic membrane has been excited by serotonin, excess neurotransmitters have to be quickly removed from the synaptic cleft to prevent that signal being confused with subsequent signals. The 5-HT transporter (5-HTT) inactivates synaptic 5-HT by a process known as reuptake, transporting it back into the presynaptic knob for repackaging in the vesicles. The 5-HTT thus exerts strong control over 5-HT functioning, depending on its efficiency. The 5-HTT gene (SLC6A4) has a polymorphic region known as 5-HTTLPR (5-hydroxytriptamine transporter-linked polymorphous region) that has short (s) and long (L) versions.[1]

---

1   Polymorphisms are the genetic variations that make us all different from one another. We all have the same genes that do the same things that make us human, but we have different versions of the genes that function more or less efficiently. The different versions of genes are called alleles (one inherited paternally, and one maternally), and it is these genetic variants that carry the polymorphism. The two major polymorphisms are single nucleotide polymorphisms (SNPs) and micro- and mini-satellites (referred to collectively as variable number of tandem repeats—VNTRs). A difference in just one nucleotide is all that differentiates one allele from another in a SNP. VTNRs differ from one another in the length of contiguous nucleotide bases that are repeated a different number

The short variant reduces the transcriptional efficiency of the 5-HTTLPR, which results in decreased 5-HTT expression and 5-HT uptake. Having even one copy of the short allele (s/s or s/L) reduces the efficiency of 5-HTT functioning.

One of criminology's most revered causal variables—low self-control—is a factor highly influenced by serotonin, as is another important factor—negative emotionality. Caspi and colleagues (1994) contend that crime proneness is defined at a minimum by low self-control (which they call low constraint) and negative emotionality—the tendency to experience many situations as aversive and to react to them with irritation and anger more readily than with positive affective states. Robert Agnew (2005) has developed a promising theory of criminal behavior that incorporates both low self-control and negative emotionality (which he calls "irritability), both of which are underlain by low serotonergic functioning. Thus, aberrant serotonergic functioning "may be a heritable diathesis for a personality style involving high levels of negative affect and low levels of constraint (self-control), which generates in turn a vulnerability to criminal behavior" (Caspi et al., 1994:188).

Criminologists also place a great deal of importance on the role of "strain" in generating criminal behavior (Agnew, 1992). Most people who experience strain (the inevitable stresses of life) do not respond by committing criminal acts, but some succumb to problems of depression or anxiety. There are risk and protective factors, both social and genetic, that render individuals either vulnerable or resilient to the negative consequences of strain. For instance, Caspi and colleagues (2003) examined the effects of the 5-HTTLPR polymorphism and maltreatment and other stressful lifetime events in a longitudinal birth cohort. These subjects were assessed at age 26 for major and minor depressive episodes. Looking at maltreatment (categorized as "none," "probably," and "severe"), subjects who were homozygous for the short allele (s/s) of the 5-HTTLPR showed a dramatic increase in the probability of a major depressive episode, moving from the "none" to the "severe" category. The probability did not increase at all for subjects homozygous for the long allele (L/L) across the maltreatment categories, and heterozygotes (s/L) were at intermediate risk. The same pattern emerged for all analyses: the L/L genotype confers protection against adversity, the s/L confers some protection, and s/s individuals are particularly vulnerable. This is an example of gene–environment interaction (GxE), in that the main effects of genotype were not significant absent stressful events (the main effects for stressful events were weakly significant, however). That is, genotype mattered primarily only in the face of environmental insults.[2]

---

of times. The more times the sequence of nucleotide bases (the DNA "letters"—ATGC) is repeated, the longer the allele.

2   It should be noted that meta-analyses of the 5-HTTLPR polymorphism and anxiety-related personality traits reveal weak effect sizes (Cohen's ds between 0.10 and 0.20). However, these studies almost invariably correlate scores on personality inventories with the polymorphism. Longitudinal studies such as Caspi et al. (2003) utilizing verified

The amygdala is a major target for serotonin. A meta-analysis of fMRI studies showed that individuals with the short variant of 5-HTTLPR tend to have heightened amygdala sensitivity—the amygdala fires sooner, stronger, and more frequently (Munafo, Brown & Hariri, 2008). Recall that the amygdala provides emotional emphasis (especially fear) to experiences that moves us to focus on risks and dangers and how to avoid them, and encodes memories for future ruminations. We would thus expect s/s and s/L individuals to avoid risks and to be hypervigilant to danger, and to be less inclined to engage in criminal behavior. We should also expect that populations with a great prevalence of individuals carrying the short allele to have a greater prevalence of anxiety and depression, as well as lower crime rates (these expectations are discussed below).

As indicated earlier, serotonin (and other monoamine neurotransmitters such as dopamine and norepinephrine) that escapes reuptake is degraded by the enzyme monoamine oxidase A (MAOA). The MAOA gene is a variable number of tandem repeats (VNTR) polymorphism repeating between two and five times, with the 3 (about 40%) and 4 (about 55%) repeats being the most common. These repeats produce low (MAOA-L) and high (MAOA-H) genotypes, respectively. The MAOA-H allele evinces high transcriptional activity compared to the MAOA-L allele, which ultimately promotes higher levels of serotonin in the synapse (Chiao & Ambady, 2007). A number of studies suggest that individuals with the low activity polymorphism are more likely to react to challenges with aggression (McDermott, 2009), and low serotonergic functioning is consistently and robustly related to impulsivity, one of the strongest correlates of criminal behavior known (Fishbein, 2001). Brain imaging studies have shown that MAOA-L men show greater activity in the amygdala and lower activity in the regulatory prefrontal areas during emotional arousal, thereby suggesting the emotional and cognitive channels that link MAOA-L to impulsive aggression (McDermott et al., 2009).

The landmark GxE (gene–environment interaction) study of MAOA of interest to criminologists is the longitudinal cohort study of Caspi and colleagues (2002). The environmental risk was verified child maltreatment, and the genetic risk was the MAOA gene. The dependent variables were a variety of antisocial outcomes, the most serious being a conviction for a violent crime by the age of 26. All self-reported measures were verified via official police and social service records, making this study a "gold standard" of reliability and validity. No main effects for MAOA were found, but there were strong GxE effects. Males with the

---

maltreatment and other real-life stressor and genes as predictors of behavior (GxE) are rare. If the s/s and s/L genotypes are only risk factors in the presence of environmental adversity, we should expect low (or even non-significant) effect sizes if GxE is not considered. GxE interaction involves the assumption that different genotypes will interact with and respond to their environments in different ways—that is, people are differentially sensitive to identical environmental influences. Genes influencing behavior and a myriad of other things (for example, IQ, weight, psychiatric conditions, height, personality, physical and psychological health) are always in interaction with the environment to produce the phenotype.

MAOA-L allele who were maltreated constituted only 12% of the cohort but were responsible for 44% of its violent convictions, the odds of such males having a violent crime conviction being 9.8 times greater than the odds of the MAOA-H non-maltreated males having one. The maltreatment/non-maltreatment groups did not differ significantly on MAOA activity, thus ruling out evocative gene–environment correlation (rGE) effects: low MAOA activity did not contribute to child maltreatment via children's evocative behavior because the two groups did not differ on the proportion carrying the risk allele.[3]

A meta-analysis of the MAOA maltreatment literature concluded that the interaction between MAOA and maltreatment is a statistically significant predictor of antisocial behavior across studies (Kim-Cohen et al., 2006). However, Widom and Brzustowicz (2006) found that while the MAOA-H allele buffered whites from the effects of childhood abuse and neglect on antisocial behavior later in life, it did not protect non-whites (mostly blacks and Hispanics) abused and neglected as children. The authors suggest that other environmental stressors may have negated the protective power of the genotype among non-whites. They also noted that non-whites had a higher percentage of MAOA-L individuals than whites.

Interestingly, it is estimated that one-third of males carry the low-activity version of the MAOA gene, which is located on the X sex chromosome. Because males only have one X chromosome, they only get one version of the gene (either high or low activity), making its effects easier to detect (Williams et al., 2009). Females, on the other hand, have two X chromosomes, so they are much more likely than males to get at least one high-activity allele of the MAOA gene. This may partially explain why females are far less prone to criminal behavior than males (see Chapter 10). The relatively high frequency of the MAOA-L allele suggests that it may confer adaptive benefits to its carriers in some environments (McDermott et al., 2009).

Serotonin plays a role in brain development prior to assuming its role as a neurotransmitter: "Serotonin acts as a growth factor during embryogenesis, and serotonin receptor activity forms a crucial part of the cascade of events leading to changes in brain structure" (Sodhi & Sanders-Bush, 2004:111). Thus, if 5-HT is not effectively metabolized, it could lead to toxic levels of 5-HT that could

---

3   The concept of gene–environment correlation (rGE) avers that genotypes and the environments they encounter are not random with respect to one another, and that genetic factors influence complex psychosocial traits by influencing the range of individuals' effective experiences. Evocative rGE refers to the way parents, siblings, teachers, peers, and all others in the social environment react to the individual on the basis of his or her evocative behavior. Active rGE refers to the niche-picking activities of individuals seeking experiences and environments compatible with their genetic proclivities. Passive rGE refers to the fact that parents provide their offspring with both genes for certain traits and environments conducive to their development. For instance, athletic parents will provide whatever genes are associated with athleticism to their offspring, plus an environment that will enable athletic skills to be practiced and honed.

result in aberrant brain development. Meyer-Lindenberg and colleagues (2006) examined various brain structures in over 200 individuals with either the low- or high-activity variant of the MAOA polymorphism using fMRI and found that compared to the MAOA-H variant subjects, MAOA-L subjects showed pronounced limbic volume reductions and hyper-responsiveness of the amygdala and hippocampus during emotional arousal. Among male subjects, there was impaired cingulate activity during cognitive tasks and a 14% increase in the volume of the orbitofrontal cortex, which the researchers attributed to deficient pruning, and thus impaired functioning. All these brain structures and mechanisms are related to impulsiveness and violence (Tancredi, 2009).

The Dopaminergic System

Figure 2.2 illustrates that dopamine underlies reward and pleasure, and in this sense we can see it as a motivator or "exciter" of behavior at the level of the organism, but at the molecular level it is generally considered an inhibitory neurotransmitter. However, depending on the type of receptor it binds with and dosage level, it is can also be excitatory. DA has many functions, particularly as a "motivator" of behavior, regulating movement, memory, emotion, and pleasure. Neurons whose principle neurotransmitter is DA are found primarily in the ventral tegmental area (VTA), the substantia nigra (SN), and the hypothalamus (see Figure 2.2). Both the VTA and the SN are involved in reward and addiction. In the hypothalamus, which links the nervous system to the endocrine system, DA functions as a neurohormone and a precursor of the hormones/neurotransmitters epinephrine and norepinephrine that serve a number of functions such as the regulation of "fight or flight" response. In the frontal lobes, DA regulates the flow of information coming in from other areas of the brain. Given DA's many vital functions, it is easy to see why scientists have been intrigued by its role in human behavioral regulation (Guo et al., 2010).

There are five subtypes of DA receptors, with the DRD2 and DRD4 subtypes being better understood than the other three subtypes (Keltikangas-Jarvinen & Salo, 2009). The dopamine D2 receptor gene (*DRD2*) is highly polymorphic, with most attention being focused on what is known as the *Taq*1A (or simply A1) single nucleotide polymorphism (SNP). This SNP[4] is the substitution of the nucleotide base thymine (in the A1 allele) for cytosine (in the A2 allele). Individuals homozygous for the A2 allele (A2/A2) have receptors with the highest binding potential for DA, A1/A1 homozygotes the lowest binding potential, and A1/A2 heterozygotes are intermediate (Hirvonen et al., 2004). The A1 allele is considered the risk allele, largely because it "is a contributor to the reward deficiency syndrome, which typifies people who need high levels of excitement

---

4   See note 1 in this chapter.

and stimulation to activate their reward system in the same capacity as those with normally functioning reward systems" (DeLisi et al., 2009:1,189).

The DRD2-A1 allele has been linked to many crime-related syndromes such as antisocial personality, ADHD, conduct disorder, serious and violent delinquency, and drug addiction (reviewed in DeLisi et al., 2009). D2 receptor antagonists (drugs that block dopamine receptors) have been used for decades to treat aggressive behavior and violent outbursts among psychotic and dementia patients, as well as for individuals with aggressive conduct disorders and borderline personality disorder (Almeida et al., 2005).

The other DA receptor of interest is *DRD4*, which is one of the most polymorphic genes known, coming in long and short forms of 48 bases that repeat between 2 and 11 times (Ding et al., 2002). The shorter the repeat, the more responsive the brain is to DA; the longer the repeat, the less responsive it is. Individuals with two or three repeats tend to be over-stimulated by events that most people (the 4Rs) find optimally stimulating, and thus they seek to tone them down or withdraw. Individuals with the 7R, especially if they are homozygous for this allele, are suboptimally aroused by those same events. Suboptimal arousal is subjectively experienced as boredom, and bored people seek to raise the level of stimuli to alleviate it, which sometimes results in criminal or other forms of antisocial behavior if paired with environments conducive to it (Raine, 2008).

As is the case with all neurotransmitters, when DA is released at the synapse it must be quickly removed after it has excited the postsynaptic neuron. The dopamine transporter gene DAT1 largely determines the magnitude and the duration of synaptic DA signaling by transporting DA back into the presynaptic knob for repackaging after it has excited downstream neurons. The DAT1 gene contains 7, 9, 10, and 11 repeat alleles, with the 9R and 10R being most common (Guo et al., 2007b). The 10R is more efficient in the reuptake process than the other major repeat (9R), which implies less DA in the synaptic cleft available for activation (Miller-Butterworth et al., 2008). Because DA activates pleasure centers in the nucleus accumbens (see Figure 2.2), its too rapid clearing from the synaptic cleft leads the person to seek more experiences that activate DA in order to experience normal levels of pleasure. These pleasures, legal or illegal, raise DA to levels which are conferred more easily with less behavioral activity on persons with less efficient reuptake transporters.

A number of studies have looked at the relationship of the DAT1-10R to risky sensation-seeking and/or antisocial behavior. For instance, Guo and colleagues (2007b) found that males who were homozygous for the 10R allele had 80–100% (depending on age category) more sex partners than males who were homozygous for the 9R version. Another study found that the DAT1-10R allele was significantly related to number of sex partners (a variable long known to be highly predictive of criminal activity, particularly psychopathy) and to antisocial behavior among a sample of 1,925 males aged 18–26 (Beaver, Wright & Walsh, 2008). Of course, we cannot consider an allele as common as the 10R to be a defective one. It is more reasonable to consider the 9R a "conservative" allele that confers lessened motivation to seek pleasure excessively or compulsively (Guo et al., 2007b).

The final polymorphism to be discussed is catechol-O-methyltransferase (COMT), which is the primary enzyme responsible for the degradation of dopamine. The COMT gene has a tri-nucleotide sequence *ATG* that produces the amino acid methionine and a *GTG* sequence that produces the amino acid valine. The SNP difference is not trivial. The valine variant degrades DA at about four times the rate of the methionine variant, which may lead val-val homozygotes to addictive pleasure-seeking (Beaver, 2009). The val-val polymorphism has been related to a variety of negative outcomes such as ADHD (Thapar et al., 2005), borderline personality disorder (Wagner et al., 2009), and schizophrenia (Lewandowski, 2007). Examining how the brain responds to these polymorphisms via fMRI scans conducted on 105 healthy male volunteers, Yacubian (2007) and colleagues monitored activity in the PFC and the ventral striatum area. They found that val-val subjects showed high levels of activity and met-met subjects showed blunted activity in anticipation of similar rewards (val-met heterozygotes intermediate). Studies such as this provide solid neurological and genetic evidence of the bases for the reward dominance theory of addiction to all kinds of things, including addiction to crime.

There are also a number of studies that have examined the interactive effects of the various polymorphisms because their effects are conditioned by other polymorphisms as well as by the environment. A study by Eisenberg and colleagues (2007) revealed that risk DRD2 allele (A1) had a statistically significant main effect on impulsiveness, but DRD4 risk allele (7R) did not. Additional analyses indicated that DRD2 and DRD4 risk alleles interacted to predict variation in impulsivity. Beaver and colleagues (2007) examined the same polymorphisms in a large data set and found that neither one had consistent main effects on antisocial behavior or conduct disorder, but all five models they explored that included the interaction of the two genes (GxG) produced statistically significantly results. Another study by DeLisi and colleagues (2008) found that after controlling for age, race, gender, and low self-control, both polymorphisms were independently predictive of the age of first criminal arrest, as was their interaction. However, this was only true for youths at low environmental risk for antisocial behavior, once again underlining the fact that we cannot fully understand gene effects without considering the environment, and that all known genetic and environmental risks should be included in studies of antisocial behavior.

Culture Matters

There is no doubt that genes and environments interact to produce effects in individuals, but what about interactions between macrocultural practices and genetics? The 5-HTTLPR and DRD4 polymorphisms have particularly interesting interactions with cultural practices over evolutionary time.

East Asian Americans (Chinese, Japanese, and Koreans) have been extolled as the "model minority" and seen as a hardworking, intelligent, successful, and law-abiding despite the horrendous treatment accorded them in the past. Although the "model minority" appellation has been challenged by some sociologists as a "myth," all objective measures of prosocial behavior place East Asians at the top of the list compared to other racial/ethnic groups (Chou, 2009), and all measures of criminal activity (arrest and imprisonment rates) place them at the bottom (Johnson & Betsinger, 2009). Even in the heyday of the Chicago school of social ecology, research in city after city showed that Asian Americans living in high crime areas had lower crime rates than any other racial/ethnic group living in the same areas (Shaw & McKay, 1972). Wilson and Herrnstein (1985:473) also pointed out that although a Chinese neighborhood in San Francisco in the 1960s had the highest rate of poverty and unemployment, the greatest percentage of substandard housing, as well as other disabilities, only five Chinese Americans were committed to prison in 1965 in the whole state of California. If we look beyond the United States to compare countries, we find that East Asian countries have lower crime rates than African, American, and European countries, and that wherever the three major races (Asians, whites, blacks) co-exist, Asians have the lowest offending rates, followed by whites, and then blacks (Eysenck & Gudjonsson, 1989; Rushton & Whitney, 2002; Walsh, 2009b).

Could the genetic polymorphisms we have looked at explain at least part of the intriguing racial/ethnic ordering of criminal and other forms of antisocial behavior? About 75% of East Asians carry at least one short allele of the 5-HTTLPR, compared with about 44% of Europeans (Chiao & Blizinsky, 2010), and only about 20% for persons of African descent carry it (Lotrich, Pollock & Ferrell, 2003). Although the 5-HTTLPR prevalence data are consistent with the hypothesis that high anxiety and harm avoidance are protective factors against crime, fewer East Asians than Europeans and European and African Americans are diagnosed with depression and anxiety disorders. To understand this anomaly (why a population with a high prevalence of an allele known to be associated with these disorders has a low prevalence of these disorders), we have to turn to gene–culture coevolution.

Fincher and colleagues (2008) note that historically high levels of environmental pathogens impose selective pressures on social behaviors on host populations. They suggest that behavioral manifestations of collectivism (as opposed to individualism) such as conformity, fear of outsiders, and ethnocentrism—all of which are aided by anxiety and harm avoidance—evolved as antipathogen defenses ("Stay away from strangers; they may be diseased"). They examined the hypothesis that individualism/collectivism scores would be associated with historically high prevalence of pathogens among over 100,000 individuals across 68 countries. They found individualism to be strongly related to historically low pathogen prevalence ($r = -0.69$), which obviously also means that collectivism is strongly related to high levels of historical pathogens.

Building on this work, Chiao & Blizinsky (2010) argued that behaviors that served an antipathogen function should serve an adaptive anti-psychopathology function as well, and that both functions are served in part by a high prevalence of the short allele of the 5-HTTLPR in the population. In their own words: "[C]ollectivist cultural values serve an adaptive function [by] reducing the probability of environmental stress, a known catalyst for negative affect, thus leading to genetic selection of the S allele within collectivist cultures" (2010:3). They also note that an active amygdala confers advantages in highly conformist groups because it serves as an early warning radar system, quickly alerting the individual to signs of disapproval in the words and facial expressions of other members of the group. Furthermore, members of collectivist cultures tend to define their self-worth in relation to the collectivity and their contribution to it, so that both success and failure are attributed to the collectivity. Thus, there is less self-blame for things that go wrong, and therefore less anxiety and depression despite the abundance of the short allele that is so salient in more individualist countries. Even in highly individualistic cultures such as the United States, individuals who belong to and are committed to collectivist-type organizations such as religious groups and who are otherwise at environmental risk (immigrants adjusting to a strange culture) for physical and mental health problems are buffered—a trouble shared is a trouble halved (Walsh, 1998).

Chiao and Blizinsky (2010) found that the most individualist countries (the US, UK, and Australia) had a lower prevalence of the short allele than all other countries, and China, Singapore, Korea, and Taiwan had the highest collectivist scores and the highest prevalence of the short allele. The correlation over all 29 countries for which genetic data were available between prevalence of the short allele and collectivism was a strong 0.70, $p < 0.0001$. Controlling for covariates such as GDP and the Gini index of income inequality only reduced the standardized beta to 0.61, $p < 0.002$. Thus, behaviors which would seem overly conformist and obsequious in individualist cultures appear to be adaptive in collectivist cultures. Chiao and Blizinsky (2010:6) conclude:

> Emphasizing social norms that increase social harmony and encourage giving social support to others, collectivism serves an "anti-psychopathology" function by creating an ecological niche that lowers the prevalence of chronic life stress, protecting genetically susceptible individuals from environmental pathogens known to trigger negative emotions and psychopathology.

Turning now to gene–culture interplay and the 7repeat allele of the DRD4, worldwide studies find that 65.1% of individuals have the 4R allele, 19.2% have the 7R, 8.8% the 2R, and the remaining 6.9% have one of the other rare repeats. There is strong evidence that the DRD4-7R allele is a young mutation that arose about 40,000 years ago and has been positively selected for (Arcos-Burgos & Acosta, 2007). Eisenberg and colleagues (2008) note that the emergence of the 7R mutation roughly coincided with the time when the first signs of rudimentary complex horticultural/agricultural societies began to emerge, and with the time when humans were exploring and expanding widely around the planet. A mutation that is positively selected means that behaviors underlain by the allele in question must have had some positive effect on the bearer's survival and reproductive success. Thus, some endophenotypes (impulsivity, restlessness, aggression, novelty-seeking) associated with this allele and with the criminality phenotype must have been selectively adaptive at certain times and in certain environments.

None other than Charles Darwin suggested one such adaptive function when he wrote almost 150 years ago: "Restless men who will not follow any steady occupation—and this relic of barbarism is a great check to civilisation—emigrate to newly-settled countries, where they prove useful pioneers" (1871:172). Darwin's observation received strong support from a study of 2,320 individuals from 39 different racial/ethnic groups which found that the percentage of 7R version ranged from near zero in populations that have remained in the same geographic region for the last 30,000 years (for example, Han Chinese, Yemeni Jews) to an average of 63% (more than three times the worldwide average) in six migratory populations of South American Indians. (Ding et al., 2002). The reported correlation between percentage of 7Rs in a population and geographic distance from the original parent population was an impressive 0.85.

We would expect individuals in groups that elect to migrate from the parent population and explore the greater world to exhibit a greater need for excitement than the average person in the parent population. To the extent that the need is a function of the 7R allele, it should be well represented among groups with a reputation for boldness, irritableness, boredom-proneness, and fierceness. Commenting on the 7R's variable distribution around the world, Harpending and Cochran (2002:12) state:

> It is probably no accident that two of the best known ethnographies of the twentieth century are titled "The Harmless People," about the !Kung who have few or no 7R alleles, and the "Fierce People," about the Yanomamo with a high frequency of 7R.

Conclusion

In this chapter we have examined a little of the neurochemistry that bubbles along in our brains. We have discussed genetic polymorphisms of the genes that produce this chemistry, which unfortunately reminds some of the depressing accusations of genetic determinism. Let us emphasize: *The power of genes takes nothing away from the power of the environment; it underlines it.* Genes certainly modulate environmental effects, but just as certainly, environments modulate genetic effects. Genes and environments are the heads and tails of our existence as they perform their exquisite *pas de deux* in the brain. As Matt Ridley (2003:6) points out:

Genes are not puppet masters, nor blueprints. They may direct the construction of the body and brain in the womb, but they set about dismantling and rebuilding what they have made almost at once in response to experience. They are both the cause and consequence of our actions. Somehow the adherents of the "nurture" side of the argument have scared themselves silly at the power and inevitability of genes, and missed the greatest lesson of all: the genes are on our side.

Far from being molecular puppetmasters, Colin Badcock (2000:71) asserts that our genes "positively guarantee" human freedom and agency. Likewise, because so many things that we do in life affect the expression of our genes, Randy Jirtle asserts that: "Epigenetics[5] introduces the concept of free will into our idea of genetics" (in Watters, 2006:34). And neuro scientist Steven Rose writes: "Individually and collectively we have the ability to construct our own futures, albeit in circumstances not of our own choosing. Thus it is that our biology makes us free" (2001:6).

Badcock, Jirtle, and Rose are able to make such a bold statement because, unlike our environments, our genes belong to us; they are *ours*. They are what make us uniquely ourselves, and thus resistant to environmental influences which grate against our natures. This view of humanity is more respectful of human dignity than the view that we are putty in the hands of fickle environments arranged by others.

---

5   Epigenetics is the study of environmental effects on gene expression, and will be discussed in later chapters.

Chapter 3
Brain Development, Abuse-neglect, and Criminality

The Importance of Early Experience

In Chapter 1 we discussed the plasticity of the brain and how it was designed by natural selection to physically capture environmental experiences in its neural networks. Environments, good or bad, conspire with our genes to mold our brains into their adult form. The delayed development of the human brain compared to non-human animals provides us with many windows of opportunity, but unfortunately it also provides for windows of vulnerability. Social scientists have long informed us that the negative experiences of childhood such as abuse and neglect can have negative behavioral consequences later in life, but they never told us why except in the most general and nebulous sense. If negative early circumstances and experiences constitute an elevated risk for antisocial behavior, we would like to know why at a fundamental neurobiological level: "If deprivation causes or promotes behavioral maladaptation, it has to do so through its influence on the central nervous system" (Wright et al., 2009:85).

According to neurobiologist Bruce Perry (2002), there are three key brain systems relevant to the ultimate evolutionary concerns of all sexually reproducing species. They are neural mechanisms that facilitate (1) responses to threats to well-being, (2) the protection and nurturing of the young, and (3) mate selection and reproduction. Although mechanism 3 is sexier than the others, it is not of particular concern to criminologists, so we unfortunately limit ourselves to discussing mechanisms 1 and 2.

There are eminent criminologists who aver that childhood experiences deserve no special place in the pantheon of causes of later behavior (for example, Sampson & Laub, 2005). We take strong issue with such an assertion. In our earliest years, when our brains are most pliable, environmental experiences chisel neural networks in ways that are not easily altered. Later experiences (Sampson and Laub's "turning points," such as educational, job, and marriage opportunities) are interpreted differently by different neural networks because their influence is channeled along the pathways laid down during childhood by experiences that can be taken all the way back to the womb. The nineteenth-century romantic poet and novelist Samuel Taylor Coleridge once wrote that: "The history of man for the nine months preceding his birth would, probably, be far more interesting and contain events of greater moment than for all the three score and ten years that follow it" (in Hepper, 2005:474). Turning Coleridge from poet to scientist, he is saying that the intrauterine environment helps to place us on a developmental trajectory that later experiences may find difficult to derail.

Prenatal Brain Development and Teratogenic Insults:
Abuse Begins in the Womb

It is important here to again emphasize that a range of mature phenotypes can arise from any given genotype depending on different developmental conditions. Brain development begins about three weeks after conception with the forming of the neural tube. From a single precursor cell (the fertilized egg), about 250,000 brain cells are produced every minute from immature cells called neuroblasts (Toga, Thompson & Sowell, 2006). These neuroblasts sprout axons with antennae that reach out to make connections with other neurons to form the various parts of the brain. As neurons are born, they must differentiate according to where in the brain they are to reside and what functions they are to perform once they get there. Thus, neurons migrate from their birthplace to their eventual home, and it is during this migratory phase of neural maturation that the brain is most vulnerable to perturbations (Prayer et al., 2006). Newly minted neurons must be able to recognize the correct path and make the correct connections in order to perform their allotted functions, and they do this guided by glial cell scaffolds and molecular messengers. Once neuron migration and connections are accomplished, the ruthless process of paring back their numbers begins, with only about half of them surviving. Those that win the battle for survival are those able to secure a supply of a class of chemicals known as neurotrophins, whose function is to stimulate and guide neurogenesis. Neurons that fail to access these life-sustaining chemicals activate their internal destruct programs and "commit suicide" (apoptosis).

The molecules informing the processes of recognition, connection, and paring are susceptible to being confused by alien molecules in their microenvironment. This confusion may become so garbled that neurons may be sent to the wrong neighborhood or be instructed to prematurely self-destruct. These alien chemicals are known collectively as teratogens, which are defined as any exogenous substance that can disrupt the development of an embryo or fetus and result in some form of birth defect. The most common of these teratogenic chemicals are associated with alcohol introduced to the embryo/fetus by its mother's drinking.

There are a number of neurological disorders that result from pregnant women drinking alcohol known as *fetal alcohol spectrum disorders* (FASD), the most serious of which is *fetal alcohol syndrome* (FAS). FAS has a number of readily identifiable physical abnormalities associated with it, but developmental behavioral scientists are most concerned with the effects of prenatal alcohol exposure on the migration and hook-up of neurons in brain areas such as the frontal lobes, amygdala, hippocampus, hypothalamus, and on the serotonergic system (Goodlett, Horn & Zhou, 2005). Fetal alcohol exposure also interferes with the myelination process (Noble, Mayer-Proschel & Miller, 2005), and is the foremost preventable cause of intellectual impairment in the world (O'Leary, 2004).

The prevalence of FASD in the United States is around 1% of live births, and for full-blown FAS about 0.33 per 1,000 (Manning & Hoyme, 2007). It is found in all ethnic and racial groups, but African American children are five times more likely to exhibit FAS than white children, and American Indian/Alaska Native children are 16 times more likely (Sokol, Delaney-Black & Nordstrom, 2003). Asian American children have the lowest rate of FAS (Meaney & Miller, 2003). Large social class differences are also found. A review of numerous studies by the National Institute of Alcohol Abuse and Alcoholism (May & Gossage, 2008) found a ratio of 13:1 between middle-class (a rate of about 0.26 per 1,000) and lower-class (about 3.4 per 1,000) rates of FAS.

The traits or behaviors associated with FAS include low IQ, hyperactivity, impulsiveness, ADHD, poor social, emotional, and moral development, and a highly elevated probability of alcoholism (Jacobson & Jacobson, 2002). Each item in this parade of deficits is linked to high levels of antisocial behavior and criminal offending independent of FAS, but FAS individuals are almost always saddled with them all. FAS individuals are not good candidates for acquiring the cognitive and emotional skills needed to gain a stake in prosocial behavior such as obtaining a good education, a good job, and acquiring prosocial friends and marriage mates.

Not all children exposed to fetal alcohol develop observable physical symptoms; much depends on when they were exposed, how much and how often they were exposed, and on their mothers' constitutions. Nevertheless, children who are exposed to fetal alcohol who do not evidence the morphological characteristics of FAS still experience many difficulties, and are at elevated risk for antisocial behavior. A review of 30 studies of children of alcoholic parents found that all studies showed a significant relationship between having alcoholic parents and criminal and antisocial behavior regardless of a FASD diagnosis (Ellis & Walsh, 2000). This probably indexes gene–environment correlation mechanisms in which parents provide offspring with a suite of genes conducive to antisocial behavior and an environment (for example, poverty, poor parenting, abuse-neglect) that are conducive to the development of antisocial behavior.

Other Teratogenic Substances

There are many other teratogens that have similar effects on neuron development and migration, such as those associated with illicit drugs, because whatever the mother ingests, so does her embryo/fetus. A common risk factor is maternal smoking. Maternal smoking has its primary risk in fetal intermittent hypoxia (intermittent reduction of oxygen available to the fetus due to vasoconstriction that may lead to cell death) (Zechel et al., 2005). Cohort studies (for example, Brennan, Grekin & Sarnoff, 1999) consistently find that maternal smoking during pregnancy predicts criminal behavior in fetally exposed offspring independent of other risk factors. A review of a number of such studies found log of the odds ratios (LODs) ranging between 1.5 and 4.0 for fetal tobacco-exposed individuals versus non-exposed individuals for various forms of antisocial behavior across diverse contexts and independent of other factors such as maternal SES and IQ (Wakschlag et al., 2002).

It has been estimated that as many as 375,000 infants born each year have been exposed to cocaine in utero, and that in some inner-city hospitals as many as half of pregnant women test positive for it (Mayes et al., 1995). A large study of neonates born in inner-city hospitals in four large American cities who were and who were not exposed to cocaine in utero found that while cocaine exposure does not result in the anatomical problems associated with FAS, it does result in serious central and peripheral nervous system symptoms (Bauer et al., 2005). Cocaine-exposed infants were 42 times more likely to have a diagnosis of hepatitis, and 15 times more likely to have a diagnosis of syphilis—statistics that starkly reflect their mothers' antisocial lifestyles and brutal lack of responsibility. Comparing the mothers of cocaine-exposed infants (n = 717) to non-exposed infants (n = 7,442) it was found that only 10.1% of the mothers of cocaine-exposed infants were married (versus 40.4% of mothers of non-exposed infants), 50.2% had less than a high school education (versus 28.7%), and only 22.7% worked in the previous year (versus 53.6%). In addition, 81.8% of the mothers of cocaine-exposed infants also smoked during pregnancy (versus 19.7% of the mothers of non-cocaine-exposed infants).

Lead and the Brain

Exposure to noxious substances in the environment outside the womb, such as lead, over which the mother has no control, has negative effects on children's brain, manifested most clearly in the reduction of IQ. The IQ decrement per one unit increase in μg/dl (micrograms per deciliter of blood) of lead is an average of 0.5 points (Koller et al., 2004). The main source of lead exposure today is lead dust from paint in older houses, which of course means that they tend to be situated in the poorest neighborhoods and inhabited by the poorest people. Toxic levels of lead (>40 μg/dl) distort enzymes, interfere with the development of the endogenous opiate system, disrupt the dopamine system, and reduce serotonin and MAOA levels (Wright et al., 2008).

An fMRI study found that brain gray matter was inversely correlated with mean childhood lead concentrations in mostly black young adults taken from the longitudinal Cincinnati Lead Study (Cecil et al., 2008). The mean childhood blood lead concentration of this sample was 13.3 μg/dl, which is well below toxic levels but far in excess of the 2006 average of 1.5 μg/dl for the general population (Bellinger, 2008). Although the gray matter lost to lead exposure was relatively small (about 1.2%), it was concentrated in the frontal lobes and the anterior cingulate cortex, which we know are vital behavior-moderating areas of the brain responsible for executive functioning and mood regulation.

Another sample (n = 250; 90% black; mean age 22.5) from the same Cincinnati Lead Study examined the relationship between childhood blood lead and verified criminal arrests. The mean number of arrests for the males in the sample who were ever arrested was 5.2. The main finding of this study was that after adjusting for relevant covariates for every 5 μg/dl lead increase there was an increase in the probability of arrest for a violent crime of about 50% (Wright et al., 2008). There are a number of other studies that have found weak to moderate effects of lead exposure on crime, particularly violent crime (reviewed in Needleman, 2004).

Lead competes with calcium for absorption in the body, so if children do not receive adequate dietary calcium, it absorbs lead instead. This is important because blood lead levels are associated with a calcium absorption gene called the vitamin D receptor gene (VDR) (Chakraborty et al., 2008). A certain polymorphism of the VDR (an enzyme known as Fok1) makes the absorption of calcium more efficient for its carriers, which is beneficial in the presence of adequate dietary calcium, but not in its absence. Unfortunately, these polymorphisms are more prevalent among blacks (who tend to live in areas where lead is most abundant) than among whites or Asians (Chakraborty et al., 2008; Haynes et al., 2003). If this polymorphism renders calcium absorption easier, and given lead's ability to mimic calcium, lead is also more easily absorbed. This creates a GxE interaction in which African Americans will tend to absorb more lead than similarly exposed members of other racial groups.

The Importance of Affectionate Bond Formation on the Brain

The importance of bond-formation and the consequences of not forming them illustrates each of Tinbergen's Four Questions introduced in Chapter 1. David Rowe (1992:402) has remarked that "the affection dimension of child rearing appears to pull in more correlates with child behavior than any other dimension." Human infants are adapted to demand the formation of strong affectionate bonds with their caregivers via contact stimuli because such bonds are a species-expectable feature of their nature, and in their absence the relevant synaptic connections are pruned (Glaser, 2000). As Cirulli, Berry, and Alleva (2003:74) put it: "Since the mutual regulation occurring between mother and infant can shape the organization of the infant's brain, disruption in the mother-infant relationship could affect brain plasticity." They go on to discuss how such disruption will negatively affect the formation of affectionate social bonds. There are many negative outcomes associated with the failure to form such bonds, including criminal and other forms of antisocial behavior (Lee & Hoaken, 2007). But why is affectionate bonding so important for humans?

The trajectory toward selective evolutionary pressures for the formation of affectionate bonds in humans was probably precipitated by simultaneous selection pressures posed by bipedalism and rapidly (in an evolutionary sense) increasing cranial size. As humans evolved bigger and smarter brains due to the demands of cultural living, hominid cranial capacity (measured in cubic centimeters—cc) increased from *Australopithecus* (M = 450 cc) to *Homo erectus* (M = 900 cc) to *Homo sapiens* (M = 1,350 cc) (Bailey & Geary, 2009). Because hominid female pelves were probably shaped by natural selection to satisfy upright posture and bipedalism (thus narrowing the birth canal) more than for increased fetal cranial size, an evolutionary conflict arose between the obstetric and postural requirements of females (Van As, Fieggen & Tobias, 2007). This resulted in extreme birthing difficulties which still persist today to a lesser extent.

The evolutionary solution to the obstetrics/posture conflict was for infants to be born at ever earlier stages of development as cerebral mass increased. Human infants experience 25% brain growth inside the womb, and 75% growth outside the womb (Perry, 2002). This means that human infants are extremely dependent on caregivers for an extended period, and that the extreme incompleteness of their brains demands and assures a greater role for the extra-uterine environment in its development than is true of any other species. The period of brain growth in the womb is called uterogestation, and the period outside the womb is called exterogestation (Van As, Fieggen, & Tobias, 2007). A species burdened with extremely altricial young must have experienced strong selection pressures for mechanisms designed to assure the young will be nurtured for an extended period. Ashley Montagu (1981:93) stresses the importance of a "continuous symbiotic relationship between mother and child" across the two gestation periods, and calls this relationship *love*. He goes on to add: "It is, in a very real and not in the least paradoxical sense, even more necessary to love than it is to live, for without love there can be no healthy growth or development, no real life." Modern science tells us that love confers enormous benefits in terms of healthy functioning in human beings through its impact on central and peripheral nervous system functioning as well as the negative consequences of not receiving it during the earliest period of life (Esch & Stefano, 2005). Whether we call it love, attachment, or bonding, it is the "foundational phase of infant brain development" because it "deeply marks the brain neurobiologically" (Narvaez & Vaydich, 2008:301).

Breastfeeding as a Proximate Template of Affectionate Bonding

The ultimate source of the human mother–infant bonding process is selection for genes underlying empathy (De Waal, 2008). The proximate mechanisms of mother–infant bonds of affection are probably organized by the birthing process and consolidated by mother–infant interaction during the immediate postpartum period. Oxytocin (OT), a neuropeptide that has been called the "cuddle chemical" that "calms and comforts," underlies these mechanisms (MacDonald & MacDonald, 2010). OT is synthesized in the hypothalamus, stimulated by events such as the birthing process, infant distress, and breastfeeding, and is conveyed to infants through breast milk and contact (Nair & Young, 2006). Breastfeeding combines the panoply of sight, sound, smell, touch, and the tangible evidence in the mother's arms that affirms her womanhood, and stimulates the release of OT, which intensifies the warm feeling that released it in a felicitous feedback loop. The OT released by breastfeeding is related to mothers' reduced sensitivity to environmental stressors, which allows for greater sensitivity to the infant. Lactating mothers show significantly fewer stress responses to infant stimuli, as determined by skin conductance and cardiac response measures, than non-lactating mothers, and the OT-generated sense of emotional warmness motivates significantly greater desire to pick up their infants in response to infant-presented stimuli (Hiller, 2004).

Breastfeeding generally reflects a mother's desire to care for and be close to her infant. The nutritional needs of infants and toddlers were provided throughout the history of the species almost exclusively by breast milk. Only in the twentieth century did the water supply became safe enough to allow for bottle feeding (Huber, 2008). One of the many positive effects of prolonged breastfeeding was demonstrated in a large study of 13,889 Belarusian breastfeeding mothers. A random half of these mothers were given incentives that encouraged prolonged breastfeeding, while the remaining half continued their usual maternity hospital and outpatient care. When the children were assessed six years later, it was found that the children breastfed for a prolonged period (>6 months) had a mean IQ almost six points higher than the control group children, and received higher academic ratings from teachers (Kramer et al., 2008). The experimental design allowed researchers to measure breastfeeding effects on IQ without biasing confounds such as the positive relationship between mothers' IQ and the probability of prolonged breastfeeding.

Kramer and colleagues could not determine whether the breastfeeding–IQ relationship was due to the constituents of breast milk or mother–child interactions and the warm kin-to-skin contact experienced during breastfeeding, or both. Tactile stimulation of infants confers enormous benefits on the infant, and copious amounts are recommended by physicians for the optimal brain development of low-birth weight infants and infants who have suffered a head injury. The positive effects of tactile stimulation on brain development are probably due to its ability to release the quiescent features of OT and the reward features of dopamine (Adams & Moghaddam, 2000).

Breastfeeding and the tactile stimulation accompanying it is an experience-expected feature of human brain development, and the failure of the infant to experience it may be viewed as the deprivation of important developmental input. The neuroscience literature is replete with studies documenting abnormal brain connectivity in children subjected to severe early socioemotional deprivation (for example, Chugani et al., 2001; Eluvathingal et al., 2006). These connection abnormalities tend to be primarily between the higher cognitive areas such as the PFC and "emotional" areas such as the amygdala, which we shall see in Chapter 11 is the primary neurological hallmark of the psychopath. The lack of frequent bodily contact with mother has to be interpreted by the infant's experience-expected mechanisms as abandonment, because the infant can only "think" with its skin. The infant's contact comfort derived from the sensitive responses of mother (and other caregivers) during times of duress tells it that everything's OK, "She's there for me, I'm safe, all's right in my world." If this contact input is not forthcoming, the infant's underspecified and miswired circuits interpret otherwise.

Nutritionally, mothers' milk confers many benefits, not the least of which is its immunological benefits. In terms of IQ enhancement, a study of 3,000 British and New Zealand children born in the early 1970s and IQ-tested in the 1990s found that subjects who were breastfed scored on average 6–7 points higher on IQ tests than non-breastfed subjects (Caspi et al., 2007). This was only true for breastfed subjects who had at least one copy of the C (cytosine) base variant of the fatty acid desaturase (FADS2) gene (90% of the sample) that codes for an enzyme that converts fatty acids into two polyunsaturated acids that accumulate in the infant brain in the early months after birth. There was no IQ increase noted for breastfed children homozygous for the G (guanine) base allele of the FADS2 gene. This is another example of gene–environment interaction, in that there was no difference in the average scores of C versus G allele individuals who were not breastfed (the gene made no difference alone), and breastfeeding made no difference for individuals with two copies of the G allele.

Unfortunately, the literature consistently shows a marked downward gradient in the rates of breastfeeding as maternal IQ, income, education, and occupational status fall. Children of lower-class women are thus more likely to be deprived of important evolutionarily experience-expected input (Glaser, 2000). A random sample of 10,519 mothers in California found that the odds of breastfeeding for the women in the highest income category was 3.65 times the odds of the women in the lowest income category (Heck et al., 2006). Data from the Department of Health and Human Services National Immunization Program survey (2004) reveal that in 2001 only 29.3% of black infants were breastfeeding at six months versus 43.2% of whites and 53.7% of Asians.

There are many studies of orphanage-reared children that bring home the importance of early tactile stimulation for developing healthy attachment. Perhaps the most interesting is one that looked at neglected (in the form of the absence of contact comfort) Romanian orphans who had been in orphanages an average of 16.6 months before being fostered to American families. After being with their American families for an average of 34.6 months, they showed significantly lower base levels of oxytocin and another important neuropeptide called vasopressin compared with a control group of American children reared by their biological parents (Wismer Fries et al., 2005). The orphans also showed significantly lower levels of these peptides after experimental exposure to the kinds of interaction with their foster mothers that normally increases their levels. In effect, these children had been reared during a period in life without the frequent tactile comfort that is an experience-expected feature of human rearing. This deprivation leads to the disruption of the neuropeptide circuitry, making it difficult to form secure relationships with caregivers and social bonds with the wider society.

Toxic Stress and the Brain

Abusive and neglectful treatment from caregivers almost certainly indexes a deficit in bond-formation. Abuse and neglect, while both painful, are different (although they tend to co-occur) and have different effects on the developing brain. Abuse is a discrete event that influences brain development at experience-*dependent* stages. That is, entrenched voltage-dependent neuronal pathways will channel subsequent experiences, even less traumatic ones, along the same pathways, further strengthening them. On the other hand, neglect is a feature of the ongoing caregiver–child relationship that deprives young children of their physical, social, and emotional needs and affectionate input in times of experience-*expected* stages of organizational maturation of the brain (Twardosz & Lutzker, 2010). As Perry and Pollard (1998:36) point out: "Experience in adults *alters* the *organized* brain, but in infants and children it *organizes* the *developing* brain." Brains organized by abuse and neglect will tend to see future events negatively, even neutral or positive ones, because they will have been relayed along the same neural pathways etched out by those early organizational events. As we have seen, well-grooved synaptic pathways established in early life become a "processing template" and are more resistant to detours than pathways laid down later in life. These pathways have been stabilized, and thus they become internal representations of how the world works which subconsciously intrude into our transactions with others across the lifespan.

Children are fairly resilient creatures if reared in the normal range of family environments, but tragically, some children are born into family environments that are far beyond the pale of species-expected environments. Children in these environments are subjected to more noise, crowding, family and neighbor conflict and instability, ambient pollution, abuse and neglect, and numerous other stress-inducing problems than are the vast majority of children. Such stressors are endemic in many inner-city environments in which children simply find themselves and have done nothing to create. Relentless stress can alter neurobiological mechanisms in such a way as to put those who experience them at an elevated risk for all kinds of antisocial behavior.

Stress is a state of psychophysiological arousal experienced when an organism perceives a challenge to its well-being. Stress is an inevitable part of life; it energizes and focuses us, and without it we would seriously handicapped in our ability to successfully cope with life's inevitable challenges. Adults who experienced average levels of stress during childhood most likely possess brains calibrated to better navigate the travails of life than those who were been assiduously protected from almost all stress. People differ in their ability to manage stress for genetic and experiential reasons that have been captured in their brain's circuitry (Perry, 2002).

While stress is functional, toxic and protracted stress damages vital brain areas responsible for memory storage and behavioral regulation, such as the amygdala, hippocampus, and PFC (Narvaez & Vaydich, 2008). Frequent activation of stress response mechanisms during childhood may lead to the dysregulation of these mechanisms, and subsequently to a number of psychological, emotional, and behavioral problems (Gunnar & Quevedo, 2007).

The stress response is mediated by two separate but interrelated systems controlled by the hypothalamus: the ANS and the HPA axis. When an organism perceives a threat to its well-being, the hypothalamus—the center of the endocrine world—directs the ANS to mobilize the body for vigorous action aided by pumping out the hormone epinephrine (adrenaline). When the organism perceives that the threat is over, the system restores the body to homeostasis.

Because the HPA axis response occurs through changes in gene expression, it is slower than the ANS response and lasts longer (Gunnar & Quevedo, 2007). The HPA axis is activated in situations that call for a prolonged rumination rather than the visceral immediacy of the ANS's preparation for fight or flight in the face of imminent threat. The HPA axis response begins with the hypothalamus feeding various chemical messages to the pituitary gland, which leads to further chemical products that stimulate the adrenal glands to release the hormone cortisol. The brain is a major target for cortisol, which, unlike the epinephrine which is part of ANS activity, is able to cross the blood–brain barrier (Van Voorhees & Scarpa, 2004). Cortisol is the fuel that energizes our coping mechanisms by increasing vigilance and activity, and is therefore functional within the normal range.[1]

Frequent HPA axis arousal may lead to upward or downward dysregulation of arousal mechanisms. Upward dysregulation is the result of overproduction of cortisol, or hypercortisolism. Hypercortisolism leads to anxiety and depressive disorders, and is most likely to be found in females who have been maltreated, because females activate significantly more neural systems associated with emotional stress and with encoding it into long-term memory than males (Van Voorhees & Scarpa, 2004). Females will thus have emotional experiences more readily available for rumination than males, and the constant pondering of those experiences increases their valence over time. Males can, of course, also develop hypercortisolism, but females are more likely to under similar circumstances. Hypercortisolism suggests a failure of the system to adjust to chronic environmental stressors, and leads to internalizing problems such as chronic depression and post-traumatic stress disorder (PTSD).

Hypocortisolism, on the other hand, suggests an adaptive downward adjustment to chronic stress, and leads to externalizing problems. It is adaptive because frequent stressful encounters habituate the organism's HPA axis to them,

---

1   There are differences between neurotransmitters and hormones that should be noted. Neurotransmitters communicate only with brain cells, whereas hormones influence every cell in the body, including brain cells. Neurotransmitters only travel across synapses; hormones travel in the bloodstream and effect target cells more slowly.

and as a consequence it does not react to further encounters as it had previously. Habituation means that both HPA axis and ANS response mechanisms have become blunted. Hypocortisolism has been linked to early onset of aggressive antisocial behavior (McBurnett et al., 2000), to criminal behavior in general (Ellis, 2005), and is more likely to be found in maltreated males than in females (Van Goozen et al., 2007). A study by O'Leary, Loney, and Eckel (2007) found that males high in psychopathic traits lacked stress-induced increases in cortisol displayed by males low in psychopathic traits. Blunted arousal means a low level of anxiety and fear—something quite useful for those committing or contemplating committing a crime. Note that while *chronically* high levels of cortisol are associated with aggression inhibition, *acutely* elevated levels and/or *chronic* extreme low levels of cortisol also tend to promote aggression (Van Goozen et al., 2007).

The development of hypocortisolism is an example of the process of allostasis, which literally means "to achieve physiological stability through change." Allostasis describes the body's attainment of equilibrium by *altering* the acceptable range of physiological set points to adapt to extreme acute stress or chronic stress rather than returning them to their previous state, as in homeostasis. According to Goldstein and Kopin (2007:111): "Adaptations involving allostasis to cope with real, simulated, or imagined challenges are determined by genetic, developmental and previous experiential factors. While they may be effective for a short interval, over time the alterations may have cumulative adverse effects." Frequent allostatic responses is termed allostatic load, which Goldstein and Kopin (2007) liken to having the heating and cooling systems running simultaneously—a situation guaranteed to hasten the wear and tear of both systems, and eventual breakdown. Likewise, Massey (2004) points out that chronically elevated cortisol also interferes with the normal operation of glutamate, the most common excitatory neurotransmitter that is vital in the formation of synaptic connections and learning. Children exposed to chronic stress will thus have fewer cognitive resources regardless of their genetic potential.

In his Presidential address to the American Sociological Association, Douglas Massey made a plea for social scientists to stop ignoring the interaction of biological and social factors if they wish a deeper understanding of how the stresses attending their favored causes of criminal behavior (poverty, abuse-neglect, and so on) manifest themselves in the actual structure and functioning of the brain. Massey (2004:22) wrote:

> By understanding and modeling the interaction between social structure and allostasis, social scientists should be able to discredit explanations of racial differences in terms of pure heredity. In an era when scientific understanding is advancing rapidly through interdisciplinary efforts, social scientists in general— and sociologists in particular—must abandon the hostility to biological science and incorporate its knowledge and understanding into their work.

Meaney (2010) asks why nature would configure a process that changes gene expression in ways that are clearly pathological from a health point of view. Allostatic load clearly reduces survival probability, but fitness is defined by reproductive success, not survival. Survival means nothing if it does not enhance fitness, and any health problems arising from allostasis have their greatest impact after optimal reproductive age. Meaney (2010:63) further notes that reduced parental investment may even be adaptive: "Environmental adversity decreases parental investment in the offspring and thus alters phenotypic development. And there is evidence that these phenotypic effects are adaptive with adverse settings." That is, offspring use parental signals subconsciously as forecasts of the type of environments they are likely to encounter in their later years, and thus their development is biased in the forecast direction via dynamic epigenetic modifications.

Epigenetics of Nurturing

Almost all the human studies of the effects of toxic stress and the role of the nurturing environment in calibrating the brain to respond adaptively to it are either retrospective correlative studies or "experiments of nature," such as the orphanage studies. True experiments can only be conducted with non-human animals. Social scientists tend to be suspicious of animal research applied to humans, correctly pointing out that culture has a huge affect on human behavior, but the effects of cultural practices on the developmental biology of the brain is precisely what this chapter is about. Biologists do not study fruit flies, rats, or monkeys because they have a consuming interest in improving the lot of such species. Rather, they hope to learn from them something useful about humans. Animal models have proven pivotal to our understanding of all sorts of human physical and psychological problems. Once a biological mechanism has been demonstrated in one species, it is almost always found to be applicable to others (Ridley, 2003). Nature is parsimonious; she does not create an entirely new genome every time a new species branches off.

One of the best of these animal studies of interest to criminologists is that of Weaver and colleagues (2004), who examined the molecular bases and behavioral consequences of different levels of maternal care among rats. The level of rat nurturing is indexed by the level of pup licking and grooming (LG) and arch-back nursing (ABN). Examining high- and low-level-nurtured pups as adults, the offspring of high LG/ABN mothers had lower HPA axis responses to stress (as well as exhibiting a number of other behaviors such as better memory and learning abilities) and were generally more socially adept than offspring of low LG/ABN mothers. A portion of the pups from each inbred stain was then cross fostered (high LG/ABN mothers fostering pups born to low LG/ABN mothers, and vice versa) to determine how much of this mother/offspring correlation is attributable to shared genes and how much to the nurturing experience. It was found that in adulthood, cross-fostered pups exhibited temperaments and behaviors resembling their adopted mother more than their biological mother, indicating that early nurturing experiences have a profound impact on adult patterns of rat behavior.

Weaver and colleagues (2004) found that high levels of LG/ABN reduce methylation of glucocorticoid receptor genes (GRs) that determine the number of hippocampal GRs an animal will have. This is called an epigenetic effect.[2] Unmethylated genes produce more receptors, which results in better feedback control of the HPA axis and greater control of HPA stress response. GRs modulate the expression of a variety of neuronal genes, and are vital to neuronal homeostasis, and thus to mental health. The behavior of rat mothers thus led to similar genetic modifications in pups, regardless of whether pups were the mother's offspring or cross-fostered, and that these alterations resulted in stable phenotypic differences in adulthood. However, because rats mature much faster than humans, their developmental sensitive periods are much shorter. The differences generated by maternal behavior in this study occurred only in the first week of life, after which maternal behavior had no discernible effects. Maternal effects on the brains of their offspring last many years.

It is difficult to look at the epigenetics of nurturing in humans because brain tissue must be examined directly, and the only way to do this is postmortem. An autopsy study conducted by McGowan et al. (2009) examined epigenetic differences in 12 male suicide victims with a history of abuse with 12 male suicide victims without such a history and 12 male controls who died of other causes. Tissue samples were taken from the hippocampus, where the neuron-specific glucocorticoid receptor (NR3C1) is most active. The receptor sites of abused suicide victims were found to be heavily methylated at the glucocorticoid promoter region's DNA, thus the protein is prevented from docking. No such pattern of methylation was found among the 12 suicide victims who were not abused or among the 12 non-suicide controls. This means that in humans as well as rats, poor and abusive maternal care results in the inability of the HPA axis to turn itself down. Consequently, the HPA axis is constantly on high alert, leading the organism to behave as if stressed under non-stressful conditions.

---

2   Methylation occurs when an enzyme called DNA methyltransferase attaches a group of atoms called a methyl group to a cytosine base which prevents the translation of DNA into messenger ribonucleic acid (mRNA transports the genetic instructions from the nucleus of the cell to the cell's cytoplasm where the protein the gene codes for is manufactured), and hence the protein the gene codes for is not manufactured (Corwin, 2004). Methylation is one among a number of processes governing gene expression collectively referred to as epigenetics. The vital role of epigenetic processes in development is becoming more obvious every day. The most important of these processes are discussed in Chapter 7 in the context of substance abuse (see especially Figures 6.1a and 6.1b).

Conclusion

This chapter shows most plainly why we take strong issue with the claim that early childhood experiences do not deserve any special place among the posited causes of antisocial behavior. We have examined how the brain develops from zygote, to embryo, to fetus, and to child in both experience-expected and experience-dependent ways. We noted the profound influence of the environmental experiences that the individual has on that development. The brain has evolved over countless millennia to be each individual's guide and compass from cradle to grave. But the brain has calibrated itself to the social experiences that were almost invariable during *Homo sapiens*'s long sojourn on the flat grasslands of the ancient African savannah. Social relationships that fostered sharing and caring were necessities of survival among nomadic hunter-gatherer bands composed of relatively close kin. Infants were breastfed and presumably cared for by all, and abuse and neglect were unlikely to have been tolerated by the group. None of the teratogens that now surround us were present to distort the brain's circuits or otherwise destroy lives in the species's early environments.

Modern life supplies so many more opportunities for a rewarding life, and few of the natural dangers that beset our ancient ancestors exist today. Yet if our early experiences inside and outside of our mothers' wombs do not conform to experience-expected processes, we are exposed to a different set of dangers. We are set on a trajectory which will expose us to negative experiences that will wire our plastic brains in experience-dependent fashion. It is important to understand how the experiences that often accompany poverty enumerated by sociologists and criminologists (ill health, poor nutrition, increased use of teratogenic substances, increased risk of abuse and neglect, and so forth) are captured in the neural circuitry of children. This understanding should lead both to a greater appreciation of the problems suffered by our most deprived citizens, and perhaps even suggest ways to ameliorate them. The neurological evidence strongly supports calls for nurturant strategies to crime control, such as paid maternal leave, nutrition programs, home visitation programs, and head start-type programs. Data from the neurosciences doubtless have more power to influence tightfisted lawmakers and a skeptical public than heartstring appeals from humanists. As Vila (1997:18) points out: "Keeping adequate resources flowing toward child development programs is a *social investment strategy that pays compound interest.*"

Chapter 4
ADHD, Comorbid Disorders, and Criminal Behavior

ADHD: Definition and Prevalence

Attention deficit hyperactivity disorder is the most commonly diagnosed behavioral disorder of childhood and adolescence (Young et al., 2009). It is defined clinically in the American Psychiatric Association's *Diagnostic and Statistical Manual of Mental Disorders* (DSM-IV; American Psychiatric Association, 1994) as a disruptive behavior disorder characterized by ongoing inattention and/or hyperactivity-impulsivity occurring in several settings more frequently and severely than is typical for persons in the same stage of development. Three major types of ADHD have been recognized. The first is the predominately inattentive type (unorganized, difficulty following instructions or conversations, easily distracted and forgetful). The second type is the predominantly hyperactive-impulsive type (constantly in motion, restless, impulsive, difficulty in following directions). The third type is the combined type, in which the symptoms of the first two types are equally in evidence, which requires at least six of nine symptoms of each of the inattentive and hyperactive-impulsive for diagnosis. Most people with ADHD fit the criteria for combined ADHD, thus we concern ourselves with this type.

The symptoms identified vary widely in their severity and frequency of occurrence, and most healthy children will sometimes manifest them. However, they cluster together to form a syndrome in ADHD children, and are chronic and more severe than simple childish high spirits. The traits and behaviors manifested by ADHD individuals that are associated with criminal behavior include impairment of executive functions, low self-control, low arousal levels, difficulty with peers, frequent disruptive behavior, academic underachievement, risk-taking, aggression (reactive aggression driven by emotional outbursts, rather than proactive aggression driven by predatory motives), and proneness to extreme boredom (Retz & Rosler, 2009). According to the DSM-IV, 3–7% of children are diagnosed with ADHD, but there is little consensus on these figures, with some estimates as high as 10%.

ADHD, Delinquency, and Criminality

There is an abundance of research that identifies a strong and robust relationship between ADHD and delinquent and criminal behavior (Gordon & Moore, 2005;

Pratt et al., 2002). Individuals diagnosed with ADHD are consistently found to be overrepresented in juvenile detention centers, jails, and prisons worldwide (Rösler et al., 2004). Gudjonsson and colleagues' (2009) review of nine studies of prevalence rates of ADHD among adult prison inmates using various diagnostic criteria in a number of countries found rates ranging from 24% to 67%, with their own study showing that 62.5% of inmates were either fully ADHD-symptomatic or in partial remission. A German study (Rösler et al., 2004) found that 45% of the inmates had some form of ADHD, compared to 9.4% of a control sample. This same study found that 85.5% of the ADHD inmates were comorbid for alcohol and substance abuse/dependence, and that 30.2% of them had either definite or possible antisocial personality disorder. Inmates with ADHD also have significantly more prison violations, such as verbal and physical aggression, destruction of property, and self-injury (Young et al., 2009).

The risk of delinquent and criminal behavior increases for ADHD individuals who are comorbid for conduct disorder (CD) and/or oppositional defiant disorder (ODD) (Comings et al., 2005). For those diagnosed with all three conditions, ADHD symptoms usually appear first, followed by ODD symptoms, and then CD. However, even in the absence of CD and ODD, ADHD remains a potent risk factor. A study of lifetime criminality among 207 white males diagnosed with childhood ADHD and free of CD found that 42% had been convicted of at least one officially recorded crime by age 38, compared with 14% of the control group (Mannuzza, Klein & Moulton, 2007).

Criminologists are familiar with ADHD and its symptoms and correlates, but few are familiar with its etiology as revealed and understood by natural scientists. Unnever, Cullen, and Pratt (2003:495) point out that ADHD research "has been conducted primarily by psychologists and biomedical researchers with few ties to the field of criminology." They further point out that because ADHD is a major risk factor for antisocial behavior, criminologists must become involved with this research because they may offer insights that are "theoretically consequential." Unnever, Cullen, and Pratt even suggest that ADHD underlies one of criminology's most revered etiological concepts—low self-control. Nevertheless, ADHD may not be a true nosological disorder as is, say, schizophrenia. Rather, it may be a normal human phenotypic variant (as its relatively high prevalence rate in many populations suggests) that happens to be unsuited to many modern social conditions (Schilling, Walsh & Yun, 2011).

The Genetics and Neurobiology of ADHD

Although the precise etiology of ADHD is not known, numerous twin, adoption, and family studies support a strong genetic component. Heritability estimates for ADHD average about 0.80 and are consistently found regardless of whether it is considered a categorical or continuous trait (Bobb et al., 2005). Of course, heritability studies show only that genes contribute a certain percentage of the variance in a trait in a population, not how much genes contribute to ADHD in any given individual (if indeed it makes any sense at all to talk about genes making direct contributions to behavioral traits independent of the environment). Neither can heritability studies tell us which genes contribute to the development of the condition. We require molecular genetic studies to do that, and such studies show that ADHD is highly polygenic, with at least 18 genes (estimates vary) with small to moderate effects being involved (Curatolo et al., 2009). The highly polygenic nature of ADHD probably explains why it is so clinically heterogeneous and why it is linked to many problems such as CD, ODD, substance abuse, and pathological gambling, as well as criminality and antisocial behavior in general.

The hunt for candidate genes implicated in any disorder involves looking at genetic polymorphisms. It is estimated that about 85% of genetic causes of most behavioral disorders are attributable to single nucleotide polymorphisms (Plomin et al., 2001). Meta-analyses have shown that the three polymorphisms most replicated in ADHD genetic studies are the dopamine receptor D4 (DRD4), the dopamine transporter (DAT1), and the serotonin transporter (5-HTT) (Bobb et al., 2005; Gizer, Ficks & Waldman, 2009). We discussed the mechanisms of these polymorphisms and how they are implicated in criminal and other forms of antisocial behavior in Chapter 2. We should emphasize that any individual genes associated with complex disorders such as ADHD are likely to have low penetrance,[1] thus many carriers will not develop the disorder.

Whatever the genes associated with ADHD may be, they are expressed in the brain, particularly the prefrontal cortex. As noted earlier, because of its many connections with other brain areas, the PFC plays the major integrative as well as the major supervisory role in the brain, and is vital to the forming of moral judgments, mediating affect, and for social cognition. ADHD is basically a disorder of neurological regulation and underarousal, making the PFC a key focus of neuroscientists. Meta-analyses of brain imaging studies show that reductions in the gray matter volume in both the left and right cortices of the PFC are the most robust and consistent brain region deficits associated with ADHD (Valera et al., 2007).

The PFC requires optimal levels of dopamine and norepinephrine (NE) to function properly. Both DA and NE are vital for long-term potentiation (LTP).[2]

---

1 Penetrance refers to the degree to which carriers of an allele will evidence the symptom or trait associated with the allele.

2 The importance of DA and NE is reflected in the medications used to treat ADHD. The most frequently prescribed drugs for ADHD are methylphenidate-based stimulants such as Ritalin and Concerta. These drugs work as DA agonists by preventing DA synaptic reuptake by occupying the DA transporters, thus increasing DA availability in the PFC and subcortical areas associated with reward and punishment. Stimulant drugs have a calming or normalizing affect on suboptimally aroused individuals by raising the activity of the brain's sensory mechanisms to normal levels. This relieves feelings of boredom because the brain is now able to be more attentive to features of the environment that it could not previously capture. Of course, stimulant drugs would have exactly the opposite effect on non-ADHD individuals (Applebaum, 2009). Another popular medication is the non-stimulant

LTP refers to long-lasting enhancement in signal transmission between neurons (pre-and post-synaptic) that have frequently fired synchronously, which in simpler terms means that LTP is crucial to long-term memory formation, and thus to learning. The efficiency of LTP depends on the efficiency of neurotransmitter activity (Johansen et al., 2009). Too little DA and NE activity leads to feelings of drowsiness, boredom, or fatigue; too much and we are stressed—either of which impairs normal PFC functioning. In short: "Imaging studies have demonstrated that patients with ADHD have alterations in PFC circuits and demonstrate weaker PFC activation while trying to regulate attention and behavior" (Arnsten, 2009:22). Not coincidentally, when the myelination of the PFC is largely accomplished by early adulthood, many ADHD symptoms, especially impulsiveness, tend to subside. Depending on the strictness of the definition of ADHD, about 25% will continue to exhibit symptoms in adulthood under a strict definition, and about 66% under a more relaxed definition (Willoughby, 2003).

The subsiding of symptoms in adulthood suggests a delay model of ADHD rather than a deficiency model in which symptoms do not subside with age, such as in autism. A longitudinal fMRI study by Phillip Shaw and colleagues (2007) scanned cerebral cortical thickness at more than 40,000 different cerebral points in 223 children with ADHD (92% combined ADHD type) and 223 closely matched for socioeconomic status, sex, and IQ. Each subject had a number of scans between the ages of 5 and young adulthood. The primary finding was that cortical thickness attained its peak in ADHD children at a median age of 10.5 years, compared to 7.5 years in the control group. The delay was most prominent in PFC areas crucial for behavioral regulation. Interestingly, the only brain area in which the ADHD group evidenced earlier maturation was the primary motor cortex. Commenting on their findings, Shaw and colleagues (2007:19,651) state that: "It is possible that the combination of early maturation of the primary motor cortex with the late maturation of the higher-order motor control regions may reflect or even drive the excessive and poorly controlled motor activity cardinal to the syndrome."

If the symptoms subside with maturation and myelination in young adulthood, why do we see so many adults diagnosed in childhood with ADHD involved in the criminal justice system? The problem for ADHD individuals is that their neurophysiological deficits place them on a trajectory of gene–environmental correlations and interactions from which it may be extremely difficult to escape. Traits such as impulsivity and negative emotionality strongly influence how others in the family, school, peer group, and workforce respond to those displaying them

---

atomoxetine. Atomoxetine is a NE reuptake inhibitor that increases both NE activity (and also facilitates DA activity) in the PFC. Both stimulant and non-stimulant drugs have been shown to increase cortical attention and facilitation with stimulant medication working better for some people and non-stimulants for others in reducing ADHD symptoms (Gilbert et al., 2006). Atomoxetine treatment targets the posterior attention system (for example, parietal lobe and thalamus) and methylphenidate targets the anterior attention system (for example, PFC and anterior cingulated cortex) (Curatolo et al., 2009).

(evocative rGE). The tendency for ADHD individuals to self-medicate with illegal stimulant drugs can also get them into trouble with the criminal justice system and throw them into the company of antisocial others. These antisocial others are typically the only kinds of people who will associate with ADHD individuals in friendship. Many ADHD children thus do not build up enough social capital (positive social relationships) to draw on when brain maturation finally catches up that would allow them pause enough to jump off the antisocial roundabout.

ADHD and Reinforcement (or Reward) Dominance Theory

We have seen that DA and 5-HT are central to reinforcement dominance theory, the major neurobiological theory focusing on the emotional expression or suppression of behavior. Crucially, both sensitivity to reward and punishment, and thus reinforcement and extinction, rely on paying attention to cues and on memories of what those cues led to on prior occasions. Attentional and memory processes rely on the LTP process, which relies on neurotransmitter activity. It is a tenet of operant psychology that behavior is governed by its consequences. During our formative years, we try out many novel things which we either retain or eliminate according to the ratio of rewards to punishments these actions produce. Experiments (and the everyday experiences of parents) show that children with ADHD impulsively tend to select small rewards that are available now over larger rewards which require waiting. This tendency has been considered a deficiency in the attention and memory systems of ADHD individuals caused largely by the failure of DA and NE signaling to induce LTP which makes such children relatively unresponsive to cues of reward and punishment that are likely to result from a particular behavioral choice.

The fight-flight-freeze system dimension of RDT has also been implicated in ADHD symptoms because, as we indicated in Chapter 2, the behavioral inhibition system and the FFFS may be thought of as a single integrated inhibition system. The BIS leads to behavioral inhibition via conditioned emotions such as anxiety/ guilt, and the FFFS via both conditioned and unconditioned (fear) emotions (Vervoort et al., 2010). Anxiety, guilt, and fear all lead to avoidance behavior in the face of punishment cues. If ADHD behavior is in part a function of a relatively unregulated seeking of pleasure due to suboptimal arousal (suboptimal DA and NE functioning), then individuals with it should display hyperreactivity of the autonomic nervous system. This should be particularly true if they are comorbid for CD or ODD because a sluggish ANS implies a low level of fear, which is a useful attribute for a criminal to possess (Ortiz & Raine, 2004). Studies have consistently shown that ADHD individuals, especially those with ADHD+CD or ADHD+ODD, display low ANS arousal as measured primarily by electrodermal responses (Crowell et al., 2006; Posthumus et al., 2009).

Activation of the inhibitory BIS thus involves endocrinal responses, which would include cortisol. West, Claes, and Deboutte (2009) hypothesized that if ADHD is partly the result of a defective BIS, then different patterns of hypothalamic–pituitary–adrenal (HPA) axis functioning, as measured by salivary cortisol levels, should be found between ADHD individuals and controls. That is, ADHD individuals should evidence lower cortisol levels as evidence of low levels of anxiety/fear than controls. The researchers found that combined ADHD type individuals showed significantly lower basal levels of cortisol relative to controls, and much lower levels under conditions of induced psychosocial stress. However, in contrast to the blunted response of combined ADHD type children, ADHD-inattentive type children showed elevated cortisol response to induced psychosocial stress. This and other similar findings led West, Claes, and Deboutte to join the increasingly loud chorus of researchers that the combined ADHD and ADHD-inattentive conditions should be studied as qualitatively distinct disorders.

ADHD, CD, and ODD Comorbidity

In addition to placing individuals at increased risk for antisocial behavior, delinquents with ADHD are more likely than non-ADHD delinquents to persist in their offending as adults. This probability rises dramatically for ADHD+CD individuals (Comings et al., 2005). CD is also a neurological disorder with substantial polygenic effects with heritability estimates ranging between 0.27 and 0.78 (Coolidge, Thede & Young, 2000). CD has an onset at around five years of age. It remains at a steady rate for girls (about 0.8% of all girls) and rises to about 2.8% at age 15, but rises steadily in boys from about 2.1% at age 5 to about 5.5% at age 15 (Maughan et al., 2004). Lynam (1996:209) has stated that the ADHD+CD combination is a "particularly virulent strain … best described as fledgling psychopathy." CD is defined as persistent serious antisocial acts, such as assaulting, stealing, setting fires, bullying, cruelty to animals, and vandalism, that are excessive for a child's developmental stage, and it is considered one of the most stable diagnoses in psychiatry (Comings et al., 2005). ADHD and CD are found to co-occur in about 50% of cases in most clinical and epidemiological studies (Waschbusch et al., 2002).

ODD is an earlier-appearing and less severe disorder characterized by behaviors such as temper tantrums and lying. Some view ODD as a less severe form of CD, while others maintain the distinction between the two but acknowledge that ODD frequently develops into CD. As Lahey and Loeber (1994:144) describe the distinction: "ODD is an enduring pattern of oppositional, irritable, and defiant behavior, whereas CD is a persistent pattern of more serious violations of the rights of others and social norms." CD and ODD are developmental and hierarchical, in that all children who meet the clinical criteria for CD also meet the criteria for ODD, but not all ODD children will develop CD. Factor analyses of the symptoms and behaviors of the two conditions produce two or three factors, with a three-factor solution labeled as "ODD," "intermediate CD," and "advanced CD" (Lahey & Loeber, 1994).

The comorbidity of ADHD with many other disorders strongly suggests that epistasis (the interaction of genes at different loci) and pleiotropy (the influence of a single gene on more than one phenotypic trait) are involved, as well as genetic heterogeneity (different genes resulting in similar phenotypes in different individuals) (Wallis et al., 2008). The genetic logic behind comorbid inheritance is rather simple, starting with the fact that each time the sex cells segregate during meiosis, the alleles on the chromosomes are not transmitted to the daughter cell with fidelity. During meiosis, the chromosomes separate and their alleles are segregated into two different gametes (this is known as the law of segregation). Because ADHD is a quantitative trait, and thus polygenic, the genes coding for proteins underlying it will most likely reside on separate chromosomes or at distant locations of the same one. Thus, the law of segregation assures that very few of them will be passed on to the next generation *in toto*. Then there is the law of independent assortment, which states that allele pairs separate independently during the formation of gametes, meaning that traits (or rather the genes underlying them) are transmitted to offspring independently of one another.

Given the laws of segregation and independent assortment, it would seem to follow that the alleles underlying comorbid disorders are located very close together. The odds of inheriting alleles for comorbid disorders are determined by genetic linkage studies and quantified by LOD (log of the odds ratio) scores. The closer two or more alleles are together on a chromosomal locus, the greater the odds that they will be transmitted together. A LOD score of 3 is considered the minimal standard of evidence for linkage—the likelihood that two genes have not separated during meiosis (Arcos-Burgos & Acosta, 2007). A LOD of 3 means the hypothesis that the genetic markers are linked is 1,000 times more likely than the null hypothesis that they are not. This value is chosen because the base-10 logarithm of 1,000 is 3 ($10^3 = 1,000$; so $\log_{10}$ of 1,000 = 3). In one study of 616 subjects, the LOD score for ADHD+CD was 5.34, for ODD+CD it was 6.68, and for ODD+ADHD it was 14.19, indicating extremely strong linkages of the genes associated with these syndromes (Jain et al., 2007).

Not surprisingly, many of the cognitive and temperamental symptoms of CD and ADHD children are similar. However, unlike non-comorbid ADHD children, CD children tend to score in the low-normal or borderline range of intelligence, are most likely to be found in impoverished families, and are significantly more likely than children without CD to have parents diagnosed with antisocial personality disorder (ASPD) (Sergeant et al., 2003). One of the psychiatric requirements for a diagnosis of ASPD is a childhood diagnosis of CD. Thus, if a parent is diagnosed with ASPD, it means that he (almost always a he) was diagnosed with CD as a child, and if his offspring is also diagnosed with CD, the cross-generation linkage is further suggestive of genetic transmission of CD (Comings et al., 2005).

A number of researchers have offered evidence that ADHD is a product of a deficient BIS, and CD is a product of a reward-dominant BAS (Levy, 2004; Quay, 1997). This double disability indicates that ADHD+CD sufferers are inclined to seek high levels of stimulation because of an oversensitive BAS, and then their faulty BIS hampers them in putting a stop to their search for pleasurable stimulation once it is initiated. Others have found that it is an overactive BAS that is primarily associated with ADHD (for example, Mitchell & Nelson-Gray, 2006), and still others (Hundt et al., 2008) aver that because the affects of the BIS and BAS on behavior are interdependent, either or both positions could be correct, depending on the individuals and the measures utilized. This is the position we find most satisfying. Whatever the case may be, Lynam (1996:22) describes the trajectory from ADHD+CD to criminality by stating that the co-occurrence of ADHD and CD:

> may tax the skills of parents and lead to the adoption of coercive child rearing techniques, which in turn may enhance the risk of antisocial behavior. Entry into school may bring academic failure and increase the child's frustration, which may increase his or her level of aggressive behavior. Finally, the peer rejection associated with hyperactivity may lead to increased social isolation and conflict with peers.

Thornberry, Huizinga & Loeber's (2004) pyramidal model of offending, which focuses on the escalation of seriousness of delinquent acts being committed as boys age, provides us with a useful model with which to view the offending patterns of ODD, CD, and ADHD individuals (see Figure 4.1). The model presents three pathways that represent patterns of offending behavior; it says nothing about clinical syndromes, but neatly conforms to Lahey & Loeber's (1994) three-factor model discussed above. The *Authority Conflict* pathway is the earliest pathway (starting before age 12), and begins with simple stubborn behavior (ODD), followed by defiance and authority avoidance. Note that the base of the triangle represents the earliest stage and contains the most boys. Some boys move into the second stage (*defiance/disobedience*), and a few more will move into the authority avoidance stage. At this point, some boys progress to one of the other two pathways, but many will go no further than authority avoidance. The *Covert* pathway starts later, and involves minor offenses in stage 1 that become progressively more serious for a few boys who enter stage 3 on this pathway. The covert pathway would consist overwhelmingly of boys who were not diagnosed with ODD or CD, but perhaps with ADHD. The *Overt* pathway progresses from minor aggressive acts in stage 1 to very serious violent acts in stage 3. The more seriously involved delinquents in the overt and covert pathways may switch back and forth between violent and property crimes, with the most serious probably fitting the criteria for ADHD+CD comorbidity.

Environmental Factors

Even if ADHD is 80% heritable, there is still 20% of the variance in ADHD symptoms that is attributable to environmental factors. The heritability coefficients

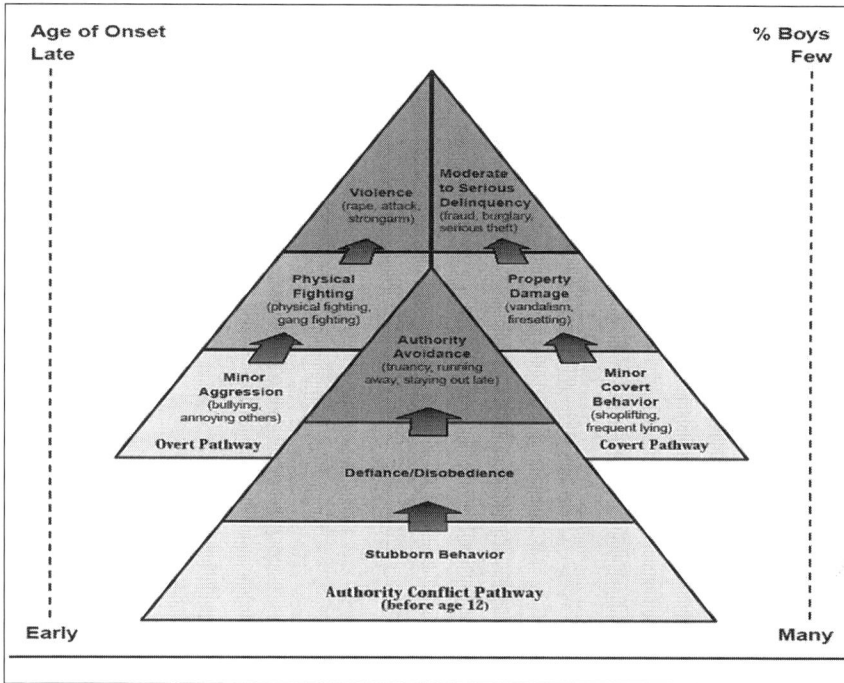

Figure 4.1   Three pathways to boys' delinquency

Source: Thornberry, Huizinga & Loeber (2004)

of CD and ODD, as well as the heritability of other ADHD comorbid conditions, are less than 0.80, thus leaving plenty of causal space for the environment. As we constantly reiterate, genes and environments are not independent entities driving behavior, because genes condition the effects of environments and environments condition the expression of genes. Genes do not directly affect complex behaviors; rather, individuals create and respond to their environments via the constant interplay of genes and the environment through the processes of gene–environment interaction and gene–environment correlation. Because genes affect differential *exposure* to environmental risks via active rGE and differential *susceptibility* to environmental risks via GxE, both processes are always operating and difficult to untangle. In other words, people self-select themselves into different environments on the basis of their genetic preferences when they are able (active rGE), and because they self-select a particular environment, they will be more susceptible to its influence (GxE) than will those there by happenstance. Once in contact with an environment inhabited by antisocial others, the environment may have unique causal effects. Failure to incorporate appropriate environmental risk factors may account for some of the inconsistent findings in biomedical research, and it is here that criminologists can make a contribution.

Environmental features identified as playing a role in the etiology of ADHD were identified by Spencer and colleagues (2002), who reported a series of LODs for ADHD individuals versus controls. The highest LOD was 8.2 for parental ADHD, which is of course genetic rather than environmental, but reported for comparison purposes. The strongest environmental factor was low birth weight (3.0), followed in order by prenatal tobacco exposure (2.9), prenatal alcohol exposure (2.5), and prenatal drug exposure (1.5). The LODs for socioeconomic status, mother's age at time of birth, and parental IQ were not significantly different from even, and are thus not implicated as possible causal factors. Later environmental factors such as family and school experiences or peer pressure do not to have any causal impact on ADHD, although, as we have discussed, they tend to exacerbate its symptoms and further move many ADHD individuals in antisocial directions via evocative and active rGE mechanisms (Coolidge, Thede & Young, 2000).

A number of other studies have also shown that while non-biological environmental factors alone cannot induce ADHD, they can lead to enhanced ADHD comorbidity with ODD and CD, and hence to delinquent and criminal behavior (Ficks & Waldman, 2009). We have already noted Lynam's (1996) description of how the behavior of ADHD children taxes parental skills and may lead to the type of coercive parenting that often leads to ODD and CD. This is an example of evocative rGE, in that the child's behavior evokes reactions from parents that magnify the child's antisocial phenotype. In other words, while there is no dispute that abused children evidence higher rates of ADHD and comorbid disorders than non-abused children, the "causal" direction is far from certain. This is particularly so since ADHD children tend to have parents who exhibit at least some of the symptoms of ADHD themselves, thus parental genes may both lead to parental abuse and exacerbate their children's ADHD (Ficks & Waldman, 2009).

Another example of gene–environment interplay is the proposal by Moffitt, Lynam, and Silva (1994) that verbal deficits place children at risk for CD. This gains some support from a study of children comorbid for ADHD and reading disorder which showed that both were caused in part by common genetic effects (Friedman et al., 2003). Neurological evidence suggests that the left frontal lobes contain the mechanisms by which children process their parents' instructions that become their internalized basis of self-control. Children with deficits in these mechanisms fail to profit from their parent's verbal instructions, and tend to develop a present-oriented and impulsive cognitive style. Lacking normal ability to connect abstract verbal commands with their own concrete behavior, such children may have to learn lessons through the more painful process of trial and error, and may thus experience more frequent punishments for their lack of compliance with instructions. As Moffitt, Lynam, and Silva (1994:296) put it:

> Children who have difficulty expressing themselves and remembering information are significantly handicapped. Dysfunctional communication between child and his parents, peers, and teachers may be one of the most critical

factors for childhood conduct problems that grow into persistent antisocial behavior in young adulthood.

Culture Matters

The relatively high rate of ADHD means that the genes underlying it have survived the weeding process of natural selection because they have conferred some benefits in evolutionary environments even if they do not in evolutionarily novel classroom and work environments (Bjorklund & Pellegrini, 2000). We have seen that there is strong evidence that the DRD4-7R allele, the most robust genetic correlate of ADHD, is a young variant that arose about 40,000 years ago, and that it has been positively selected for (Arcos-Burgos & Acosta, 2007). Positive selection means that traits and behaviors underlain by the genes in question have had some positive effect on the bearer's survival and reproductive success. Yet this is difficult to reconcile with many ADHD symptoms that signal low levels of engagement with peers, such as the inability to follow rules and low self-control. This kind of behavior would seem to be an impediment to reproductive success in any society, but chronic criminals tend to have high levels of mating success (see Chapter 11) even though they possess characteristics unlikely to be welcomed in any community. The point is that one does not have to interact and be found acceptable in "decent society" in order to meet, mate, and have offspring.

No one claims that the full ADHD phenotype is an adaptation. The continued existence of the ADHD individuals at relatively high rates only suggests that *some* endophenotypes[3] (energetic, unpredictable, novelty-seeking) of ADHD may have been selectively adaptive, but not all of them. ADHD-like behaviors such as restless boldness and curiosity meant exploring beyond known boundaries, and would have made such individuals valuable to a band roaming the savannah—the individual took the risks, and the group reaped the benefits. ADHD children often show neurological deficits, but ADHD children who also carry the DRD4-7R do not show these deficits (Harpending & Cochran, 2002)—this allele may be a "cause" of ADHD independent of neurological deficits. One study comparing ADHD children with and without the 7R allele found that children with the allele had better cognitive performance and better prognoses for long-term outcomes

---

3   Endophenotypes (endo = "within" [the phenotype]) are essential subunits of a complex chain leading from genotype to phenotype. Each link in the chain may have only minor effects on the phenotype, and then only if combined with other relevant endophenotypes and the right environmental variables. Reducing the ADHD phenotype to its constituent and less complex endophenotypic parts such as impulsiveness or inattention makes it easier to identify and study their genetic basis than if we tried to map the more amorphous phenotype itself (Glahn, Thompson & Blangero, 2002). This is so because intermediate traits (the endophenotypes) "sit closer to the genotype in the development scheme" (Gottesman & Hanson, 2005:268).

than ADHD children without it, suggesting that the: "allele may be associated with a more benign form of the disorder" (Gornick et al., 2007:379). This again shows the heterogeneity, and hence the polygenic nature, of ADHD.[4]

Williams and Taylor (2006) offer an evolutionary model of ADHD based on the DRD4-7R allele using computer simulations to explore the possible value of unpredictable and novelty seeking behavior in hunter-gatherer environments. They hypothesized that the restlessness and impulsiveness associated with the DRD4-7R allele prompted increased exploration of new behaviors and new territories that enhanced the fitness of those carrying it, and thanks to those individuals, of the group as a whole. Their simulations were supportive of their model. In light of what we have said about ADHD and reproductive success, it is interesting to note that among the high-prevalence 7R allele Yanomamo, the strutting, violent, energy they display that would land a person in hot water in Western societies has excellent fitness payoffs. Males who have killed the most in inter-village warfare have an average of three times as many wives and children as those who have killed least or not at all (Buss, 2005).

Thom Hartman's (2000) hunter versus farmer theory of ADHD also asserts that many of the subtraits of ADHD such as impulsivity and novelty-seeking were assets when our ancestors were nomadic hunter-gatherers. Hartman theorizes that good hunters were hyper-vigilant to all incoming stimuli, continually monitoring the environment, flexible in their strategies and able to respond immediately to new sights and sounds. In today's classroom and work environments, we call this trait "distractibility." Impulsivity also allowed a hunter to rapidly identify and seize opportunities without taking time to plan and consider (which, of course, can be quite dangerous). With the advent of agricultural and industrial modes of life, different traits that Hartman called "farmer" traits, such as prolonged and purposeful linear thinking and focusing on tasks until they are completed, became more socially useful. We might say that humans as well as their animals became more "domesticated" with the advent of farming. Today, the hunter phenotype possessing some ADHD traits without CD comorbidity may become firefighters and police officers, while the tamer farmer phenotype prefers the quiet, plodding, cerebral lifestyles of the accountant or computer analyst. Hartman gives a number

---

4   Although the association of the DRD4-7R allele with ADHD is the most replicated association in molecular genetic studies of ADHD (Bobb et al., 2005), there have been some failures to replicate. We should expect such failures given the polygenic nature of ADHD and the low penetrance rate of individual genes for quantitative traits. Genes are modified not only by environmental input but also by the interactions with one or more other genes at different loci. A study by Carrasco et al. (2006) found that neither the DRD4-7R nor the DAT1-10R polymorphisms (both indicating low dopaminergic functioning) had a statistically significant effect on ADHD, but individuals who possessed both polymorphisms were significantly more likely to be diagnosed with ADHD (LOD = 12.7) than subjects possessing neither or only one of these alleles. This large effect was attributed to epistasis (GxG).

of examples of how many of the symptoms of ADHD would make a person a better hunter in prehistoric times, but are largely maladaptive and disvalued in today's "farmer's" world.

Eisenberg and colleagues (2008) tested the theory using data from the Ariaal tribe of Kenya. This tribe split in two groups some time around 1972, with some members retaining their traditional nomadic life and the others settling down to an agricultural life. Both factions of the tribe were tested for the DRD4-7R allele, with approximately 19.4% of each faction carrying it. The study found that the nomadic "hunter" members with the allele were generally healthier than those without it, while among the "farmer" members, those with the allele were generally less healthy. In other words, there was a GxE interaction such that the DRD4-7R allele conferred an advantage in one environment and a disadvantage in another, just as the hunter versus farmer hypothesis predicts. Eisenberg et al. (2008:6) note that the ADHD-like traits conferred by the DRD4-7R would allow "nomadic children to more readily learn effectively in a dynamic [non-school] environment, while the same attention span interferes with classroom learning." They also note that the allele is advantageous for warrior with "a reputation for unpredictable behaviour that inspires fear," but less well suited in sedentary environments where predictability and bonhomie are valued.

Conclusion

In this chapter, we have looked at ADHD and two of its many comorbid disorders, CD and ODD. These diagnoses did not exist in the halcyon days of the 1950s and 1960s, when the typical behavior of such children would be met at home and school with paddle and pain. It is thus tempting to dismiss these syndromes as simply reflecting the medicalization of high spirits and rough-and-tumble, as well as our evolving desire to treat rather than punish. Yet the genetic and neuroimaging data show that ADHD children are clearly departures from the norm. But we are not suggesting that ADHD represents some form of hopeless pathology that leads its victims down the road to inevitable criminality, particularly in cases where CD is not present. Nevertheless, childhood ADHD is very much an important risk factor for adult criminality. Commenting on what they had learned from 30 years of data from their longitudinal cohort study, Moffitt and colleagues (2001:238) wrote that: "it is clear that the four problems of neuro-cognitive deficits undercontrolled temperament, weak constraint, and attention-deficit hyperactivity constitute a core aetiological risk for the most persistent, sever forms of antisocial behaviour." Note that they list ADHD as a separate risk factor from the other three problems, which are typically considered core symptoms of combined ADHD type.

Perhaps the symptoms were less noticeable and covered up in times when there was less tolerance for ADHD-like behavior and wrathful responses to it. The ever-increasing numbers of children being diagnosed with ADHD most likely reflects teachers' growing intolerance for disruptive classroom behavior in the absence of their ability to administer meaningful punitive responses to it. Environmental factors as simple as attitude changes push more children over the risk threshold for being labeled with these disorders, since many ADHD children (absent comorbidity for CD) have above-average IQs and are creative, so perhaps the symptoms of ADHD are only problematic in the modern context in which children are expected to sit still for long periods learning subjects that they find boring. While acknowledging that ADHD is problematic in modern society, that it has real neurological foundations, and that parents are probably right in the current social context to choose to medicate their ADHD children, Jaak Panksepp (1998) asserts that ADHD-like behaviors are observed in the young of all social species, and it is called "rough-and-tumble" play. Panksepp suggests that we as a society should provide more opportunities in schools for the young (especially boys) to indulge in their biological need for rough-and-tumble play—"More recess, less Ritalin" sounds like a good rallying cry for a drug-free delinquency reduction program.

Chapter 5
The Age–crime Curve, Puberty, and Brain Maturation

The Regularity of the Age–crime Curve

Nagin and Land (1993:330) have described the age–crime curve as "the most important regularity in criminology." "Age–crime curve" refers to the statistical count of the number of known crimes/delinquent acts committed in a population over a given period and mapped according to age categories. The curve reflects a sharp increase in offending beginning in early adolescence, a peak in mid-adolescence, and then a steep decline in early adulthood, followed by a steadier decline thereafter. The peak may be higher or lower at different periods, and the peak age may vary by a year or two, but the peak remains. There are debates over whether the peak represents the prevalence of offending (the number of people in the population who have offended) or the incidence of offending (the increased frequency of offending among chronic offenders), but regardless of which is correct, the peak remains. Figure 5.1 illustrates these curves from different countries and different historical periods.

The pattern represented by the curve has been noted in all cultures where statistics are gathered and at all times. Even before the urge to count and tabulate everything came over the human species, Plato and Aristotle were condemning the obnoxious behavior of Athenian teens. Then there is William Shakespeare's lament in *The Winter's Tale* that adolescence is a period of "getting wenches with child, wronging the ancientry, stealing, fighting" (Act III, Scene III). In 1913, Charles Goring noted the constancy of the age–crime curve and concluded that it was "a law of nature" (in Gottfredson & Hirschi, 1990:124). Laws of nature describe regularities of nature; they do not explain why these regularities happen, although criminologists have been trying for a long time. The age–crime curve has puzzled those criminologists who have labored under the sociological dogma that biology is irrelevant to understanding human behavior. Hirschi and Gottfredson (1983:554) have even stated that "the age distribution of crime cannot be accounted for by any variable or combination of variables currently available to criminology." Shavit and Rattner (1988:1,457) share this opinion when they write that the age peak in delinquency remains "unexplained by any known set of sociological variables."

Nevertheless, some criminologists have tried to explain the phenomenon, but their attempts have been a country mile away from convincing. Greenberg (1985), for example, offers a "strain" explanation and wants us to believe that because the pocket money parents give to their children is insufficient for their

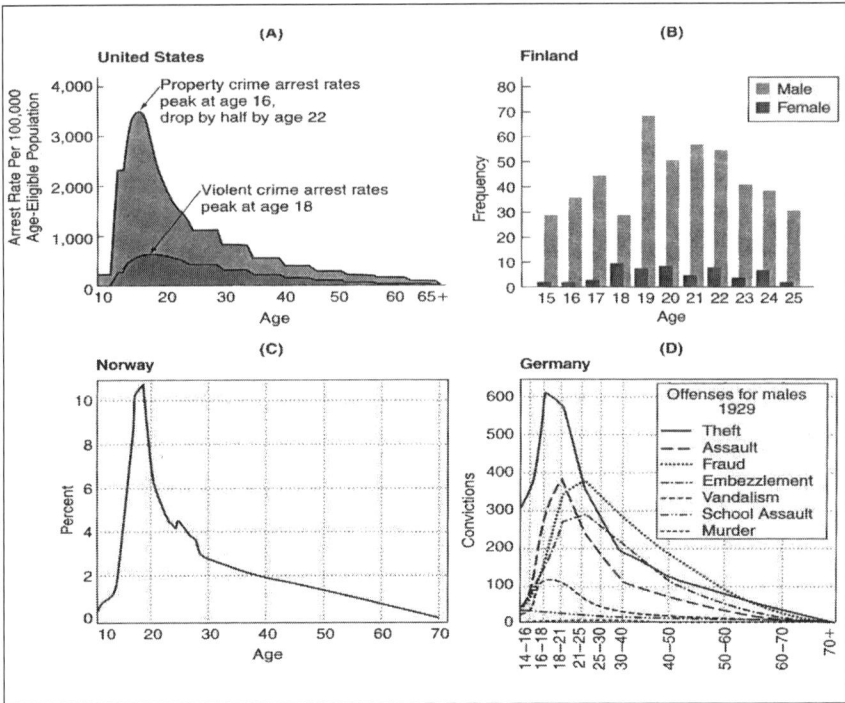

Figure 5.1   Illustrating the age–crime curve in different countries

Source: Ellis & Walsh (2000), p. 109

needs, they rob and steal to make up the difference! It escapes him that adults with families to support and mortgages to pay with salaries that may be inadequate are subjected to considerably more financial strain than adolescents, but very few resort to crime to "make up the difference." Another "explanation" that improves only a tad on Greenberg's is Akers's (1998:338) belief that: "Age-specific [crime] rates differ because individuals are differentially exposed to the learning variables at different ages." Sampson (1999:447) responded to this by pointing out that it: "seems rather incongruous [that] teens are suddenly able to reverse course after more than a dozen years of anti-delinquent learning ratios." Sampson is saying that presumably children have been exposed to prosocial "learning variables" for their entire lives, but all this suddenly counts for nothing as they turn to different sources of learning that lead them in antisocial directions.

These different learning sources are peers. Mark Warr (2002) attempts to explain the onset and increase in delinquency during adolescence by increased peer association and influence, and the decrease of delinquency in early adulthood by lessening peer association and influence. He notes that the decreasing influence of peers is compensated for by the increasing influence of girlfriends, wives, children, and employers. No one doubts that the number of delinquent friends an individual has is a powerful predictor of the individual's own antisocial behavior, but birds of a feather do flock together. An "explanation" in terms of peer influence only describes what it purports to explain—it portrays situations that correlate with the onset and the desistence of offending. It does not explain why the influence of peers suddenly becomes so powerful in adolescence, or why it so often leads to antisocial behavior.

Explanations in Terms of Personality Change

Many psychological theories aver that age-related levels of antisocial behavior reflect normative age-related changes in key personality traits from adolescence to adulthood. Personality is developmentally dynamic rather than static, although in general terms it is stable. That is, personality does not change dramatically over the life-course (for example, from introvert to extrovert), but rather its dynamism reflects maturational changes as it becomes increasingly solidified with age (Blonigen, 2010). Two of the most prominent of these traits are conscientiousness and agreeableness. Conscientiousness is composed of a number of subtraits that range from well-organized, disciplined, scrupulous, orderly, responsible, and reliable at one end of the continuum to disorganized, careless, unreliable, irresponsible, and unscrupulous at the other (Lodi-Smith & Roberts, 2007). Conscientiousness is important to success in the workforce and climbing the class ladder—two things that that the typical criminal is notoriously unable to do legitimately. Conscientiousness has a mean heritability coefficient of 0.49 (Bouchard et al., 2003).

Agreeableness is the tendency to be friendly, considerate, courteous, helpful, and cooperative with others. Agreeable persons tend to trust others, to compromise with them, to empathize with and aid them. This list of subtraits suggests a high degree of concern for prosocial conformity and social desirability. Disagreeable persons simply display the opposite characteristics—suspicion of others, unfriendly, uncooperative, unhelpful, and lacking in empathy—which all suggest a lack of concern for prosocial conformity and social desirability. A pooled heritability estimate of 0.48 for agreeableness has been reported (Jang et al., 1998).

Conscientiousness and agreeableness are positively correlated, but far from perfectly (about 0.39; Witt et al., 2002). A person can be very conscientious at work but thoroughly disagreeable socially (think of the Machiavellian white-collar criminal). Conversely, one can be most agreeable to everybody but lackadaisical at work (think of the happy-go-lucky ritualist of Mertonian strain theory). From a meta-analysis of personality and antisocial behavior, Miller and Lynam (2001:780) describe the personality of the typical criminal in terms of agreeableness and conscientiousness thus:

Individuals who commit crimes tend to be hostile, self-centered, spiteful, jealous, and indifferent to others (i.e., low in Agreeableness). They tend to lack ambition, motivation, and perseverance, have difficulty controlling their impulses, and hold nontraditional and unconventional values and beliefs (i.e., are low in Conscientiousness).

Blonigen's (2010) review of a number of studies of age-related changes in personality traits related to antisocial behavior found medium to strong effect sizes. A reduction in negative emotionality (the tendency to interpret and react to stimuli with negative rather than positive affect) and an increase in conscientiousness stood out as the strongest changes. There were also moderate to large increases in agreeableness and constraint (cautious and restrained) and small to moderate decreases in neuroticism (emotional instability). Blonigen (2010:94) states that although there were considerable differences in the magnitude of these findings across different studies, they represent "clear congruence in the patterns of change in personality across a number of independent samples, which demonstrates moderate to large mean-level [changes in personality] from late adolescence to early adulthood."

Blonigen (2010) also takes issue with sociological arguments such as those made by Sampson and Laub (2005) that informal social controls that kick in with the acquisition of a job and a "good" marriage can account for desisting from antisocial behavior in early adulthood. He avers that such arguments are made without acknowledging the reciprocal relationship between social roles and personality traits (intelligent and conscientious people get good jobs, and agreeable people with positive emotionality are congenial marriage partners). Put otherwise:

self selection and social influence are "corresponsive" in their effect on personality such that social roles serve to accentuate features of an individual's personality that were already present ... this process reflects ... a "niche-picking" process in which individuals chose roles consistent with their personality make-up. (Blonigen, 2010:96)

This niche-picking argument is supported by a study of 1,036 sibling pairs that found genetic factors accounted for 64% of the variance in delinquent peer affiliation (Cleveland, Weibe & Row, 2005). A longitudinal study of peer group deviance using data from 469 monozygotic (MZ) and 287 dizygotic (DZ) twin pairs followed from age 8 to 25 found that as twins matured and created their own mini-worlds (active rGE) genes played an increasingly larger role in peer choice (Kendler et al., 2007). The heritabilities of peer group deviance across five age categories rose from 0.138 in the 8–11 age group to 0.462 in the 22–25 age group. Shared environment effects declined from 0.27 in the youngest group to 0.143 in the oldest group, and non-shared effects stayed relatively stable at 0.342 and 0.352, respectively.

Although we sympathize with the empirically well-demonstrated personality change argument, it still does not tell us why we observe these changes, any more than the peer group influence argument tells us why peer groups have their effects and why adolescents are susceptible to them. Just as we cannot explain a variable with a constant, we cannot explain a constant (the age–crime curve) with a variable. With penetrating insight, Gwynn Nettler (1984:104) informs us that: "To explain the 'age effect' one has to abandon sociological and sociopsychological theories of crime causation and revert to physiology, to ways organisms differentially function with age." In other words, the invariance of the age–crime curve must be explained by something which itself is invariant, and that is age-specific developmental biology.

Neurobiological Explanations for the Age–crime Curve

Social influences on behavior during adolescence are experienced in the context of the profound neurological and endocrinal changes that render adolescents vulnerable to risky behaviors that could involve them in the criminal justice system. This risk vulnerability is seen in the fact that the three most frequent causes of death among adolescents are, and have been for decades, accidents, homicide, and suicide (Heron, 2010). The inaugural event for all these changes is the onset of puberty, an invariant age-dependent physiological factor. Puberty is the developmental stage that occurs around 11 years of age for girls and 12 for boys in the modern Western world, marking the onset of the transition from childhood to adulthood and preparing us for procreation. Sisk and Zehr (2005) remind us that puberty is a brain event. When certain "permissive signals" are received from the environment and internally, the hypothalamic–pituitary–gonadal (HPG) axis activates neurons that initiate a series of chemical events that lead to the production of the sex hormones responsible for the emergence of secondary sex characteristics. For a variety of reasons, these permissive signals are arriving much earlier in modern times than was heretofore the case (Gluckman & Hanson, 2006).

Whereas puberty is a well-defined period containing well-defined biological events, adolescence is ill defined because there are no analogous biological markers that indicate its end. Adolescence is a period of social limbo in which individuals no longer need the same parental care as children, but are not yet ready to take on the roles and responsibilities of adulthood. Socially defined adulthood means taking on socially responsible roles such as acquiring a steady job and starting one's own family that mark individuals as independent members of society. If puberty marks the onset of adolescence, then socially defined adulthood marks its end. The legal definition of adulthood as 18 years of age rarely matches socially defined adulthood today. Puberty signals reproductive ability, but not social readiness to assume the responsibility of parenthood. Gluckman and Hanson (2006:29) state that this constitutes "the first time in our history as a species [that] biological maturation well precedes psychosocial maturation." This mismatch formed by the decreasing age of puberty combined with the increasing time required to prepare for today's complex workforce has led to a large "maturity gap" which provides fertile soil for antisocial behavior (Moffitt, 1993).

Adolescence is a normal and necessary period in the human lifespan. There is much to learn about being an adult in modern societies, and adolescence is a time to experiment with a variety of social skills before putting them into practice in earnest, and a time of sorting out what aspects of the previous generation to retain and what to discard. Adolescents are thus *re*-socialized to a somewhat different culture because they need to experiment with skills needed to live in their own generation, not that of their parents. This is the underlying reason why the adolescent peer group become an extremely important source of behavioral learning.

Although rebellious teens are often a source of parental despair, if teens are to become capable of adapting to new situations, it is necessary to temporarily strain the emotional bonds with parents that served their purpose well in childhood. Adolescents who do not assert themselves hinder their quest for independence. Adolescents must leave their childhood nests and mate with their own generation and explore their place in the world. Leaving the nest is fraught with risk, but it is an evolutionary design feature of all social primates, as males seek out sexual partners from outside the rearing group. Fighting with parents and seeking age peers "all help the adolescent away from the home territory" (Powell, 2006:867). This parent–child conflict rarely results in permanent fracturing of the bond, and it has often been found that moderate conflict with parents leads to better post-adolescent adjustment than either the absence of conflict or frequent conflict (Smetana, Campione-Barr & Metzer, 2006).

The Role of Steroid Hormones

Natural selection has provided adolescents with the necessary tools to engage in all this experimentation, such as the huge increase in testosterone (T) that accompanies puberty (Felson & Haynie, 2002). T is an anabolic steroid that increases protein synthesis and is primarily secreted in male testes (small amounts are secreted in the female ovaries and in the adrenal glands of both sexes). Figure 5.2 illustrates T fluctuations across the lifespan. T organizes the male brain in utero (see Chapter 10) so that it will respond to the pubertal surge of T in male-typical ways. After T *organizes* the male brain, there is little difference between the sexes in levels of T until puberty, when the third surge of T (there is a small one in males shortly after birth, as seen in Figure 5.2) *activates* the male brain to engage in male-typical behavior (Ellis, 2005). It very much looks like the evolved purpose of the pubertal T surge, in addition to preparing us for procreation, is to facilitate the behaviors—risk-taking, sensation-seeking, sexual experimentation, dominance contests, self-assertiveness, and so on—that cause so much consternation. None of these behaviors are necessarily antisocial, although they can easily be pushed in that direction in antisocial environments. Nor does anyone claim a causal role

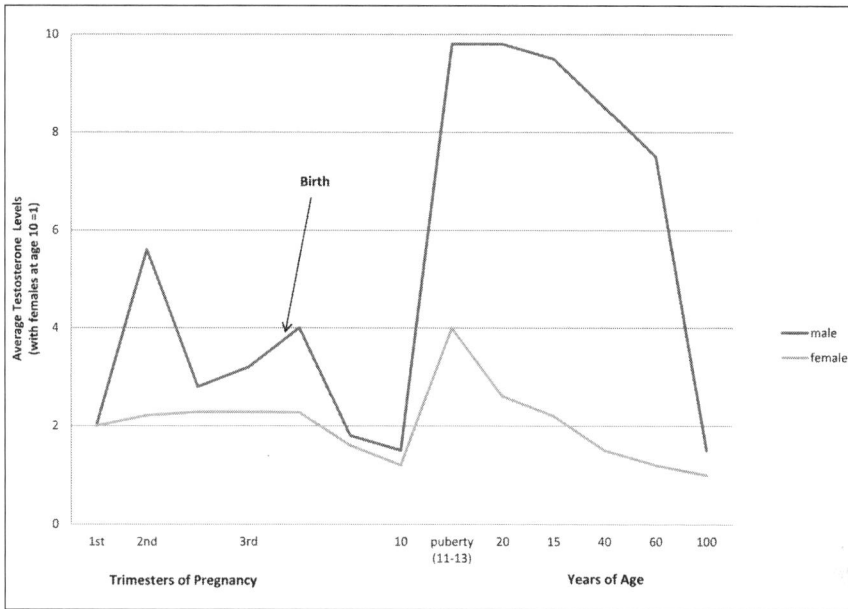

Figure 5.2   Testosterone levels of human males and females from conception to old age

Source: Ellis & Walsh (2000)

for T in these behaviors. Although T levels are highly heritable, at least 40% of the variance is attributable to environmental factors (Booth et al., 2006). T levels rise and fall to help organisms meet the challenges they confront. The "need" to conform to risky behavioral patterns, to seek dangerous sensations, and to engage in dominance competitions with other males certainly qualify as challenges that would require raising T levels to meet them (Mazur, 2005).[1]

Adolescent risk-taking does not mean that teenagers lack the reasoning capacity to evaluate danger. In purely rational terms, the reasoning of 15-year-olds is on par with adults, in that they are just as able to perceive risk and estimate vulnerability,

---

1   The effects of T on body morphology and on behavior are not simply a function of T levels. Most T in the blood is not free to activate tissue because it is bound to sex hormone-binding globulin (SHBG). Males apparently have about half the level of female SHBG, thus is might be said that males not only have about 10 times more T than females, they actually might have about 20 times the "free" (unbound) levels of T (Ellis et al., 2008). The effects of T also depend to a great extent on the efficiency of the androgen receptors (ARs). The AR gene is polymorphic, coming in short and long forms of a C-A-G repeats, with the short repeat more efficiently utilizing T (Perrin et al., 2008). We discuss the AR gene further in Chapter 8.

but teens tend to discount their perceptions and risk estimates because of poor impulse control and poor emotional regulation, not poor logical reasoning (Reyna & Farley, 2006). Adolescents can act just like adults under most conditions, but fall back on emotions and on cues from their peers when under stress. Logical decisions relating to risky behavior are easily undermined among adolescents when emotions are in the driver's seat and similarly emotion-driven peers occupy the passenger seats. The neurobiological data show the physical reasons for the adolescent surge in sensation-seeking and the propensity to favor short-term hedonism over more reasoned long-term goals.

The Adolescent Brain

While the T surge explains some of the changes in adolescent behavior, the problem of impulse control and emotional regulation suggests that teens are not fully able to access areas of the brain that allow adults to react to stress and danger in more controlled ways. The neurobiological data show the physical reasons for the adolescent surge in sensation-seeking and the propensity to favor short-term hedonism over more reasoned long-term goals. Studies using fMRI have shown that compared to children and adults, adolescents have exaggerated nucleus accumbens activity feeding into the PFC, thus perhaps hampering the PFC's ability to guide emotions (Eshel et al., 2007; Galvan et al., 2006).

Adolescence is accompanied by increases in neurotransmitters that excite motivation, and a reduction in those that inhibit it (Collins, 2004; Walker, 2002). Adolescents are thus provided with all the biological tools needed to increase novelty-seeking, sensation-seeking, status-seeking, and competitiveness. All these changes strongly suggest that the mechanisms of adolescence are adaptations forged by natural selection precisely to function in risky and competitive ways (Spear, 2000; White, 2004). Mid-adolescence and early adulthood is a period of intense competition among males for dominance and status among many primate species, aimed ultimately at securing more mating opportunities than the next male. As Martin Daly (1996:193) put it: "There are many reasons to think that we've been designed to be maximally competitive and conflictual in young adulthood."

In addition to the changes in neurotransmitter ratios, the pubertal hormonal surge prompts the increase of gene expression in the brain to slowly refine the neural circuitry to its adult form (Sisk & Zehr, 2005). The PFC undergoes a wave of synaptic overproduction just prior to puberty, followed by a period of pruning during adolescence and early adulthood, and these changes are particularly significant in the PFC: "Significant changes in multiple regions of the prefrontal cortex [occur] throughout the course of adolescence, especially with respect to the processes of myelination and synaptic pruning" (Steinberg, 2005:70). The process of myelinating the adolescent PFC is far from complete, which accounts for the "time lapse" between the adolescent perception of an emotional event in the limbic system and the rational judgment of it in the PFC. The relative low level of

PFC myelination has also been implicated in the weaker decision-making skills of adolescents (Beckman, 2004). Myelination depends partly on activity-dependent interaction between neurons and glial cells (Fields, 2005). The steep growth of white matter (myelinated axons) also depends to a great extent on testosterone in males, but not in females (Perrin et al., 2008). Even within the structure of the PFC itself, the ventral regions that are the foundation of emotional evaluation mature earlier than the dorsal and lateral regions that underlie executive functions (Romer, 2010).

Functional MRI studies (for example, Monk et al., 2008) have shown that adolescents exhibit greater limbic activation in response to angry and fearful faces than to happy and neutral faces, whereas adults show the opposite. A number of other imaging studies (for example, Casey et al., 2010) have demonstrated less functional connectivity between the PFC–amygdala network in response to fear cues in adolescents compared to children and adults. Other fMRI studies have shown exaggerated nucleus accumbens response in adolescents compared to children and adults when receiving a reward, as well as significantly greater limbic–PFC imbalance in adolescents compared to children and adults (Somerville, Jones & Casey, 2010). These data indicate that adolescents pay greater attention to negative emotional states than adults.

Ernst, Pine, and Hardin (2006:299) sum up much of this literature and explain risky adolescent behavior in terms of an imbalance between areas in the brain associated with approach/avoidance behaviors (the BAS/BIS systems): "The propensity during adolescence for reward/novelty seeking in the face of uncertainly or potential harm might be explained by a strong reward system (nucleus accumbens), a weak harm-avoidance system (amygdala), and/or an inefficient supervisory system (medial/ventral prefrontal cortex)." The explosion of earlier studies such as these led to four major conclusions relating to the adolescent brain from the 2003 neuroscience conference of the New York Academy of Sciences. These conclusions are summarized by White (2004:4):

1. Much of the behavior characterizing adolescence is rooted in biology intermingling with environmental influences to cause teens to conflict with their parents, take more risks, and experience wide swings in emotion.
2. The lack of synchrony between a physically mature body and a still maturing nervous system may explain these behaviors.
3. Adolescents' sensitivities to rewards appear to be different than in adults, prompting them to seek higher levels of novelty and stimulation to achieve the same feeling of pleasure.
4. With the right dose of guidance and understanding, adolescence can be a relatively smooth transition.

The first three conclusions have helped criminologists to understand the link between teenage behavior and the brain, and the fourth gives cause for optimism, since this is the outcome for the vast majority of individuals who temporarily slip off the prosocial tracks in their youth. There are *physical* reasons for the immature and sometimes antisocial behavior of adolescents. The immaturity of the teen brain combined with a teen physiology on fast-forward facilitates the tendency to assign faulty attributions to the intentions of others. In other words, a brain on "go-slow superimposed on a physiology on fast-forward" explains why many teenagers "find it difficult to accurately gauge the meanings and intentions of others and to experience more stimuli as aversive during adolescence than they did as children and will do so when they are adults" (Walsh, 2002:143). As Richard Restak (2001:76) put it: "The immaturity of the adolescent's behavior is perfectly mirrored by the immaturity of the adolescent's brain."

Puberty and Delinquency

Because T is related to seeking and maintaining dominance and status, if the social context is such that obtaining dominance and status requires acts of antisocial bravado, then T becomes a useful facilitator. One of the mediating mechanisms by which T does this is by reducing fear (Van Honk, Peper & Schutter, 2005), which helps to explain why high T levels are found in high sensation-seekers (Zuckerman, 2007). But T is only one link in a chain of interacting biological and social variables which push behavior one way or another. T is only an accomplice in an aggressive act; it is not the perpetrator. The perpetrator is the whole organism making use of its entire toolbox in an effort to achieve the biologically relevant goal of dominance, which itself is the handmaiden of the ultimate goal of all life— reproductive success.

Although the relationship between T and violent aggression is strong among non-human animals, it is much weaker among humans, among whom there are layers of cultural and cognitive buffers mediating the relationship. Reviews of the literature (for example, Ellis, 2005) report average correlations between T and criminality to be a modest 0.20–0.25. The interplay between T and social context is illustrated in a longitudinal study of 1,400 boys which found that T levels were unrelated to conduct problems for boys with "non-deviant" or "possibly deviant" friends, but conduct problems were greatly elevated among boys with high T who associated with "definitely deviant" peers (Maughan, 2005). Given the responsiveness of T to experience, this relationship might reflect high-T boys self-selecting into deviant peer groups, or in the activities of deviant peer groups raising the T levels of boys engaging in them.

A longitudinal study that assessed multiple measures of antisocial behavior and repeated measures of T among males followed from age 12 to 21 found that males who had an official criminal record at age 21 had higher T levels at age 16 than males without a record, and that those with the highest T levels from ages 13 to 20 were the most delinquent (Van Bokhoven et al., 2006). Males with the highest T levels were also higher in both reactive and proactive aggression. All males in the study were from lower-socioeconomic status families, and were thus vulnerable to antisocial behavior for other reasons, but because SES was a constant, it could not be construed as a source of variance in the T–antisocial behavior relationship.

Several studies show generally that the earlier the onset of puberty, the greater the level of problem behavior for both girls and boys, which may suggest the interplay of T and adolescent brain changes (Haynie, 2003). For instance, Cota-Robles, Neiss, and Rowe's (2002) study of 5,550 Anglo American, African American, and Mexican American boys found that early maturing boys in all three groups reported higher levels of both violent and nonviolent delinquency than other boys. An earlier study found that T level predicted future problem behavior, but only for boys who entered puberty early (Drigotas & Udry, 1993). Felson and Haynie (2002) found that boys who experienced early onset of puberty were more likely to commit a number of delinquent and other antisocial acts than other boys, but also that they were also more autonomous, better psychologically adjusted, and had more friends.

Adolescence and Moffitt's Developmental Theory

Most adolescents, of course, do not engage in major life-defining antisocial acts. Biglan and Cody (2003), for instance, found among youths aged 12–20 that 18% of them accounted for 88% of criminal arrests and 66% of drunk driving arrests. Thus, there is only a small subset of youths who are of major concern. Cohort studies in the United States and abroad have consistently shown that although about one-third of adolescents acquire a delinquent record, a small proportion commit a vastly disproportionate percentage of the offenses. It is also consistently found that high-rate offenders begin their criminal careers in childhood and continue long into adulthood (Farrington, 1996). Data such as these have long suggested that there are two primary trajectories of offending with their own developmental histories.

Terrie Moffitt's (1993) biosocial developmental theory provides the best theoretical context to explore the differences between high- and low-rate adolescent offenders. The theory posits dual pathways to offending: one that begins in early childhood and continues well into adulthood, and the other in which offending is limited to the adolescent years. Moffitt called the first pathway the life-course-persistent (LCP) pathway, and the second the adolescent-limited (AL) pathway. Moffitt does not claim that all offenders fit snugly into one or the other of these categories, or that LCP offenders literally offend across their entire lives. The model is simply a convenient typology into which the great majority of offenders fit.

Moffitt proposes that neuropsychological and temperamental impairments initiate a cumulative process of negative person–environment interactions for LCP offenders that result in a life-course trajectory that propels them toward ever-hardening antisocial attitudes and behaviors. The impairments most often mentioned—low IQ, hyperactivity, inattentiveness, negatively emotionality, and low impulse control—are consistently and robustly found to be correlated with criminality (Agnew, 2005; Moffitt & Walsh, 2003). These impairments arise from a combination of genetic and environmental effects on nervous system development that are exacerbated by ineffective socialization because problem children tend to have ineffectual parents. Moffitt describes the antisocial trajectory of LCP offenders as one of:

> biting and hitting at age 4, shoplifting and truancy at age 10, selling drugs and stealing cars at age 16, robbery and rape at age 22, fraud and child abuse at age 30; the underlying disposition remains the same, but its expression changes form as new social opportunities arise at different points of development. (1993:679)

Behavioral consistency across time is matched by cross-situational behavioral consistency: LCP offenders, "lie at home, steal from shops, cheat at school, fight in bars, and embezzle at work" (Moffitt, 1993:679).

Adolescent-limited offenders have a different developmental history which puts them on a prosocial trajectory that is temporarily derailed at adolescence. AL youths are statistically normal, and we may view their offending as adaptive responses to conditions and transitional events that temporarily divert them from their basically prosocial life-course trajectories. In other words, they are responding to the social and biological changes of adolescence in a totally normative way, including disengaging from parents and bonding with peers. That is, AL offending is a group social phenomenon that does not reflect any kind of stable personal deficiencies. These youths may turn their envious eyes on LCP offenders, who have ostensibly gained independence and have obtained a modicum of the resources (cars, nice clothes, access to sex partners) that signal mature status. Because the behavior of LCP offenders seems to bring desired results, AL delinquents are drawn to them and mimic their behavior. Many studies of friendship patterns and popularity find that the most popular boys are sociable, athletic, and cooperative, but about a third of the most popular boys are antisocial youths who are frequently disruptive and belligerent and "central members of prominent classroom cliques" (Rodkin et al., 2000:21). Studies also show that as youngsters age into adolescence, they begin to admire good students less and aggressive antisocial peers more (Bukowski, Sippola & Newcomb, 2000). AL delinquents internalize the idea that antisocial behavior, popularity, and independence go together, and thus receive validation for their oppositional behavior.

It is important to note that for LCP delinquents, *stable* antisocial traits precede association with delinquent peers and exemplify active rGE, but for AL offenders, association with delinquent peers precedes the development of *temporary* antisocial traits. This suggests that association with delinquent peers may be necessary to initiate delinquency for AL offenders, and that there is little or no genetic influence on delinquency for them at a time in life when peer influence is very important. As AL offenders mature neurologically and become freer to structure their environments consistent with their genetic preferences, they realize that a criminal record will limit their future options. They begin to knuckle down, take on responsible roles, and desist from further offending. Unlike LCP offenders who have burnt their bridges to the prosocial world, AL offenders have accumulated a store of positive attachments (they elicit positive responses from others) and academic skills (they are intelligent and conscientious) which provide them with prosocial opportunities such as a good marriage and a good job. In short, AL offenders desist from antisocial behavior because, in Moffitt's (1993:690) words, they are "psychologically healthy," and "Healthy youths respond adaptively to changing contingencies."

Moffitt's theory has been widely tested; a review of these studies conducted ten years after the theory was first proposed found strong support for it (Moffitt & Walsh, 2003). Overall, these studies show that LCP offenders almost always had childhood temperament problems identifiable at age 3 years, and that they were more likely to have weak family bonds, low verbal IQ, and the psychopathic traits of callousness and impulsivity. LCP were much more likely to commit serious violent crimes such as robbery, rape, and assault, while AL boys typically committed offenses such as petty theft and public drunkenness. Although LCP boys constituted only 7% of the cohort, they were responsible for more than 50% of all delinquent acts committed by it.

Culture Matters

While the biological changes of puberty are universal, the behavioral "storm and stress" of these changes is not. A culture's level of socioeconomic development, its customs and child-rearing practices, all influence how adolescence is perceived, experienced, and responded to. We have already noted the wide gap between biological and social maturity in developed countries. Moffitt (1993:692) views the maturity gap as largely responsible for the high prevalence of juvenile offending in Western societies: "adolescent-limited offending is a product of an interaction between age and historical period." The cohort contained only a small number of males who avoided any antisocial behavior during childhood and adolescence. Moffitt's theory predicts that teens who abstain from any form of antisocial behavior would be rare, and they must have either structural barriers that prevent them from exercising antisocial behavior, a smaller than average maturity gap, or unappealing characteristics that cause them to be excluded from teen social group activities. The most obvious reason for why some adolescents do not offend, from her perspective, is that they do not experience the maturity gap to the same degree as most young people do. Abstainers may experience late puberty and/or early initiation into adult roles and responsibilities—throwbacks to an age in which puberty arrived later and less preparation was needed to enter the job market. Moffitt also speculates that abstainers may belong to religious and cultural groups in which youths are given early access to adult privileges and adult accountability.

The meaning of adolescence also varies across cultures. In individualistic cultures where individuals are expected to become autonomous and independent, there is likely to be more intergenerational turbulence than in collectivist cultures (Trommsdorff, 2002). Most adolescents in these cultures fit into what would be the "throwback" category in Moffitt's theory. Moreover, the autonomy and independence so valued in Western societies is not as valued in collectivist/ communitarian/paternalistic societies; rather, being integrated into a group is more valued in such societies (Choudhury, 2009). As we noted in our discussions of the 5-HTTLPR and DRD4 polymorphisms in Chapter 2, because of many centuries of gene–culture co-evolution, most of the inhabitants of China, Japan, and Korea carry the alleles that predispose them to adapt successfully to collectivist cultural values. In those cultures, older people, especially the elderly, tend to be respected and revered as fonts of wisdom, not as people from whom the young should distance themselves.

Parental warmth is also apparently affected by collectivism versus individualism. Chen and Farruggia (2002) propose that individualism leads to a greater propensity to place the needs of self over the needs of others. Consequently, parents in an individualistic society may expend less care (time constraints involved in working mothers also figure into this) and affection on their children than parents in collectivist cultures. In such situations, adolescents turn to their peers to form affectionate ties with others, and spend more time with them. Gang theorists have long maintained that gangs function as surrogate families, and that the children most likely to be attracted to gang life are those reared in single-parent homes lacking in affection and supervision. Gang members often display their belonging to and affection for the gang through initiation rites, secret gang signals, special clothing, "colors," and tattoos, all of which shout out loud: "I belong!" "I'm valued!" As one researcher described the function of gangs: "The gang serves emotional needs. You feel wanted. You feel welcome. You feel important. And there is discipline and there are rules" (Bing, 1991:12).

Other societies hold ritual ceremonies (rites of passage) that are publicly witnessed, marking the entry in adulthood. These ceremonies are typically initiations into adult roles of responsibility, having to do with work and family roles—productivity and fertility as those roles are practiced in that society (Chen & Farruggia, 2002). There are no clear-cut publicly witnessed initiation ceremonies in Western societies where the young can say "Now I'm a man" (or woman) and be publicly acknowledged as such. In addition, and importantly, in cultures with less adequate nutrition and medical care, children will enter puberty later. In such cultures, the young are also expected to work and take on reproductive responsibilities very soon after puberty, thus we do not see the disjunction between biology and culture which has the potential to make the transition from childhood to adulthood difficult for a significant proportion of Western children.[2]

---

2   There are obviously also individual differences among adolescents within the same culture that can explain why some do not engage in antisocial acts. Moffitt finds abstainers to be less well adjusted than adolescents who experiment with delinquency. At age 18, these abstainers described themselves as extremely self-controlled, fearful, interpersonally timid,

Conclusion

This chapter has examined the age–crime curve and the so-called *Sturm und Drang* of adolescence—a period that begins at adolescence and which has no readily definable end. It is marked by a huge surge in hormone steroids that initiate the development of the secondary sexual characteristics as well as some equally dramatic brain changes. Teenage brains seem to be wired for action, risk-taking, and competition because there is an imbalance between the brain's rational and emotional systems. It was noted that culture plays a very large part in how adolescence is experienced and expressed, and that the biggest cultural influence in Western societies is the disjunction between biology (earlier onset of puberty) and society (a longer period between puberty and obtaining socially responsible roles).

It was noted that the vast majority of adolescents who commit antisocial acts (most of which are relatively minor) will desist as their brains slowly attain their adult form and opportunities arise to acquire responsible adult roles. Even though the power of informal social control in Western societies is lacking relative to those of more collectivist societies, and thus condemns them to suffer higher levels of youthful antisocial behavior, perhaps many consider this an acceptable price for the greater freedoms enjoyed in those societies. Whatever one's opinion on that, it is comforting to end this chapter by again quoting the New York Academy of Sciences' fourth conclusion from its conference on the neuroscience of the adolescent brain: "With the right dose of guidance and understanding, adolescence can be a relatively smooth transition" (White, 2004:4).

---

socially inept, and latecomers to sexual relationships. Abstainers were the type of good and compliant students who become unpopular with peers (Bukowski et al., 2000) and fit the profile reported for youth who abstained from drug and sexual experimentation in a historical period when it was normative (Shedler & Block, 1990; Walsh, 1995). Although their teenage years had been troubling, abstainers became successful in adulthood. They retained their self-constrained personality as adults, had virtually no crime or mental disorder, were likely to have settled into marriage, were delaying children (a desirable strategy for a generation needing prolonged education to succeed), were likely to be college-educated, held high-status jobs, and expressed optimism about their own futures.

Chapter 6
Substance Abuse Disorders, Epigenetic Plasticity, and Criminal Behavior

Alcohol Abuse and Dependence

Humans have an inordinate fondness for alcohol and other mind-altering substances; we gulp, sniff, inhale, and inject with a gusto that suggests sobriety is a difficult state to tolerate. We drink to be sociable, to liven up our parties, to loosen our tongues, to feel good, to sedate ourselves, and to anesthetize the pains of life. Alcohol allows us to reinvent ourselves as superior people; the worried and the insecure become carefree and confident, the timid courageous, the diffident brash, and the wallflower flirtatious. The downside is the toll it takes in return, because alcohol is the greatest substance abuse threat there is. No other correlate, with the possible exception of gender, is as closely related to crime as alcohol abuse. Alcohol is linked to about 85,000 deaths a year, versus the "mere" 17,000 fatalities attributable to other illicit drugs (DrugWarFacts, 2008). City police officers spend more than half of their law enforcement time on alcohol-related offenses. Estimates are that one-third of all arrests in the United States are for alcohol-related offenses, and that about 75% of robberies and 80% of homicides involve a drunken offender and/or victim (Schmalleger, 2004). About 40% of other violent offenders in the United States had been drinking at the time of the offense (Martin, 2001). The cost of alcohol abuse in terms of crime, health, family and occupational disruption is staggering. Crimes associated with alcohol and drugs combined were estimated to have cost the economy over $205 billion in 2005 (Miller et al., 2006).

Alcohol is a depressant drug that affects our behavior by inhibiting the functioning of the higher brain centers. As we ingest more alcohol, our behavior increasingly becomes less inhibited as the neocortex surrenders control to the emotions of the more primitive limbic system. Raw basic emotions are then expressed without benefit of first being channeled to the PFC for rational consideration. Alcohol abusers who experience this surrender may be classified as problem drinkers if they are able to recognize their problem and are able to stop drinking in the face of social, marital, and occupational problems. Those who continue to drink despite such problems may be considered alcohol-dependent (alcoholic).

Alcoholism is a chronic condition marked by progressive incapacity to control alcohol consumption despite psychological, social, and physiological disruptions. It is a state of altered cellular physiology caused by the repetitive consumption of alcohol that manifests itself in physical disturbances when alcohol use is suspended (withdrawal symptoms). Alcoholics do not necessarily drink to achieve a "high," but to avoid the physiological pains of alcohol withdrawal, which can be more life-threatening than withdrawal from narcotics. Although only about 14% of frequent alcohol users descend into the hell of addiction (Bierut et al., 2010), non-alcoholics who abuse alcohol constitute the majority of criminal justices problems because there are a lot more of them. The acute effects on violent behavior are much greater than the chronic effects—the immediate effects of impaired judgment experienced by anyone who drinks to much rather than the results of long-term effects on the physiology of individuals who are alcoholics (Giancola et al., 2010). Nevertheless, it is a rare chronic offender who is not also a chronic abuser of alcohol and other kinds of mind-altering substances.

The Genetics of Alcoholism

Cascades of family, adoptee, and twin studies lead to the conclusion that vulnerability to alcohol addiction is strongly related to genetics. If millions of people can drink every day without it seriously affecting their lives, it means that those unable to control their drinking must have some sort of congenital liability. Estimates of the heritability of alcoholism range between 0.49 and 0.64, indicating considerable variance in the reinforcement properties of alcohol across individual genotypes (Bevilacqua & Goldman, 2009). A bewildering number of genes synthesize and regulate the neurotransmitters and enzymes implicated in alcoholism. For instance, a large meta-analysis of 2,343 lines of evidence from peer-reviewed journals identified 316 alcohol addiction-related genes and 13 addiction-related pathways (the molecular routes and interactions among neurotransmitters and enzymes to produce the effect) to alcohol addiction (Li, Mao & Wei 2008). Thus, "Genetic vulnerability to alcoholism is likely to be due to numerous genes of small to modest effects on many neurotransmitter systems (for example, opioid, serotonin, dopamine, gamma-aminobutyric acid [GABA], glutamate, and cannabinoid) and signal transduction pathways within the mesolimbic dopamine reward pathways" (Enoch, 2006). These same polymorphisms also affect traits marking vulnerability to criminal behavior (Hall, 2006).

Moussas, Christodoulou, and Douzenis (2009:3) state that "Antisocial behaviour is considered not only to be related more than any other behavioural disorder to alcohol dependence, but it also may predict it." This does not mean that alcoholism and criminality are synonymous. It does mean that there are sufficient genetic, neurobiological, and environmental similarities between them that one can be used as a strong predictor of the other. For example, a large study of twins found that factors accompanying externalizing disorders such as antisocial personality disorder and conduct disorder accounted for 71% of the genetic liability to alcoholism (Kendler et al., 2003). This similarity is reflected in reward dominance theory in criminology and the "craving brain" concept in alcoholism theory. There is an old saying among alcoholics that is a metaphor for the "craving brain": "One drink is one too many, but a hundred drinks are never enough." This seemingly contradictory statement informs us that a single drink activates the pleasure centers in the nucleus accumbens by activating dopamine, but that one drink leads to such a craving for more that no amount will satiate.

One line of thought is that the craving brain is a reward-dominant brain, because the craving for alcohol (or other drugs) is unopposed by serotonin (Yacubian et al., 2007). Alcohol initially increases serotonin, but then rapidly decreases it, thereby allowing for the reduced impulse-control capacity of the PFC (Badawy, 2003). The craving brain concept is common to all craving behaviors (eating, gambling, sex, drugs, smoking), not just to alcoholism, which is why few people are addicted to just one substance or behavior, and why individuals easily addicted are also ripe candidates for criminal behavior (Ellis, 2003).

But addiction is not only about hedonic pleasure, because we all receive gratification from the natural pleasures (eating, drinking, sexual activity, bonding) that natural selection has built into us to assure that we like doing things that contribute to our survival and reproduction efforts. The euphoria obtained from unnatural (that is, evolutionarily novel) pleasures hijacks the brain because they involve much greater dopamine signaling at the synapse, thus usurping neural circuits that control responses to natural rewards. As Hyman (2007:10) explains: "unlike natural rewards, addictive drugs always signal 'better than expected.' Neural circuits 'over-learn' on an excessive and grossly distorted dopamine signal."

"Better than expected" is a subjective appraisal of bodily states arising from neural firing patterns. Dopaminergic neurons transmit signals by phasic firing (short transient bursts of several signals) or tonic firing (low signaling over a longer period). The patterns of phasic/tonic firing are thought to determine the salience of a reward signal (Tsai et al., 2009). A reward that is "better than expected" results in increased DA firing, and one that is "worse than expected" results in less firing. Natural rewards that are "just as expected" do not alter the homeostatic rates of DA neuronal firing. It has been proposed by many addiction researchers that the transition from casual use of alcohol and other drugs to addiction reflects the shift from "better than expected" to "worse than expected" (Wand, 2008).

There are many "closet alcoholics" who never run afoul of the law and who seem agreeable to many people, thus the "alcoholic = crook" formulation does not always hold up. Researchers have long noticed this, and have divided alcoholics broadly into *Type I* and *Type II* alcoholics. As Crabbe (2002:449) describes the two types: "Type I alcoholism is characterized by mild abuse, minimal criminality, and passive-dependent personality variables, whereas Type II alcoholism is characterized by early onset, violence, and criminality, and is largely limited to males." The distinction made between Type I and Type II alcoholics is reminiscent of Terrie Moffitt's distinction between adolescent-limited and life-course-persistent offenders discussed in the previous chapter. Type II alcoholics can be likened to LCP offenders. They start drinking (and using other drugs) at a very early age and rapidly become addicted, and have many character disorders and behavioral problems that *precede* their alcoholism. Type I alcoholics are akin to

AL offenders. They start drinking later in life than Type IIs, progress to alcoholism slowly, and are much better candidates for maintaining sobriety. Type Is typically have families and careers, and if they have character defects, these are typically induced by the alcohol, and not permanent (Crabbe, 2002). The heritability estimates reported above (0.49–0.64) are based on Type I and Type II alcoholics combined, but for Type II alcoholics, heritability is about 0.90 and less than 0.40 for Type I alcoholics (McGue, 1999). Environmental factors are thus much more important to understanding Type I than Type II alcoholism (Crabbe, 2002). Fishbein (1998) proposes that Type II alcoholics have inherited abnormalities of the serotonergic and dopaminergic systems (probably the risk alleles of the DRD2 and 5-HTTLPR polymorphisms) that may be driving both their drinking and their antisocial behavior.

Addiction is a form of alcohol-induced neural plasticity. The acute changes in brain chemistry induced by alcohol are the reason why we feel the pleasurable mood changes that make drinking so reinforcing. Although alcohol is ultimately a brain-numbing depressant, at low dosage it is a stimulant because it raises dopamine levels in the nucleus accumbens. It also reduces anxiety, worry, and tension by increasing the levels of the neurotransmitter gamma-aminobutyric acid by increasing its release and by enhancing its binding to GABA receptors. GABA is the major inhibitory neurotransmitter—when it occupies a receptor, it dampens the neuron's electrical activity. The effect of alcohol-enhanced GABA expression is "reduced anxiety about the consequences of aggressive [or any other behavior not normally evoked when sober] behavior" (Martin, 2001:41). Alcohol ingestion also inhibits the release of glutamate, the most prevalent excitatory neurotransmitter, which accounts for alcohol's inhibition of cognitive and motor skills and its sedative effects.

As previously noted, the process of allostasis maintains the stability of a physiological system outside of its normal homeostatic range. Allostatic adjustments to GABA receptors in response to excessive activation involve reducing the number of functional GABA receptors. This results in the lessened ability of the GABAergic system to counteract the glutamatergic excitation of neurons, thus upsetting the normal fine balance between excitation and inhibition of the central nervous system. This is the reason that for those who are seriously dependent on alcohol, even short abstinence from alcohol can result in anxiety attacks, tremors, convulsions, insomnia, and memory loss, and why abstinence is so difficult to maintain (Heinz, 2006).

Epigenetics and Substance Abuse

Additional nuances on the interplay of nature and nurture are provided by the science of epigenetics. The prefix "epi" means "on" or "in addition to," thus epigenetics means "on or in addition to the genes." A broad definition of epigenetics is "any process that alters gene activity without changing the DNA sequence" (Weinhold, 2006:163). Epigenetic modifications affect the ability of the DNA code to be read and translated into proteins by making the code accessible or inaccessible (Gottleib, 2007). DNA itself only specifies for transcription into messenger RNA (mRNA), which has to be translated by transfer RNA (tRNA) and assembled by ribosomal RNA (rRNA). The genes are switched on and off by signals from the organism's internal chemical environment and/or by its external environment, according to the challenges it faces.

Epigenetics highlights genomic plasticity, similar to the idea of neural plasticity. Neural plasticity is developmental because it allows for novel responses as the brain is physically calibrated to environmental events; the same applies to genomic plasticity. No one proposes that the genome possesses the level of plasticity that the brain does, but epigenetics provides the software by which organisms respond genetically to their environments without changing the DNA hardware. Epigenetic modifications of DNA are more vulnerable to environmental factors than the DNA itself because there is no intracellular repair system for epigenetic errors similar to the system that repairs nucleotide copying errors in the DNA (Kubota et al., 2010). Genome plasticity, like brain plasticity, is therefore both good and bad according to the environments it is exposed to. Because epigenetic processes regulate gene expression according to what the organism does or ingests, the epigenetics of substance abuse is of major importance to social scientists who want a deeper understanding of this major crime correlate.

The epigenetic regulation of genetic activity is accomplished by two main processes: DNA methylation and acetylation (also called histone modification). Acetylation involves a groups of atoms called an acetyl group attaching itself to histones (see Figures 6.1a and 6.1b), which has the effect of "loosening" or "relaxing" them, which increases the likelihood of genetic expression. Conversely, deacetylation (the removal of the acetyl group) has the opposite effect (Lopez-Rangel & Lewis, 2006). DNA methylation occurs when a group of atoms called a methyl group is attached to a cytosine base which prevents the translation of DNA into mRNA, and hence the protein the gene codes for is not manufactured (Corwin, 2004). To apply a criminal justice metaphor to these processes, acetylation is a mechanism that aids and abets gene expression, and methylation arrests it. Methylation can produce stable, even permanent, changes in genetic functioning, but acetylation is labile and reversible (Powledge, 2009).

Epigenetic Mechanisms of Drug Addiction

Understanding how drugs (including the drug alcohol) alter brain chemistry provides criminologists with a better understanding both of why addiction is so difficult to beat and of the importance of gene–environment interactions. As is the case with alcoholism, multiple genes, enzymes, and transcription factors are involved in drug addiction, with over 100 genes known to be changed with repeated cocaine exposure (Madras, 2006). There are at least three models of the pathway

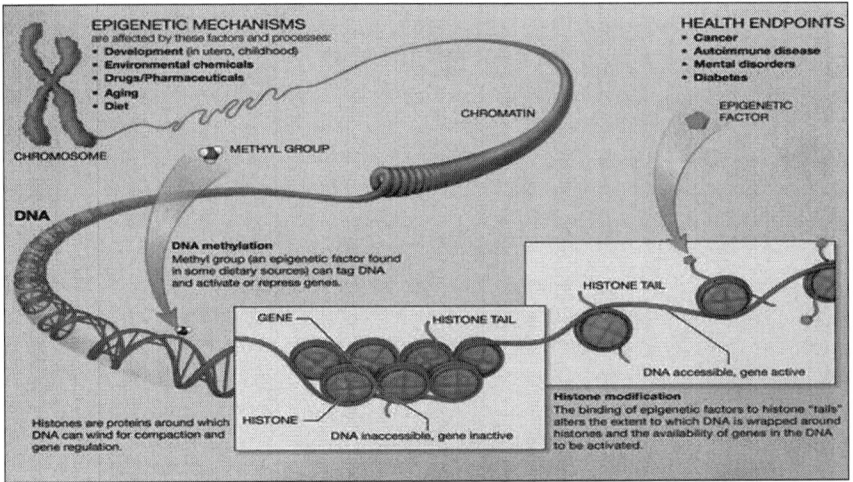

Figure 6.1a   DNA methylation and acetylation

Source: <http://www.drugabuse.gov/NIDA-notes/NNvol121N4/gene.html>

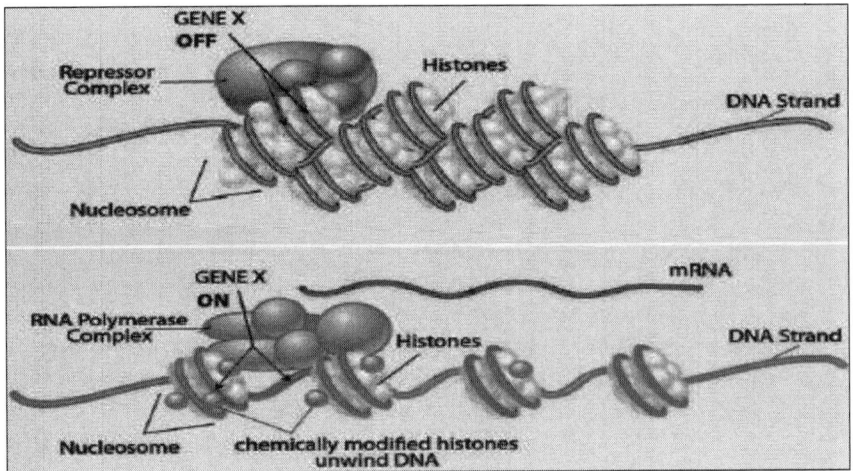

Figure 6.1b   Illustrating DNA methylation (top) and acetylation (bottom)

Source: <http://www.drugabuse.gov/NIDA-notes/NNvol121N4/gene.html>

from use to addiction, indicating that individual differences in susceptibility must be considered. All three models have in common the role played by dopamine signaling, and all point to weak executive functioning (impulsivity, low self-control), which implicates the roles of the PFC and the serotonergic system (Ahmed, Graupner & Gutkin, 2009).

We couch our discussion of epigenetic mechanisms in terms of cocaine addiction because it has the largest average heritability coefficient (0.67) of all commonly abused substances (Bevilacqua & Goldman, 2009). However, only about 15–16% of users become addicted, just slightly more than the percentage of users of alcohol who become addicted to alcohol (Robinson & Berridge, 2003). The bare outline of what cocaine does is that it releases DA in the pleasure centers and then blocks its reuptake into the presynaptic knob. This blockage leaves DA signaling at DA receptors for much longer than the milliseconds it resides there in response to natural rewards. When DA stays in the synaptic gap and is not taken back up for repackaging, it is eventually broken down by enzymes. The exposure and destruction of excess DA at the synapse leads to depletion of the neurons' supply, leaving the abuser unable to feel much pleasure from natural rewards. This is an abnormal state of affairs for which the brain tries to compensate. Because these mechanisms of compensation (allostasis) that lead to the hell of addiction are complex, in the spirit of the old adage "A picture is worth a thousand words," we present out discussion with reference to Figures 6.1a and 6.1b.

In the upper left-hand corner of Figure 6.1a we have a chromosome, which is a structure of protein and long chains of DNA containing numerous genes. This combination of DNA and proteins is called chromatin. The primary protein components of chromatin are called histones, which are the spools shown in the figure around which the DNA is wound. Histones play an important role in gene regulation. As shown in Figure 6.1b, a nucleosome is DNA wrapped around histone protein cores. Figure 6.1a shows a methyl group attaching itself to the DNA, and the top diagram in Figure 6.1b illustrates what happens when it does. The initial process of reading the DNA code for a given substance is called transcription, and is carried out in the cell nucleus by an enzyme called RNA polymerase (RNAP). When a protein needs to be manufactured, RNAP runs along the DNA strand, "reading" the recipe for that protein, and fashions a complementary strand of mRNA which leaves the nucleus and enters the cell's protein factory. When a methyl group attaches to a cytosine base (tagged as "repressor complex" in Figure 6.1b), it prevents the code from being read—no transcription order, no protein.

The opposite effect is illustrated in the bottom part of Figure 6.1b. Here we see RNAP doing its job in reading the recipe for "gene X" and clipping off the transcribed strand of mRNA. The right-hand insert of Figure 6.1a shows how one of a family of enzymes called histone acetyltransferaces (HATs) transfers an acetyl group of atoms that bind to lysine at the histone tail. This is thought to work by reducing lysine's attraction to the negatively charged phosphate backbone of DNA. The reduced electrostatic charge loosens the chromatin, enabling the RNAP to transcribe a gene (Renthal & Nestler, 2009). Conversely, another group of enzymes called histone deacetylases (HDACs) removes acetyl groups, thus reinstating the electrostatic attraction and repressing chromatin activity. Chronic cocaine use has been shown to induce histone acetylation in the nucleus accumbens by reducing HDAC functioning (Oh & Petronis, 2008). The optimal expression of genes is in large part a function of establishing a balance between the "on–off" enzymatic functions of HATs and HDACs (Tsankova et al., 2007).

The Allostatic Effects of Cocaine on the Nucleus Accumbens and Associated Centers

When cocaine is ingested, it activates neurotransmitters that send their messages to the various brain areas associated with reward and addiction, such as the nucleus accumbens (providing the pleasure and assigning salience), the PFC (providing the feedback), and the hippocampus (remembering how good it feels). Recall that messages from multiple dendrites are assembled in the cell body of the receiving neurons and a "decision" is made whether or not to pass the message on. A molecule called cyclic adenosine monophosphate (cAMP) is synthesized from adenosine triphosphate, the source of energy in all cells, a member of a group of intracellular molecules called "second messengers." These second messengers convey the messages from neurotransmitters (the first messengers) from the cell's membrane to its internal machinery. Chao & Nestler (2004:103) state that: "one of the best established molecular mechanisms of addiction is the upregulation of the cAMP second messenger pathway." It is through the actions of second messengers such as cAMP that long-term patterns of gene expression occur that change synaptic strength. Another way of putting it is that cAMP potentiates long-term memory, which is what addiction is all about.

The upregulation of cAMP results in the activation of a gene transcription factor (proteins that bind to genes and turn them on) called cAMP response element-binding protein (CREB), which in turn recruits one of the family of HATs (CREB-binding protein—CBP) to facilitate gene expression. CREB promotes the transcription of a number of genes implicated in addiction through its role in chromatin remodeling, which many addiction researchers consider to be the molecular process that underlies to transition from social use to addiction (Kalivas & O'Brien, 2008). Repeated exposure to cocaine (via the cAMP-CREB pathway) activates genes to produce a protein called dynorphin, which inhibits dopamine release in the ventral tegmental area, thus contributing strongly to certain aspects of tolerance (Madras, 2006).

Another transcription factor called delta FosB (ΔFosB) has effects opposite to those of CREB, leading to reverse tolerance—hypersensitivity to cocaine. This leads to many long-lasting structural changes in the reward circuitry of the nucleus accumbens that appear to promote the outflow of DA, glutamate, and other neurotransmitters. A single dose of cocaine will elevate chromatin acetylation for a short time, but with each intake of cocaine, ΔFosB slowly accumulates in the brain and will remain active long (sometimes for many weeks) after the effects of CREB have faded. This buildup converts acute brain responses to cocaine use into stable, and perhaps permanent, allostatic adaptations that signal the transition from abuse to addiction. Increasing levels of ΔFosB also change the neuroarchitecture by increasing brain-derived neurotrophic factor (BDNF). BDNF supports the survival of existing neurons, dendrites, and synapses, and encourages the growth and differentiation of new ones. In response to increased ΔFosB, BDNF increases and sustains extra dendritic branches and spines (synaptic sites on the dendrites) on neurons in the nucleus accumbens and PFC, which results in increased sensitivity and drug-seeking behavior (Nestler, Barrot & Self, 2001).

Opponent Process and Incentive Sensitization

The interplay of CREB and ΔFosB is an example of the psychologists' opponent process theory of motivation working at the intracellular molecular level. The theory maintains that emotions are oppositely paired, and that experiencing one emotion will engage its opponent (euphoria–dysphoria, fear–relief, and so on) after the termination of the stimulus that evoked the initial emotion is dissipated. The theory also avers that when one emotion is evoked in response to a stimulus, the other is automatically suppressed. This opponent process is deemed necessary so that the body can return to emotionally neutral homeostasis. Solomon (1980:693) provides an example of how extreme fear automatically engages its opponent—extreme elation—at the end of the stimulus that brought on the fear (parachute jumping):

> During their first free-fall, before the parachute opens, military parachutists may experience terror: They may yell, pupils dilated, eyes bulging, bodies curled forward and stiff, heart racing and breathing irregular. After they land safely, they may walk around with a stunned and stony-faced expression for a few minutes, and then usually they smile, chatter, and gesticulate, being very socially active and appearing to be elated.

However, repeated exposure to the stimulus will result in a lower level of the initial reaction and a stronger opposing reaction, and the individual will "crave" the next jump—not for the fear, but for fear's opponent: relief. According to the opponent-process theory of drug addiction, addiction is the result of the emotional pairing of pleasure (euphoria) associated with the drug, and pain (dysphoria) associated with withdrawal. The addict initially experiences high levels of pleasure and low levels of dysphoria from withdrawal. Drugs are positive reinforcers at this point; that is, they are taken because they provide pleasure. The hedonic process is of rather short duration, and over time, CREB-induced tolerance is reached and the addict requires increasing doses to achieve the same high. Not only is more of a substance required, the addict receives less and less pleasure from ingesting it. This is the transition from "better than expected" to "worse than expected."

We might ask why addicts continue to use if they are no longer positively reinforced by doing so. They do so because they are negatively reinforced (relieved from aversive stimuli). As the positive reinforcer (pleasure) decreases, withdrawal symptoms that accrue from not taking the drug increase, and this provides motivation to take the drug again. This negative process mediated by ΔFosB builds up strength slowly, decays even more slowly, and generates resistance to tolerance. Tolerance means that allostatic processes have changed the hedonic set point to a new and higher level, diminishing the effects of the drug. Once the set point has been established and the addict increases his or her cocaine consumption, the hedonic set point is pushed even further, leading to yet more consumption. Thus, it is seeking negative reinforcement (taking more cocaine to deal with the pleasure center's inability to deal with a hedonic set point that keeps escalating) rather than positive reinforcement that drives addiction. In short, the capacity of drugs to alleviate some aspects of dysphoria caused by the hedonic allostasis of the mesolimbic reward system is what sustains addictive behavior.

The incentive-sensitization model of addiction also maintains that addiction is caused by neuroadaptations resulting from long-term drug use, but focuses more on the brain's sensitization to cocaine as opposed to the development of tolerance. The model also suggests that the adaptations underlying sensitization are stable, and possibly permanent. As the phrase "incentive sensitization" implies, hypersensitization (ΔFosB at work) makes the stimulus to which the brain has been sensitized highly salient, and thus the incentive to pursue it compulsively. All natural rewards have incentive salience, but sensitization of the reward system by cocaine and other drugs results in the pathological enhancement of incentive salience so that drugs are sought, often at the expense of ignoring the natural rewards of food, sex, and social relationships. The model shows how drug cues (a hypodermic needle, an old drug buddy, or even a "Just say no!" poster) can trigger compulsive drug-seeking, drug-taking, and relapse, even after many months of abstinence (Robinson & Berridge, 2008).

Robinson and Berridge (2008) distinguish between "liking" a drug and "wanting" a drug, and show that the neural substrates for incentive-sensitization that attributes salience to wanting and liking are separate, although they may be strongly linked in the early stages of drug use. In other words, the pleasurable effects of a drug ("liking") can be disassociated with the compulsive seeking of it ("wanting"), and that wanting, not liking, is the key to addiction. They further propose that the brain becomes more and more sensitized to drug wanting even as drug liking (it is no longer positively reinforcing) diminishes, or even disappears. It is important for the model that one understands that "sensitization" refers to the increasing effects on the reward system that a drug has with repeated exposure. It does not mean that the initial effects (such as euphoria) become progressively stronger. Sensitization refers to hypersensitivity of the motivational system to seek drugs (Robinson & Berridge, 2008). Sensitization increases the responsiveness of DA to activating stimuli (cues that remind the person of drugs) in sensitized individuals above the level that was previously the case. However, this responsiveness does not translate into more pleasure for the individuals; rather, they experience less pleasure due to allostatic reduction in DA receptors in response to previous DA receptor flooding. Administering the drug can alleviate some of the negative affective symptoms that accompany abstinence, but it cannot reproduce its former pleasurable effects. Note that this does not apply to casual users, because infrequent use does not lead to allostatic adjustments.

Drugs and Crime

There is no doubt that drug use, abuse, and addiction is strongly related to criminal behavior. The US Office of Drug Control Policy's Arrestee Drug Abuse Monitoring (ADAM) Program tests urine samples from arrestees for the presence of drugs other than alcohol. Figure 6.2 shows that the great majority of arrestees test positive for at least one kind of illicit drug. Clearly, these data show that illicit drug abuse is strongly associated with criminal behavior, but is the association a causal one? Criminologists often use identical reasoning to explain both criminal and drug-abusing behavior, suggesting that neither one causes the other, but rather that both are "caused" by factors they have in common.

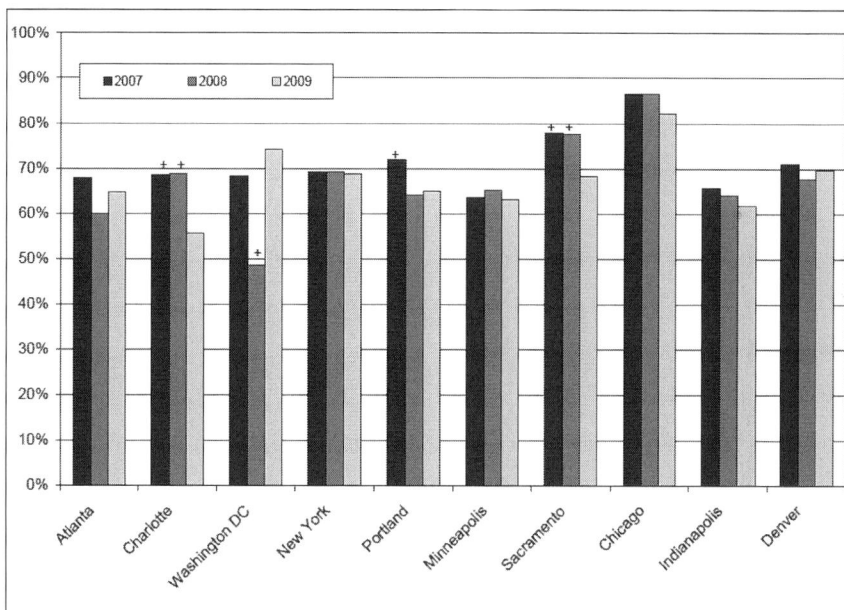

Figure 6.2   Adult arrestees testing positive for various drugs 2007–2009

Source: Office of Drug Control Policy (2010). ADAM II 2009 Annual Report

A large body of research indicates that drug abuse does not appear to initiate a criminal career, although it does increase the extent and seriousness of one (Menard, Mihalic & Huizinga, 2001; Quinn & Sneed, 2008). The typical drug addict is not an innocent victim driven into a criminal career by drugs, although this may occasionally be true. Rather, chronic drug abuse and criminality are part of a broader propensity of some individuals to engage in a variety of antisocial behaviors. A large number of studies have shown that traits characterizing antisocial individuals such as ADHD/CD comorbidity, impulsiveness, and high scores on the Hare Psychopathy Checklist also characterize drug addicts (Fishbein, 2003; McDermott et al., 2000).

The reciprocal nature of the drugs–crime connection is explained by Menard, Mihalic, and Huizinga (2001:295) as follows:

> Initiation of substance abuse is preceded by initiation of crime for most individuals (and therefore cannot be a cause of crime). At a later stage of involvement, however, serious illicit drug use appears to contribute to continuity in serious crime, and serious crime contributes to continuity in serious illicit drug use.

Much of the criminal behavior surrounding drug addiction, however, is not a function of the pharmacological nature of the drugs themselves as in alcohol, but rather of the behaviors engaged in by addicts to secure resources to feed their habits. Despite what we said above, there are many individuals who may have led fairly straight lives after adolescence who somehow became ensnared by drugs. In other words, these individuals may have shared the genetic vulnerabilities for addiction with many chronic criminals, but they may also have genetic or environmental factors that protect them against criminal behavior, such as a hyperactive ANS and a loving and supportive family.

Culture Matters

Different cultures view and react to different substances in different ways that encourage or discourage the likelihood of individuals using, abusing, or becoming addicted to them. Some societies, such as the contemporary United States, demonize drugs to such an extent that they may spend many millions of dollars in "wars" against them in ways that virtually guarantee that drugs will be related to criminal behavior. We cannot help noting that our earlier "war" on alcohol (prohibition) was an invitation to every petty criminal in the United States to become rich supplying what legitimate businesses could not. No one wants to defend the use of these substances that can literally be killers, but culture matters in terms of the overall effects of the substances and in terms of our understanding of addiction to them.

Given that only a relatively few users of addictive substances become addicted to them, it is obvious that drugs alone do not cause addiction. Although it is true some individuals are "sitting ducks" for addiction for genetic reasons, there are numerous cultural, economic, and situational contexts implicated in the process whereby a sitting duck becomes a dead duck. Sitting ducks must be exposed to the drug, be induced to self-administer it, and be socially reinforced for doing so. It is not a case of a homicidal drug, but rather of an individual using it to commit suicide (or at least to play Russian roulette) with it. To steal a catchphrase from the National Rifle Association: "Drugs don't addict people, people addict people." Of course, the drug is the instrument with which "people addict people."

For the many reasons that adolescents turn to antisocial behavior and then desist with maturation, they also turn to and then desist from drugs. Adolescence is a particularly vulnerable time to be experimenting with drugs because of the resculpting going on in the brain during that developmental period. The likelihood of drug addiction or alcoholism is increased the earlier the onset of use. For instance, someone who starts drinking or taking drugs at age 16 or younger is two to three times more likely to become addicted than someone who starts at 18 or older given the same level of genetic vulnerability (Koob & Le Moal, 2008). Yet this is the time when adolescents are most open to experimenting with all kinds of things, especially antisocial things. The pattern of drug abuse broken down by age in Figure 6.3 is a mirror image of the age–crime curves presented in Chapter 5. Although it is true that adolescents are more sensitive to the reinforcing properties of drugs and less sensitive to the negative properties (as they are to stimuli in general), drugs still have to be available before they can take them.

The counterculture of the 1960s and 1970s largely precipitated today's drug problem. Ask almost anyone who reached their majority in the earlier decades and they will tell you that they were ignorant of the presence of illicit drugs in their environments, and perhaps most were not even aware of their existence at all. How different things are today. The Drug Enforcement Administration (2003) estimates that the majority (about 55%) of today's youth have used some form of illegal substance, and that such experimenting serves as some kind of unofficial rite of passage. Certain drugs may even serve to define social groups ("usness"), as witnessed by the psychedelic movement of the 1960s and 1970s and today's rave/clubbing phenomenon defined primarily by 3,4 methylenedioxymethylamphetamine (MDMA), a horribly long chemical term for what the clubbers call "ecstasy." The sociable nature of ecstasy-centered raves is understandable when we note that taking MDMA causes the surge of serotonin (the natural antidepressant) and oxytocin (the "cuddle chemical"). Many friendship groups and sexual relationships are formed at raves. Moore and Miller (2008:7) describe the experience of one of their young research respondents to his clubbing experience: "The music, dancing, the feeling/energy doing pills gives you, enjoying myself and seeing other people I know and care about enjoying themselves, sense of community and feeling special!"

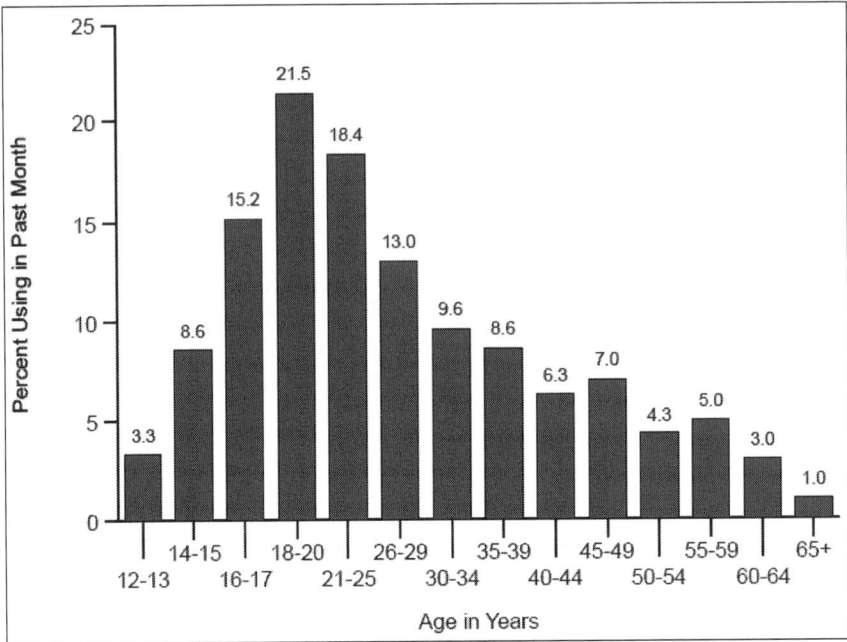

Figure 6.3   Self-reported illicit drug use in past month by age category in 2008

Source: Department of Health and Human Services, National Survey on Drug Use and Health, 2009 (http://www.samhsa.gov/data/nsduhlatest.htm)

The attraction of this drug at a time when teens need a little confidence-booster and are strongly susceptible to peer pressure is easy for teens to appreciate. The downside, however, is not. As with all drugs that lead to "better than expected" over stimulation of neurotransmitters, there will eventually be an allostatic downgrading of the systems involved. The long-term use of ecstasy can transition a person from "ultrasocial to antisocial" behavior, as the title of one neuroscience article on the role of oxytocin in drug abuse phrased it (McGregor, Callaghan & Hunt, 2008:358). Other neuroscience studies (for example, Kish et al., 2010) have demonstrated significantly decreased serotonin binding in chronic (usually defined as four or more years) MDMA users versus controls.

There are also many cultural factors to be considered when evaluating the relationship between alcohol and criminal behavior. One factor is: "defining a drinking occasion as a 'time-out' period in which controls are loosened from usual behavior and a willingness to hold a person less responsible for their actions when drinking than when sober by attributing the blame to alcohol" (Martin, 2001:146). If one's culture defines alcohol as a good-time elixir in which there is often a loss of control over behavioral inhibitions, one is granted cultural "permission" to do just that. If culture tells individuals they are less responsible for their behavior when "under the influence," this too grants permission to do things they might not otherwise do, intoxicated or sober. Such loss of inhibition regularly occurs with binge drinking (defined as the consumption of five to ten drinks in a relatively short time). Binge drinkers are typically college-age single young adults who drink solely to get drunk. An American study found that 40% of college students reported at least one episode of binge drinking in the previous two weeks (Johnson, O'Malley & Bachman, 2000), and a Russian nationwide study found that almost one-third of the men admitted binge drinking at least once a month (Pridemore, 2004). The cultures of both American college students and Russians in general have a high level of tolerance for engaging in heavy drinking.

Psychosocial stress is also strongly related to both the onset of alcohol/drug dependence and to relapse. Childhood stressors such as harsh and inconsistent parenting, rejection, physical, sexual, and emotional abuse have all been associated with increased vulnerability to addiction and relapse (Enoch, 2006). When we think about where substance abuse and addiction are most prevalent, we find that they are in the same stress-filled neighborhoods where child abuse/neglect, violence, and crime are also the most prevalent—in the most run-down and deprived areas of our cities. These are the areas where the social ambience is dominated by the worst families in them, families that Anderson (1999) calls "street families" (as opposed to "decent families"). It is in these areas that oppositional cultures hostile to almost everything in mainstream culture flourish and in which living for kicks and for "the moment" are valued.

We have seen that the HPA axis regulates the body's response to stress. Alcohol and drugs can directly activate the HPA axis, resulting in the release of hormones such as cortisol. These hormones act on the mesolimbic DA system that mediates the rewards associated with alcohol and drugs (Goeders, 2002). Thus, and counter-intuitively, drugs of abuse can both stimulate the HPA axis to increase the perception of reward *and* at the same time function as self-medications to alleviate stress. People living in stressful environments may become locked into a complex, vicious cycle of HPA axis activation (boosting the pleasure) leading to further substance abuse to alleviate the negative effects (fear, anxiety) of HPA axis activation, which again activates the HPA axis and keeps the whole process recycling. Such a vicious circle: "results in gross impairment of the normal stress response and other signaling mechanisms in the brain [certain subdivisions of the amygdala], results in a state of anxiety and internal stress" (Wand, 2008:119).

Conclusion

Alcohol and drug abuse are common in our society and around the world, and both are highly related to criminal behavior. Criminologists are well aware of the havoc in the lives of abusers and addicts, as well as the burden to society wrought by them, but they are less aware of the mechanisms of addiction. We believe it to be imperative that criminologists have at least a nodding acquaintance with the processes of hedonic allostasis in order to understand addiction and to appreciate the hell that it is for the addicted. We also need to recognize that although DNA is indeed the "molecule of life" and worthy of the reverence accorded it, like any other molecule it is subject to modifications which lead to different gene expression, and thus to different phenotypes. Multiple lines of evidence have converged at the conclusion that addiction involves a genetic predisposition involving many genes coupled with these allostatic modifications in the brain resulting from substance abuse as the brain strives to accommodate itself to chemical invasion. There is also a need for us to have an understanding of the mechanisms of tolerance and relapse. Numerous chemical compounds both within and outside the neuron other than those we have identified play their roles in inducing addiction. We have only identified some of the most important ones in a truly complex epigenetic process.

We have also shown once again that one should beware of looking at parts in isolation from the whole. While it is fascinating and necessary to explore molecular mechanisms, the sociocultural context in which they exist and play out cannot be ignored. Cultural norms and societal shifts most assuredly matter in the use and abuse of these substances, and in addiction to them. However, we should also be aware that although everyone shares (to varying degrees) in those cultural norms and societal shifts, they obviously do not affect everyone the same way. Very few people without genetic vulnerability (and it appears that it is the same genetic vulnerability to antisocial behavior in general) become addicted. But there are many biological pathways to addiction, and they all interact with environmental experiences captured by the incredible plastic brain.

Chapter 7
Intelligence, Nature/nurture, and Criminal Behavior

What is Intelligence?

Learning is the mechanism by which organisms adapt to their environment in ways that could not possibly be specified a priori by their genes. Human learning makes use of symbols—letters, words, pictures, formulas, and so on—that stand for various aspects of the environment and the relationships among them. Because of its increasing importance in modern societies, intelligence issues are becoming ever more socially relevant:

> Intelligence has a profound effect on the structure of society, not necessarily because it is the most highly valued of individual differences—although conceivably it is—but rather because it may have the widest and most stable distribution among all the traits that are valuable in industrialized nations. (Gottfredson, 1986:406)[1]

As valuable as intelligence doubtless is, we must not confuse it with moral worth. As Herrnstein and Murray (1994:21) point out: "one of the problems of writing about intelligence is how to remind readers often enough how little IQ scores tells you about whether the human being next to you is someone you will admire or cherish."

The root word of "intelligence" is *intelligo* ("to select among"). Intelligence thus implies the ability to select from among a variety of elements and analyze, synthesize, and arrange them in such a way as to provide satisfactory, and sometimes novel, solutions to problems the elements may pose. Definitions of

---

1 Mackintosh (2000:379) asks, if intelligence is so important in human affairs, "why does it still vary so much in the population, when, according to Fisher's fundamental theorem, at equilibrium the additive genetic variance should be zero?" That is, all important traits and characteristics evolve to genetic fixity. But intelligence *has* gone to fixity in the sense that all human beings are intelligent. That intelligence varies from person to person no more violates Fisher's theorem than people having varying arm lengths. Humans can no more be expected to have the same *level* of intelligence than the same arm length, height, nose size, eye color, or efficiency of their kidneys, even though humans are at genetic fixity for the presence of arms, noses, eyes, and kidneys. That is, while these organs are inherited, they are not heritable. It is doubtless true, however, that intelligence was less important in less complex cultures where status was ascribed rather than achieved.

intelligence vary, but most conform broadly to David Wechsler's (the originator of many of today's intelligence tests) definition as:

> The aggregate or global capacity of the individual to act purposefully, to think rationally, and to deal effectively with his environment. It is aggregate or global because it is composed of elements or abilities (features) which, although not entirely independent, are qualitatively differentiable. (in Matarazzo, 1976:79).

The terms "aggregate" and "global" recognize that different mental tests measure different cognitive abilities, but also that there is a factor common to them all, uniting the various abstracting functions. Psychometricians call this common factor *Spearman's g*, or simply *g*, which is the principal component derived from factor analysis of a variety of mental tests. Spearman's *g* ("*g*" for "general" intelligence) is the only independent factor common to all "intelligences," and factor loadings (the correlation between a test and the general factor) on *g* across a number of mental tests are mostly in the range 0.50–0.90 (Deary, Spinath & Bates, 2006). Thus, there is no measure of learning ability that is independent of *g*, and psychometricians appear to agree that *g* conforms to what both they and laypersons mean by intelligence (Buschkuebl & Jaeggi, 2010).

Although the National Academy of Sciences (Seligman, 1992), the American Psychological Association's task force on intelligence (Neisser et al., 1995), and a mountain of empirical studies have concluded that IQ tests are not biased, remarkably there are still some who believe that they are. Like the proverbial trial lawyer, these naysayers shout louder and louder as their case gets weaker and weaker, and the only evidence they bring to the bench is that certain groups consistently show lower average scores than other groups, and since all groups "should" be equal, the tests are *ipso facto* biased. The reliability and validity of IQ tests sit head and shoulders above all other psychometric measures of human traits and abilities, so accusations of bias are generally not made on these grounds. Rather, they are typically posed in terms of children from lower-SES families being less likely to have the kinds of intellectual experiences that prepare them for dealing with items on IQ tests.

This argument confuses crystallized and fluid intelligence. Crystallized intelligence is heavily dependent on acquired knowledge, while fluid intelligence reflects the ability to analyze problems in novel ways, and "the ability to cope with new situations for which previously acquired knowledge is only minimally useful" (Buschkuebl & Jaeggi, 2010:266). Fluid intelligence is therefore an "on-the-spot" cognitive *process*, and crystallized intelligence is the stored *product* of learning. Most items on modern tests rely heavily on items that tap into fluid intelligence to minimize the effects of acquired knowledge, but lower-SES children consistently score lower on these tests than they do on "culturally loaded" tests (Loehlin, 2000). This is because culture-free tests tap heavily into fluid intelligence and are more *g*-loaded than tests of crystallized intelligence. The higher a test's *g*-load (the more it depends on the common *g* factor rather than on a specific content domain) the greater its complexity, and the more *g*-loaded a test, the higher is its heritability (Lubinski, 2004).

The crystallized/fluid distinction tells us why intelligence is not learned in the traditional sense of the word. If IQ were acquired through learning, it would increase dramatically across the life-course as knowledge increases, but it does not. IQ is remarkably stable across the life-course with test–retest correlations as high as 0.94 over a ten-year span (Deary et al., 2000), and remains stable even as a person acquires vast storehouses of knowledge from childhood to old age. A 60-year-old may have acquired the knowledge to pontificate on esoteric subjects that would have mystified him or her at age 15, but despite huge increases in knowledge, his or her IQ would differ minimally at 60 from what it was at 15. It is fairly well agreed upon that fluid intelligence stops developing during adolescence—around 14–16 years of age (Deary, Johnson & Houlihan, 2009). This does not mean that intelligence is determined at birth and impervious to change; stability does not mean fixity.

Neurobiology and Intelligence

Whatever intelligence is, it involves neurobiological processes requiring the participation of chemicals that drive nerve impulses, the amount, concentration, and metabolism of which, as well as brain fiber architecture, vary from person to person and are under appreciable genetic control (Chiang et al., 2009). Variability in brain mechanisms implies differences in measured IQ. Intelligence is among the most heritable of human traits, with estimates ranging from 0.50 in childhood to 0.80 in old age (Neubauer & Fink, 2009). If genes did not contribute to variance in a trait, it would be logically and empirically impossible to calculate a heritability coefficient. However, it is important to note that heritability estimates provide only statistical, not biological, evidence for genetic influence on a trait—it is a descriptor, not an explanation.

Figure 7.1 presents weighted average interclass correlations on IQ among many thousands of individuals of different kinship pairings. Most of the correlations are based on 111 behavior genetic studies of childhood and adolescent IQ by Bouchard and McGue (1981). The adult correlations were derived from various sources provided in Bouchard (1998). The pattern of correlations is consistent with that which would be predicted on the basis of broad polygenic inheritance—the greater the degree of genetic relatedness between pairs, the higher the correlation between their IQs. Note that the correlations between pairs of full siblings and pairs of dizygotic twins fall dramatically from childhood to adulthood, reflecting the decreasing influence of shared environment on genetically influenced traits as we age. Conversely, the correlations between pairs of monozygotic twins, regardless of whether they were reared together or apart, remain stable from childhood to adulthood. Also note that the correlation between MZ twins reared apart (0.72) is significantly larger than that between DZ twins reared together (0.60). We

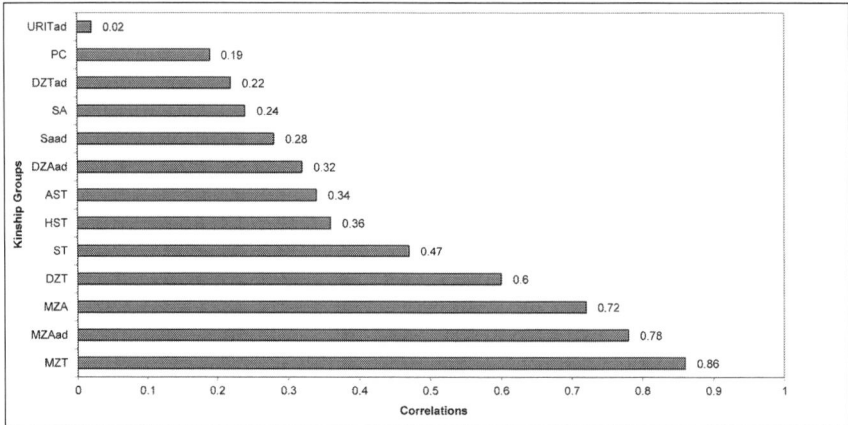

Notes: URItad = Unrelated Individuals tested as adults. PC = Parent/adopted child. DZTad = DZ twins reared together tested as adults. SA = Siblings reared apart. Saad = siblings reared apart tested as adults. DZAad = DZ twins reared apart tested as adults. AST adopted siblings reared together. HST = Half-siblings reared together. ST = Full siblings reared together. DZT = DZ twins reared together. MZA = MZ twins reared apart. MZad = MZ twins reared apart tested as adults. MZT = MZ twins reared together.

Figure 7.1   Weighted average interclass IQ correlations by kinship group

Source: Adapted from Bouchard & McGue (1981) and Bouchard (1998)

are aware that adoption agencies attempt to place siblings (twins or otherwise) in similar SES homes, but as Lykken (1995) points out, the SES correlation between placement families of adopted siblings is on average 0.30, while the SES correlation for DZ twins reared together is a perfect 1.0.

Despite evidence of high heritability, molecular genetics has still not identified specific genes related to intelligence. No one expects to discover genes with large effect sizes; the expectation is to find a large number of genes each with small effect sizes (Craig & Plomin, 2006). Nevertheless, molecular geneticists have relentlessly continued their search for a variety of candidate genes using a variety of sophisticated techniques. A large number of SNPs and VNTRs have been suggestively linked to IQ. One of the most familiar is the val[158] met polymorphism of the COMT gene we encountered in Chapter 2 (Ohnishi et al., 2006). Another candidate is the cholinergic muscarinic 2 receptor gene (CHRM2). Certain SNPs on the CHRM2 gene have been found to significantly correlate with performance, but not verbal, IQ (Dick et al., 2007). None of these polymorphisms are genes "for" intelligence, they are polymorphisms involved in brain functions involved in information processing. A genome-wide study of 500,000 SNPs from 7,000 schoolchildren who had taken a battery of IQ tests illustrates just how elusive the search has been and how small the contribution of any single polymorphism must be (Butcher et al., 2004). Butcher's team arrived at six SNPs that were significantly related to *g*, but their aggregate effect only significantly correlated 0.11 with *g*.

One way of defining intelligence physically is to examine the operation of nerve impulses reflected in the speed and accuracy of information processing in terms of reaction time (RT). The premise of RT is that higher-IQ people possess brains that are able to quickly spot, differentiate, and respond to relevant stimuli faster than lower-IQ people. The three principal tests of RT are as follows:

1. **Simple RT** measures the time (in milliseconds) it takes to recognize and respond to stimuli.
2. **Recognition RT** involves responding to the correct stimuli and ignoring distracters.
3. **Choice RT** involves matching responses by pressing the letter key corresponding to the stimulus appearing on a screen while ignoring distracters.

Correlations between RT and IQ range between -0.25 and -0.50 (higher IQ = shorter reaction time), with the largest correlations associated with the more challenging RT tasks (Deary, 2003).

Higher correlations are found in more sophisticated measures of brain activity such as cerebral glucose metabolism. Cerebral glucose metabolism is measured by PET scans which reveal metabolic functioning as the brain takes up positron-emitting glucose. A computer reveals colorized maps of the brain identifying the parts activated while engaged in some task as the energy supplied by the glucose is metabolized. Glucose metabolic rates at various brain-slice levels have been correlated with scores on Raven's Advanced Progressive Matrices, a highly *g*-loaded test of abstract reasoning. Depending on brain-slice level and brain hemisphere, correlations ranging between -0.44 and -0.84 are found, which means that high-IQ subjects expend less brain energy when performing intellectual tasks and possess brains that are speedier, more accurate, and more "energy-efficient" than low-IQ subjects (Gray & Thompson, 2004).

Further evidence for the biological substrate of intelligence is supplied by structural and functional MRI studies. A structural MRI study of MZ and DZ twins found *g* to be related to the amount of gray matter in the brain, and that the amount of gray matter is highly heritable, with a mean heritability of -0.88 (Glahn, Thompson & Blangero, 2007). Posthuma and colleagues (2002), among others, have showed that the association between brain volume and *g* is mediated by common genetic factors—the same genes that influence brain volume influence *g*. A twin study using structural MRI found correlations between various brain volume regions (total brain volume, neorcortex white matter, and prefrontal cortex) and cognitive skills (verbal IQ, performance IQ, processing speed, and reading ability) ranging between 0.32 and 0.89 (Betjemann et al., 2010).

Jung and Haier (2007) formulated a theory of intelligence called the Parieto-Frontal Integration Theory (P-FIT) based on 37 neuroimaging studies. P-FIT suggests that intelligence is related to how efficiently information processing is shunted around the brain and how well the relevant brain areas communicate with one another. Jung and Haier assert that there is no single brain location where intelligence is situated, and place their emphasis on brain areas that multiple neuroimaging studies had found to be related to IQ. Based on this information, they concluded that most of these brain areas are found clustered in the frontal and parietal lobes (recall that the parietal lobes function to integrate sensory information, among a number of other things). This fits in nicely with the body of research showing that the parieto-frontal network is activated under conflict situations and when response selection is required (Brass & von Cramon, 2004). Resolving conflicting possibilities by making the correct selection is exactly what one engages in during IQ testing.

Dennis Garlick's (2002; 2003) neuroplasticity model of intelligence argues that individuals inherit different genetic set-points for brain plasticity (not differential intelligence per se), and that environmental factors then provide the necessary input to realize their intellectual potential. Garlick argues that low-IQ individuals have brains that do not adapt as well to environmental conditions as do the brains of high-IQ individuals. The model posits that intelligence is "created" when neural connections in the brain are forged and strengthened by environmental input, and more or less of it will be created according to the differential capacity of individuals' neurons to adapt. Garlick argues that there is a critical period in which the developing brain fine-tunes its ability to adapt to novel phenomena. This period begins in infancy, when the human brain is most plastic (when it is most able to make new neural connections in response to experience), and ends around mid-adolescence—when fluid intelligence is said to stop developing.

A ten-year longitudinal MRI study of more than 300 children and adolescents found strong evidence for Garlick's model. Shaw and colleagues (2006) showed that an identical pattern of brain maturation occurred in all subjects (the cortex gets thicker, peaks, and then gets thinner with pruning), but also that the rate of these brain changes differed significantly according to IQ levels. The cortices of subjects with the highest IQs started out thinnest, quickly got thicker, peaked relatively late, and thinned very quickly. Average and below-average subjects experienced these same changes, but at slower rates, suggesting that rapid brain changes reflect a high degree of neural plasticity and that greater neuroplasticity suggests a more agile mind and higher IQ. But just how malleable is intelligence? How much can it be gained or lost in the normal range of environments?

Environmental Influences on Intelligence

Because genes are expressed to different degrees in different environments and at different times, heritability coefficients will vary across samples. Heritability coefficients quantify trait variation in a population attributable to genetics, but genes cannot do anything without an environment, and the extent to which they express themselves depends on its quality. Rowe, Jacobson, and Van den Oord (1999) and Turkheimer and colleagues (2003) found heritabilities for IQ of 0.74 and 0.72 respectively in advantaged (high-SES) environments, and 0.26 and 0.10 respectively in disadvantaged (low-SES) environments. This does not mean that genes contribute more to IQ in more advantaged environments. Intelligence is like a flower: it needs cultivating to thrive. In advantaged environments, parents typically endeavor to cultivate the intellectual potential of their children, but for a variety of reasons parents at the lowest level of SES are less likely to be willing or able to do so, thus it does not blossom. Disadvantaged environments ("poor soil") suppress the expression of genes associated with some traits and permit the expression of genes associated with other (usually undesirable) traits, and advantaged environments ("fertile soil") operate in the opposite direction.

A more intuitive example to illustrate is provided by height, which is highly heritable ($\approx$ 0.80). Despite being ethnically identical and separated by an arbitrary boundary, North Koreans are on average two to three inches shorter than South Koreans (Schwekendick, 2009). This difference is environmental. North Korea is highly disadvantaged—poverty, malnutrition, and general oppression are rife— whereas South Korea is advantaged. Thus there are large environmental effects on height despite its high heritability, because individuals' heights can vary considerably depending on environmental perturbations. However, within the populations to which they belong, most of the variance is genetically influenced because the environment is roughly similar. In other words, while heritability values would be similar *within* both North and South Korea, the mean height difference *between* them is entirely an environmental effect. Johnson (2010) demonstrates how this is also true of intelligence—how the environment affects the mean population value without affecting the variance.

The most solid evidence for environmental influence on intelligence comes from genetic research, because if genes account for say 50% of the variance in IQ scores, then the environment must account for the other 50%. It is as difficult to get a firm grasp on environmental influences as it is on genetic influences, because the "environment" encompasses everything not encoded in the DNA. Like the effect sizes of specific genes, the effect sizes of specific environmental factors, unless they are truly horrendous, are likely to be small. We saw earlier that the combined effect on IQ of breastfeeding and tactile stimulation in two large longitudinal studies is 6–7 points, but only in infants with the "right" fatty acid desaturase allele. We also saw how exposure to lead dust decreases IQ, and how protracted stress can lead to neuron death.

Adoption studies provide some evidence of environmental effects, but they tell us nothing about malleability per se because we cannot know what children's IQs would have been had they not been adopted. A French cross-fostering study by Capron and Duyme (1989) merits attention because of its unique design despite is small sample size (only 1 in every 600 children in the sample was "cross-fostered"). The study compared adoptive parent/adopted child pairs from both extremes of SES. All children were relinquished at birth, and the mean age of IQ testing was 14 years. High-SES parents were senior executives and professionals, and low-SES parents were farm workers and "diverse unskilled." The marginals in Table 7.1 show that children born to high-SES parents, regardless of the SES of adoptive parents, have higher IQs (M = 113.55) than children born to low-SES parents (M = 98.0), and that children adopted by high-SES parents, regardless of the SES of biological parents, have higher IQs (M = 111.6) than children adopted by low-SES parents (M = 99.95). The cases that fall on the main diagonal of the table constitute examples of positive rGE reflected in the difference of 27.2 points between children both born to and adopted by high-SES parents (M = 119.6) and children both born to and adopted by low-SES parents (M = 92.4). All mean comparisons were large enough to be statistically significant despite the small sizes of n.

Table 7.1   Mean IQ levels of adopted children by parental SES

SES of biological parents	SES of adopted parents		
	High	Low	Total
High	119.6 (n =10)	107.5 (n = 8)	113.5 (n =18)
Low	103.6 (n =10)	92.4 (n = 10)	98.0 (n =20)
Total	111.6 (n = 20)	99.95 (n = 18)	105.3 (n = 38)

Source: Adapted from Capron & Duyme (1989)

Consider the secondary diagonal of the table containing instances in which rGE is negative. Children born to low-SES parents adopted by high-SES parents show a lower mean IQ (103.6) than children born to high-SES parents adopted by low-SES parents (107.5), despite an average of 14 years' exposure to high- and low-SES environments, respectively. These findings indicate that the reaction range (the limit of increment or decrement) for IQ within the normal range of human environments is about 12 points.

The IQ–crime Connection

As the quintessentially human characteristic, it is no surprise that intelligence has long been considered an important correlate of criminal behavior. Claims of test bias and the assumed eugenic implications of IQ testing following World War II led to the virtual disappearance of IQ from the criminological literature from the 1930s to the 1970s, even though many well-known studies continued to demonstrate a negative relationship between IQ and crime. A number of recent reviews of studies from around the world have characterized the relationship as ubiquitous and robust (for example, Ellis & Walsh, 2003).

The US National Longitudinal Survey of Youth (NLSY) looked at a variety of relationships between IQ and lifetime outcomes, including the fact that 93% of the males in the sample who had ever been interviewed in a correctional facility over a ten-year period had IQs in the bottom half of the IQ distribution. Furthermore, of those subjects located at the bottom 20% of IQ (IQ $\leq$ 87), 62% had been interviewed in jail or prison at some point over the study period, compared with only 2% from the top 20% (IQ $\geq$ 113)—a ratio of 31:1 (Herrnstein & Murray, 1994:376). Despite such evidence, many criminology textbooks still imply that there is little evidence to support the claim of average IQ difference between offenders and non-offenders (Wright & Miller, 1998).

IQ may be related to crime and delinquency more strongly than suggested by a simple comparison of mean IQ levels of offenders and non-offenders. Offenders' IQs are typically compared with the general population mean of 100. We tend to forget that the general population includes a fairly large number of offenders, as well as individuals with such low IQs that they are largely incapable of committing crimes. The difference in IQ between offenders and normally functioning non-offenders (the mean of which is around 103–5) is actually greater than the 8–10 points typically reported.

A related problem is that many IQ studies are conducted with delinquents rather than with adult criminals. We know that almost all teenage boys commit some act which could get them into trouble with the law, and also that most delinquents do not become adult criminals (Moffitt, 1993). Criminals who offend most frequently and most seriously tend to begin their antisocial careers prior to puberty and to continue them long after the typical delinquent has desisted from offending. Delinquents who desist in early adulthood have accrued enough social capital to allow them to do so, much of that by virtue of their cognitive abilities. It has been pointed out that the IQ difference between non-offenders and adolescent-onset offenders is typically only one IQ point, but the same comparison with life-course-persistent offenders reveals a difference of around 17 points (Gatzke-Kopp et al., 2002; Moffitt, 1993). Simple arithmetic tells us that pooling these two very different groups hides the magnitude of the IQ difference between non-offenders and the most persistent and serious offenders in our midst, and thus the true strength of the relationship between IQ and criminality.

David Wechsler's (1958:176) statement that "The most outstanding feature of the sociopath's test profile is the systematic high score on the performance as opposed to the verbal part of the scale" sparked another way of examining the relationship between IQ and antisocial behavior. IQ scores are typically rendered in terms of an individual's full-scale IQ (FIQ). FIQ is the average score obtained by summing scores on verbal IQ (VIQ) and performance IQ (PIQ) and dividing by two. Most people have closely matched VIQ and PIQ scores, with a population average of 100 on each sub-scale. People who have either VIQ or PIQ scores significantly in excess of the other (VIQ > PIQ or PIQ > VIQ) are considered intellectually imbalanced. Correlating full-scale IQ with offending is problematic because offenders are almost always found to have significantly lower VIQ, but not lower PIQ, than non-offenders (Walsh, 2003). Miller (1987:120) concludes the following about the PIQ > VIQ imbalance: "This PIQ > VIQ relationship was found across studies, despite variations in age, sex, race, setting, and form of the Wechsler scale administered, as well in differences in criteria for delinquency."

In the general population of American males, it has been estimated that 18% are VIQ > PIQ-imbalanced, 66% are balanced (VIQ = PIQ), and 16% are PIQ > VIQ-imbalanced. A discrepancy of 12 points or more is considered a significant imbalance at $p < 0.01$ (Kaufman, 1976). It is consistently found that VIQ > PIQ-imbalanced individuals are significantly *under*-represented in criminal and delinquent populations, and that PIQ > VIQ individuals are significantly *over*-represented. Averaged across eight studies, V > P boys are under-represented in delinquent populations by a factor of about 2.6, and P > V boys are over-represented by a factor of about 2.2, rendering an LOD of about 5.7 (Walsh, 2003). A VIQ > PIQ profile would appear to be a major predictor of prosocial behavior, especially among adults. Barnett, Zimmer, and McCormack (1989) found that that only 0.9% of prison inmates had such a profile, compared to the 18% of the general male population—a 20-fold difference. Using FIQ to assess the role of cognitive ability in explaining antisocial behavior provides another example of how researchers can arrive at an incomplete picture of the nature of the relationship.

IQ, Status Attainment, and Criminal Behavior

IQ is considered a risk factor for antisocial conduct differentially expressed under different social conditions. Environmental factors engage individual risk factors for committing crimes at different thresholds. Two or three generations ago, when most families were intact, when there was a higher level of moral conformity, and when entry into the workforce demanded less academic preparation, relatively low-IQ individuals were more insulated from criminal behavior. Things are different today, when low-IQ individuals are likely to be from single-parent homes and to live in neighborhoods in which morality is a joke. They also have difficulty obtaining legitimate work in a society in which academic preparation is long and arduous. Social control mechanisms are thus almost entirely absent in their lives, so the threshold at which they will cross the line to engage in criminal activity is considerably lower.

There are a number of theoretical explanations for the IQ–antisocial behavior relationship, but we examine it here only in the context of status attainment in the anomie/strain tradition. This tradition maintains that people turn to crime to fulfill their status requirements because they cannot or will not fulfill them legitimately. The "American Dream" is defined in terms of financial success, which generally requires a well-paid occupation, which in turn generally requires a good education. Intelligence is, of course, causally prior to educational and occupational success—intelligence is a major "cause" of one's SES. In anomie/strain theory, however,

SES seems to be viewed as *sui generis*—an uncaused first cause that is socially "inherited" and does not require any explanation beyond that.[2]

To discuss intelligence as a determinant of individuals' SES is sociological heresy because it violates Durkheim's dictum that only social facts can explain social facts. Yet outside sociology, the weak affect of parental SES on offspring SES in the United States is considered a truism: "The net impact of measured family background on economic success is easy to summarize: very little. This conclusion holds across different data sets with different model specifications and measurements and applies to both occupational status and earnings" (Kingston, 2006:121). The evidence in support of the position that SES is achieved rather than ascribed in modern societies is overwhelming. For example, one study examined sixty years of data from males who had lived in poor high-crime neighborhoods in Boston when growing up and who were interviewed when they were 25, 32, 47, and 65 years of age. It was found that although parental SES was significantly related to offspring occupational status (r = 0.17) at age 25, it dwindled to a non-significant 0.079 by age 65. Only years of education (-0.410) and IQ (-0.347) were related to occupational success at age 65 (occupational status reverse coded) (DiRago & Vaillant, 2007).

A longitudinal study of 4,298 British males found that meritocratic factors (intelligence, aspirations, motivation, and possession of educational qualifications) assessed when subjects were 11 and 16 years old accounted for 48% of the variance in occupational status at age 33. All measured background variables (parental SES, type of housing, type of school, and parents' aspirations) combined accounted for only 8% of the variance. Based on this sixfold difference in the proportion of variance explained, the authors concluded that: "occupational selection in Britain appears to take place largely on meritocratic principles" (Bond & Saunders, 1999:217). Another British longitudinal study (Nettle, 2003) followed a cohort of all children born in Britain in one week in 1958 to the age of 42. All children had their mental abilities tested at the age of 7. At the cohort age of 42, there were 11,419 remaining subjects for whom mental ability test scores were available. The primary finding of this study was that childhood intellectual ability is associated with class mobility in adulthood uniformly across all social classes of origin. Nettle found an IQ difference of 24.1 points between those who attained professional status and those in the unskilled class, regardless of the class of origin. Nettle concluded that "intelligence is the strongest single factor causing class mobility in contemporary societies that has been identified" (2003:560).

---

2   Some sociologists maintain that parental SES "causes" offspring IQ—that is, it is a reproduction of parental class advantage or disadvantage in the offspring generation. The correlation between parental SES and children's IQ is in the 0.30–0.40 range, which is understandable since a proportion of the genes underlying the traits that contributed to parents' SES is transmitted to offspring. The real test, however, is the correlation between offspring IQ and their own adult SES, which, as we see in the body of this chapter, is substantially larger.

An American behavioral genetic study examined VIQ, grade-point average (GPA), and college plans (CPL). Partitioning the variance of these measures into genetic, shared environment, and non-shared environment components, the three heritability coefficients were VIQ = 0.536, GPA = 0.669, and CPL = 0.600; the shared environment coefficients were VIQ = 0.137, GPA = 0.002, and CPL = 0.030, and the non-shared environmental variances were 0.327, 0.329, and 0.370, respectively (Nielsen, 2006). Shared environment is everything shared by siblings as they grew up, including parental SES. The shared environment also captures other factors sociologists appeal to as explanations of important life outcomes, such as neighborhood and school characteristics. The variance explained in these three vital components of occupational success by SES of origin are miniscule compared with the proportions explained by genes and non-shared environment. The results support the behavior genetic "law" that states that as we age, the effects of shared environment (in this case, childhood SES and all the baggage that comes with it) on phenotypic traits fade to insignificance while genes and non-shared environments become more salient.

Charles Murray (2002) tackled the issue using data from the National Longitudinal Survey of Youth and asked the question: "How much difference would it make to income inequality if, magically, every child in the country could be given the same advantages as the more fortunate of our children" (2002:140). To answer the question, he created a "utopian sample" of sibling pairs to compare with a control sample of sibling pairs from the same data set. The utopian sample (n = 733 sibling pairs) was composed of siblings who were born in wedlock, had not experienced parental divorce by age 8, and who grew up in families with a median income of $64,586 in year 2000 dollars. The control sample (n = 1,075 pairs) consisted of all sibling pairs failing one or more of the criteria for inclusion in the utopian sample.

Murray compared life outcomes of siblings in both samples on median family income, marital status, and out-of-wedlock childbearing, both across samples and within them, when subjects were 30–38 years old. The within-sample comparisons were by IQ level broken down into five categories, ranging from 120+ to <80. The sibling pairs in the utopian sample enjoyed a considerable family background advantage over the control sample, in that across each IQ category, the "utopians" made more money, were more likely to be married, and were less likely to have children born out of wedlock. However, the within-subsample differences based on IQ levels were hugely greater than the between subsample differences. For instance, the median family income in the 120+ IQ category was $70,700 in the utopian versus $65,100 in the control sample, and $23,600 and $18,400 respectively in the <80 IQ categories of both samples. Thus, family advantage amounted to an income advantage of $5,600 in the high-IQ category and one of $5,200 in the low-IQ category, but within samples, high-IQ siblings enjoyed a median income that was $47,100 more than their low-IQ siblings in the utopian sample, and $46,700 more in the control sample. These data show that income inequality will exist in a meritocratic society even if, as Murray says, "by some miracle" we could equalize first-generation family income, convince women not to give birth out of wedlock, and prevent divorce during children's formative years. The intellectual abilities of the second generation will reproduce inequality by earning less, giving birth out of wedlock more and divorcing more—all of which is predictable from their IQ alone.

Other Individual Determinants of Legitimate Success

A certain level of intelligence is a necessary but not sufficient condition for legitimate occupational success. There are doubtless blue-collar workers with IQs one, two, or even three standard deviations above the mean, but there just as surely is no one in the professional classes with an IQ even close to one standard deviation *below* the mean. Intelligence is a better predictor of what one cannot do than what one can. A person with a slightly above average IQ (say 110) can become a lawyer, physician, or university professor (except perhaps in the more quantitative areas such as mathematics and physics) if he or she is ambitious, highly motivated, and conscientious. Talent plus effort are the twin pillars of occupational success, with effort perhaps being more important in most cases. As the famous Thomas Edison quote reminds us: "Success is 10 percent inspiration and 90 percent perspiration."

We can subsume everything in the "effort" end of the equation under the rubric of conscientiousness. Employers can be expected to favor high levels of conscientiousness in their employees and perspective employees. Conscientiousness is more important in high-autonomy jobs than in low-autonomy jobs because it "affects motivational states and stimulates goal setting and goal commitment" (Schmidt & Hunter, 2004:169). In an intergenerational study following subjects from early childhood to retirement, Judge and colleagues (1999) found that conscientiousness measured in childhood predicted adult occupational status $(r = 0.49)$ and income $(r = 0.41)$ in adulthood, which were only slighter less than the correlations between "general mental ability" (GMA) and the same variables (0.51 and 0.53, respectively). Schmidt and Hunter's (2004:170) analysis of GMA and personality variables in attaining occupational success concluded that "the burden of prediction is borne almost entirely by GMA and conscientiousness."

We can conclude that rather than being victims of an "unfair" social system, those who choose illegitimate routes to the "American Dream" lack either intelligence or conscientiousness, or both, among a number of other things. The whole notion of criminal behavior as the result of "strained" individuals righteously hitting back at a society that has denied them opportunities to obtain status and resources legitimately is pooh-poohed by Vold, Bernard, and Snipes (1998:177), who wrote:

> It is not merely a matter of talented individuals confronted with inferior schools and discriminatory hiring practices. Rather, a good deal of research indicates that many delinquents and criminals are untalented individuals who cannot compete effectively in complex industrial societies.

Culture Matters

Just as the micro environment influences the intellectual talents of those who specifically experience them, the broader macro environment of culture has influences on the general population. Perhaps the best evidence of this is the Flynn effect. Flynn (2007) has shown that the mean IQ of the populations of all countries studied increased by 21 points from 1932 to 2000. Because gene pools cannot have changed to account for IQ changes of this magnitude, the effect must be environmental. This does not mean that our grandparents were blithering idiots. They had just as much "raw" intelligence as any other generation, but according to Flynn, it was of a more concrete sort, anchored in everyday reality. The bulk of the IQ increase has been limited to similarities ("In what way is a rabbit like a dog?"), which increased by 24 points, whereas the vocabulary, arithmetic, and information components increased by only 3 points in 55 years (Flynn, 2007). Flynn attributes the increase in similarities scores to the increasing use of "the categories of science" that has freed the mind from the concrete and allows us to understand abstractions. The largest IQ gains have concentrated at the lower end of the distribution, as the environment has improved to allow for more of us to realize our intellectual potential.

According to Dickens and Flynn (2001), the high heritability of IQ (strong genetic effects) coupled with large secular IQ gains (strong environmental effects) provide us with a paradox that requires reconciliation. Flynn (2007:90) avers that the direct genetic effect on IQ is only about 36%, with 64% resulting from the indirect effects of genes interacting with the environment. The interplay of genes and environments result in what Dickens and Flynn (2001:349) call the "multiplier effect." They state that "genes can get matched with environments of corresponding quality only through genetically-influenced traits." That is, a match between parents and offspring (parents provide genes and environment) results in what may be a small genotypic advantage at birth being magnified ("multiplied") into a large phenotypic advantage at adulthood by a lifetime of accumulating passive, evocative, and active rGE effects on the plastic brain.

In earlier times, the multiplier effect suppressed the power of environmental effects: "The match between genes and environment [rGE] means that environmental factors, however potent, to a large extent just reinforce the advantage or disadvantage that genes confer. So the match masks the potency of environmental factors" (Dickens & Flynn, 2001:351). Across the time that the Flynn effect has been working, the masking has slipped because of the better environments to which successive generations have been exposed, and thus: "The potency of environmental factors stands out in bold relief" (Dickens & Flynn, 2001:351).

Many cultural explanations for the Flynn effect have been offered, ranging from increased educational opportunities, test-wiseness, and changes in fertility patterns (smaller families) to the sheer complexity of modern life. For instance, computer video games have provided a measure of mental stimulation to practically all children in modern societies that more cerebral children obtained from simply reading in the past, and even today's TV shows, according to Flynn (2007), demand more cognitive involvement than the offerings of yesteryear. In the same way that molecular genetics posits a role for numerous genes with small effect sizes, the Flynn effect is probably caused by a combination of all of these and other environmental factors with small effects.

Richard Lynn (2009) provides the most empirically sound explanation for the Flynn effect attributable to a single variable with a large effect size. Lynn notes that the rise in IQ has been matched by a corresponding increase in the Development Quotients (DQs) of children over the same period. DQs are measured in infants by tests that assess motor (holding up the head, sitting, standing, walking, jumping) and mental development (word utterance, curiosity, naming objects, responding to requests). Lynn notes that the malnutrition and mineral deficiencies that caused rickets, anemia, and many other environmentally induced problems prevalent in the 1930s had all but disappeared by the 1970s in developed societies, and are virtually unknown today. Lynn also notes that height and head size have increased during the period, and that DQ is significantly related to IQ (about 0.53 when corrected for unreliability). Lynn claims that these data rule out other proposed explanations for IQ gains such as those mentioned above, since increased DQs occur prior to exposure to these things. However, a better-prepared brain is a brain more able to take advantage of these later experiences.

The Flynn effect appears to have ended in developed nations (as well as height gains), implying that we seem to have wrung all the juice out of the environment that we can (Sundet, Barlaug & Torjussen, 2004). As we equalize environments, the more people will be differentiated by their genes; this truism is the central maddening irony of egalitarianism. We might even be witnessing a decline in mean IQ in developing countries since the high point achieved in 1998, although the Flynn effect is still in evidence in developing countries (Teasdale & Owen, 2008).

Conclusion

Intelligence has a huge impact on life outcomes, including one's risk for engaging in criminal behavior, via its impact on education, occupation, and income, and thus on SES. We have briefly discussed the nature of intelligence as currently understood by psychologists, geneticists, and neuroscientists and found that although it is known to be highly heritable and strongly associated with aspects of brain structure and function, no genes with strong effects sizes have been identified. We have emphasized that intelligence is a phenotypic trait developed through the constant interplay of genes and environment, and have offered evidence for this, primarily the Flynn effect. It is surely good news that modern sociocultural environments are more conducive to everyone realizing their full intellectual potential than earlier environments were.

We emphasized that low IQ is a risk factor that may be more potent today because of many different sociocultural changes over the past few decades. Very few well-paying jobs are left for those with less than adequate intellectual preparation, as factory jobs have either moved overseas or are occupied by robots. The moral scene has also shifted, as numerous girls and women give birth out of wedlock, thus greatly increasing the probability that they and their offspring will live a life of poverty, as well as undermining opportunities for their children's intellectual growth. Many souls who find themselves in the grip of criminality are there because in so many ways they are not intellectually or temperamentally prepared to compete for legitimate work opportunities, not because some disembodied entity called "society" has denied them such opportunities.

Chapter 8
Schizophrenia, Brain Development, and Criminal Behavior

The Toll of Mental Disorders

The World Health Organization defines mental disorders as "clinically significant conditions characterized by alterations in thinking, mood (emotions), or behaviour associated with personal distress and/or impaired functioning," and adds that they "are not variations within the range of 'normal', but are clearly abnormal or pathological phenomena" (in Brookman, 2005:87). Mental health disorders take a heavy toll on individuals, families, the community at large, and on the criminal justice system. In the United States in 1955, 339 per 100,000 individuals were in state mental hospitals, but in 2001, only 20 per 100,000 were (Lamb, Weinberger & Gross, 2004). This large decrease in hospitalized patients left jails and prisons as surrogate mental hospitals to absorb much of the mentally ill population. Robinson (2005) reports that there are now about 3.5 times more mentally ill people in American prisons and jails as there are in psychiatric hospitals. Only the most severely mentally impaired are hospitalized today, with most others being able to function adequately in the community with proper medication and support (Lurigio, 2001). This transfer of responsibility from hospitals to jails rode in on the coattails of the development of antipsychotic drugs, concerns about patients' rights, and the movement to deinstitutionalize them.

Table 8.1 presents highlights from a Bureau of Justice Statistics report on the mental health problems of prison and jail inmates (James & Glaze, 2006). This study found that 24% of state prison inmates, 14% of federal prison inmates, and 21% of jail inmates had a recent history of mental health problems. The 2006 study did not address probation and parole populations, but a 1999 Bureau of Justice Statistics report indicated that 547,800 (about 14% of the total) probationers/parolees had some form of mental disorder (Ditton, 1999).

There are many different forms of mental disorders, but we will concentrate on schizophrenia because it is the illness most strongly associated with criminal behavior (psychopathy is not considered an illness; psychopaths are able to function well, if not morally, in society). Schizophrenia is the most widespread of the psychotic disorders (disorders in which the person loses contact with reality), and affects about 1% of the world's population (Cannon, 2009). The disorder affects males and females equally, but has an earlier age of onset in males (around mid-adolescence, versus late twenties to early thirties for females). As a rule, the earlier the onset of the disease the more severe the impairments, and like

Table 8.1   **Prevalence of mental health problems of prison and jail inmates**

Selected characteristics	% of inmates in			
	State prison		Local jail	
	With mental problem	Without mental problem	With mental problem	Without mental problem
Criminal record				
Current or past violent offense	61	56	44	36
3 or more prior incarcerations	25	19	26	20
Substance dependence or abuse	74	56	76	53
Drug use in month before arrest	63	49	62	42
Family background				
Homeless in year before arrest	13	6	17	9
Past physical or sexual abuse	27	10	24	8
Parents abused alcohol or drugs	39	25	37	19
Charged with violating facility rules[*]	58	43	19	9
Physical or verbal assault	24	14	8	2
Injured in a fight since admission	20	10	9	3

Note: [*]Includes items not shown.
Source: James & Glaze (2006)

other psychiatric disorders that emerge during adolescence, this probably reflects aberrations in the maturational changes that normally take place in the brain (Paus, Keshavan & Giedd, 2008).

Schizophrenia comes in a variety of subtypes that are categorized according to the symptoms patients manifest. Some schizophrenics are rigid, unresponsive, slow-moving, and sometimes totally immobile (catatonic), some are unkempt, illogical, disorganized, and frenetic (hebephrenic/disorganized), and some are hostile and distrusting (paranoid). The disease most recently came to the attention of the American public through the movie and book *A Beautiful Mind* about the life of John Nash, a brilliant mathematician, and the case of Andrea Yates, the mother who drowned her five children in a bathtub to "save them from the devil"

(Javitt & Coyle, 2004). Both Nash and Yates were schizophrenics, yet both had radically different life outcomes.

Symptoms

Schizophrenia is a progressive disorder with symptoms that are relatively mild and often unnoticed by others when they first appear, but become more severe over the course of weeks, months, and sometimes years. Many subtle manifestations of the disease such as motor and attentional problems, as well as social difficulties, are noted in the childhood behavior of many individuals who are later diagnosed with schizophrenia (Fatemi & Folsom, 2009).

The symptoms of schizophrenia are divided into "positive" and "negative." Positive symptoms include delusions (beliefs with no basis in reality), thought disorders (using nonsense words and sentences), hallucinations (hearing, seeing and smelling things that are not there), and movement disorders (slow movements and repetitive gestures). Negative symptoms include anhedonia (the inability to experience pleasure), the inability to express other emotions, low energy levels, social withdrawal, and poor hygiene. The severity of these symptoms varies widely across individuals, which is why schizophrenia is seen as a spectrum disorder rather than something one has or has not.

Full-blown schizophrenia is so far removed from the everyday experience of most of us that we have to resort to analogies to try to obtain a subjective understanding of the schizophrenic experience. We have all experienced vivid, scary dreams from which we are relieved to awaken. When we awake, we are aware that we were dreaming, and our neural signals begin to respond normally to stimuli outside our private worlds. Schizophrenics, however, remain in their private worlds, in which the distinction between dreaming and waking reality is blurred. When dreaming, our neurons are making random connections unrelated to any external stimuli; we call these random connections "noise." During sleep, there are no perceptions of external stimuli, so the brain does the best it can to generate order from the random noise by drawing on past experiences stored in its memory banks. But because the brain impulses are haphazard, randomly darting from one memory to another, the images generated are less than coherent (Dixon, 2005). With all this disconnected neural activity buzzing around in their heads, schizophrenics experience delusions and hallucinations, and as a consequence have difficulties filtering information and focusing their attention on real environmental stimuli (Dixon, 2005).

Genetics and Schizophrenia

Schizophrenia is a complex multi-determined condition which has spawned many different etiological models. Some models emphasize distal causes (for example, genetics, viruses, fetal teratogenic insults), and others more proximate mechanisms, such as aberrant neural signaling. These models and theories are not contradictory; rather, they are non-mutually exclusive models that tend to reinforce one another while recognizing that any one nominated model does not explain all cases. As Cannon (2009:565) put it:

> It remains unclear whether any of the putative causal factors in schizophrenia are necessary, sufficient, or both, either to the syndrome overall or particular clinically defined subgroups. All or the vast majority of etiological factors are likely to be contributing factors that are neither necessary nor sufficient in isolation but that aggregate together in determining disease risk, as is specified in the neurodevelopmental theory of schizophrenia.

Cannon's astute appraisal of the etiology of schizophrenia fits any behavior, trait, or syndrome addressed in this book, and clearly shows why Tinbergen's four questions are "musts" for any exploration of the human condition. The theory Cannon specifically mentions—the neurodevelopmental model—is a classic diathesis-stress model, and will be addressed later. One thing that we have known for a long time is that genetics plays a large part in schizophrenia.

The risk for developing symptoms of schizophrenia advances dramatically with greater propinquity of genetic relatedness to someone who has the condition. Behavior genetic studies of schizophrenia show a concordance rate of about 50% for MZ twins and about 15% for DZ twins, which yields a heritability coefficient of approximately 0.70. A meta-analysis of studies described as "methodologically superior," Sullivan, Kendler, and Neale (2003), arrived at a heritability estimate of 0.81. While this is indicative of a large genetic effect, given that MZ twins share 100% of their genes and (most generally) 100% of their rearing environment, one would expect to see a higher concordance rate. Because we do not, something other than raw DNA and common environment must be playing a significant role. We note, however, that concordance rates for schizophrenia are almost identical for MZ twins regardless of whether they are reared together or apart, which suggests that any environmental influences on the condition occur prenatally or perinatally.

The search for specific genes that predispose individuals to schizophrenia has not been productive, so the focus has shifted to looking at epigenetic processes, as a possible answer to both the etiology of schizophrenia and the relatively high discordance rates found between MZ twins. One study of phenotypic discordance for a number of traits among healthy MZ twins found that as twins got older, they diverged considerably, with 50-year-old twin pairs averaging four times the epigenetic differences of 3-year-old twin pairs, indicating that epigenetic alterations occur and accumulate throughout life (Fraga et al., 2005). Kaminsky and colleagues (2009) examined methylation patterns in MZ and DZ twins and found discordance in both groups, although there was significantly greater discordance among DZ twins, suggesting that the DNA sequences themselves can affect methylation patterns. In vivo and postmortem studies have demonstrated that a number of genes associated with schizophrenia are particularly susceptible to DNA methylation and histone modification (Gavin & Sharma, 2010).

Wong and colleagues' (2010) longitudinal study concentrated on epigenetic modification in the "usual suspects"—widely studied genes (DRD4, 5-HTT, and MAOA) that operate at the interface of nature and nurture. The researchers found a number of interesting methylation patterns in these genes over a five-year period (ages 5–10 years), with both MZ and DZ co-twins diverging. Most interestingly, they found that while gene expression was changing with age, MZ twins were changing in the same direction, but DZ twins were diverging in the opposite direction. This phenomenon may partially account for the consistent finding that the correlations between pairs of MZ twins across a variety of traits (for example, IQ) stay quite stable with age, while the correlations between DZ pairs fall rather dramatically, as we saw in Chapter 7. The fact that divergence occurs at all in MZ twins reared in the same home also indicates that many epigenetic events are stochastic (Feinberg & Irizarry, 2010).

There is a strong consensus among researchers into schizophrenia that although no single genetic polymorphism or set of polymorphisms have been identified as either necessary or sufficient to cause schizophrenia, the condition cannot occur without genetic vulnerability (Fatemi & Folsom, 2009). Polymorphisms of nine genes have been repeatedly associated with schizophrenia, but frustratingly, no single gene has been replicated in every study, which underlines the causal heterogeneity of the condition (Fatemi & Folsom, 2009). The first plausible etiological model of schizophrenia (as opposed to the egregiously wrong and cruel assertion that "cold mothers" caused schizophrenia and just about every other mental disorder back in the days of crude environmental determinism) was the dopamine hypothesis.

Over the past three or four decades it has been convincingly shown that schizophrenics, and even non-schizophrenics who are at genetic at risk for the condition, show abnormalities of PFC functioning, namely a disturbance of the signal-to-noise ratio (S:N) during information processing. Signaling is the inter-neuronal communication of meaningful (as opposed to nonsense) information; noise is the random firing of neurons, which may be seen as akin to the background crackling in old radio sets that distorts the signal. If the S:N is much above normal, communication between brain regions is interrupted, leading generally to aberrant responses.[1] Dopamine signaling in the PFC is a critical factor in modulating the S:N, and consequently in how persons interpret synaptic activity. As discussed

---

1   We say "generally" because a certain amount of neuronal noise is actually good for us, since it sometimes leads to creative thoughts (but only for the prepared). It is a cliché to associate mental illness with creativity, but many creative people in the arts and sciences have had more than a touch of mental illness. Manzano and colleagues (2009:1) define creativity as: "the ability to produce work that is at the same time novel and meaningful, as opposed to trivial or bizarre." They assert that neural noise may spark creative thoughts precisely because it is "outside the box" of normal reality, but it must also be connected to

in Chapter 2, variation in DA signaling is mediated by the enzyme COMT that degrades DA. Because DA has a significant effect on the PFC S:N, the COMT gene is a susceptibility gene for schizophrenia (Winterer & Weinberger, 2003). Interestingly, differences in methylation patterns between MZ twins who are discordant for schizophrenia are evident in the COMT gene and the dopamine D2 receptor gene (Rutten & Mill, 2009). Further strengthening the DA hypothesis is the fact that DA antagonist drugs work in alleviating positive symptoms (delusions, hallucinations, movement disorders) in most schizophrenics by blockading D2 receptors, and that the effectiveness of different drugs is directly related to how well they block DA (Garrett, 2009).

However, DA antagonists fail to work in about one-third of cases, even though these cases receive as much DA blockage as those for whom the drug works (Garrett, 2009). This suggested that more than DA is at work to produce the aberrant S:N. After it was found that the drug of abuse PCP (phencyclidine) caused schizophrenia-like symptoms by inhibiting a type of glutamate receptor called the N-methyl-D-aspartate (NMDA) receptor, glutaminergic functioning became a major focus of research. Because neurotransmitter systems interact, changes in one system are expected to result in changes in another. It is thus not surprising that other neurotransmitters also play a role. Furthermore, because glutamate is the most common of all neurotransmitters and plays a pivotal role in neural communication, and because NMDA receptors play a key role in the development of neural pathways and in pruning neural connections, glutamate has to play a large part in the schizophrenic condition (Javitt et al., 2008).

Administering glutamate agonists (drugs that binds to a cell's receptor and mimic the action of glutamate—the opposite of an antagonist) helps to relieve both positive and negative symptoms, whereas DA blockers only alleviate positive symptoms. PET studies show that positive symptoms are associated with *hyper*-stimulation of D2 receptors, hence DA antagonists will alleviate positive symptoms. On the other hand, negative symptoms are associated with *hypo*-stimulation of D1 receptors. Dopamine functioning thus results in different symptoms depending on which receptors it activates in what areas of the brain (Patel et al., 2010). Further evidence of the pivotal role of glutamate is found in the fact that about 75% of schizophrenics smoke (and usually cigarettes with high nicotine content), as opposed to about 23% of the general population. This is seen as an effort at self-medication, because nicotine increases glutamate release, as well as increasing DA in the dorsolateral PFC where DA is depleted in schizophrenics (Garrett, 2009). The lower DA activity in this frontal area is known as hypofrontality, and can be seen in neuroimaging and assessed by attention tasks, on which schizophrenics do very poorly.[2]

---

reality—the creativity must arise from its insightfulness, originality, and unexpectedness, not from some random, disconnected departure from the ordinary.

2   Hypofrontality is most often assessed with the Wisconsin Card Sorting Test (WCST). The WCST measures the ability of the patient to display neural flexibility

Other neurotransmitters and receptors have also been implicated to one degree or another in accounting for schizophrenic symptoms, particularly the GABAergic and serotonergic systems. The promiscuous multiplication of all these putative causal factors is frustrating to those who want to know "Which one is it?" Noting that neural circuitry and neurotransmitter systems are fully integrated and that focusing on one transmitter system alone is misguided, Benes (2009:1,004) writes that: "If one asks whether it is dopamine, GABA, or glutamate that is responsible for disturbances in cortical information processing in schizophrenia, the rational response should be 'All of the above!'"

The One-two Hit in Schizophrenia: The Neurodevelopment Model

Studying schizophrenia proximally thus involves altered neurotransmitter systems and neural circuitry, but what is it distally that may account for these alterations? The neurodevelopmental model unites genetics, epigenetics, immunology, and the two critical periods of brain development (prenatal/perinatal and adolescence) in a comprehensive attempt to show how these many factors combine to produce the symptoms associated with schizophrenia. The model asserts that schizophrenia results from abnormal in utero brain development due to any number of factors; this is hit number one. Hit number two comes when the brain is being remolded into its eventual adult form during adolescence. Fatemi and Folsom (2009:528) write:

> According to this [neurodevelopmental] model, early developmental insults may lead to dysfunction of specific neural networks that would account for premorbid signs and symptoms observed in individuals that later develop schizophrenia. At adolescence, excessive elimination of synapses and loss of plasticity may account for the emergence of symptoms.

The fact that premorbid behavioral abnormalities could be present years before schizophrenic psychosis develops meant that there had to have been a "first hit" of some kind, and the transition from childhood premorbid features to overt psychosis occurring around adolescence meant that there also had to be a "second hit." The first hit that "primes" the psychotic pump is most likely to occur during embryonic development. There are a number of environmental candidates for delivering the first hit. For instance, there is a 10% increase in the risk of

---

(how well a person can shift cognitive sets to achieve a goal based on feedback from the environment) in the face of rule changes over the course of the testing period. As the rules change, the patients must learn them, and scores on the test are based on the mistakes made during the learning process. The WCST is used in assessing all kinds of neural degenerative diseases as well as schizophrenia. Numerous neuroimaging studies have shown changes in brain activation in various PFC areas while undergoing testing with schizophrenics showing hypofrontality.

developing schizophrenia among children born during January–March in the northern hemisphere, a time when many viral infections are present (Krause et al., 2010). Mednick, Machon, and Huttunen (1988) documented that the risk for schizophrenia increased 50% for individuals whose mothers were exposed during the second trimester to a virulent type of influenza during the 1957 epidemic in Finland. Another study found a 10- to 20-fold increase in risk for schizophrenia in a New York City cohort who were born to mothers who contracted rubella (a type of measles) during pregnancy (Brown, 2006). A number of other teratogenic agents (nicotine, alcohol, drugs, and so forth) leading to aberrant neural migration and/or other neurological insults have also been identified as risk factors.

Because a wide variety of infectious agents have been linked to schizophrenia, a lot of recent research has focused on the immune response, since the immune system responds to all pathogens (Meyer & Feldon, 2009). When the immune system detects a foreign substance in the host body, it mobilizes a horde of specialized cells to launch an attack on it. These cells release a class of proteins called cytokines that carry signals from cell to cell near the location of the antigen (the foreign body) and alter cell functioning to initiate the immune response. The overall effect of this immune process is to trigger inflammation. If a pregnant woman contracts an infectious disease or ingests noxious substances, her immune system will release cytokines that can enter fetal circulation. The importance of this observation is that cytokines play a role in the proliferation, differentiation, and survival of neurons, and they also influence neurotransmission by modulating neuronal and glial cell functioning. As Depino (2006:7,777) explains: "cytokines released by the maternal immune system (and/or the placental or fetal immune system) in response to infection may be responsible for the interaction between maternal infection during pregnancy, altered neuronal development, and mental diseases."

Muller and Dursun (2010) note that many genes of interest to schizophrenia researchers are related to immune system functioning, further indicating that a dysfunctional immune response plays a major role in priming the schizophrenia pump. Muller and Dursun (2010:1) further note that many studies of immunological response in schizophrenics have shown "a blunted activation of type-1 immune response and a reciprocal overactivation of the type-2 response (in certain cases switching to an autoimmune response)." Type-1 and type-2 immune responses are hypersensitivity responses, type-1 being largely associated with allergies, and type-2 being a delayed response. Type-2 hypersensitivity results in antibodies which identify and attack antigens on the hosts own cells and destroy them, but they also destroy the host cell as well (the autoimmune response). It is important to note again that numerous individuals have been exposed during embryonic/ fetal gestation to pathogens that initiated the same immune response without developing lasting effects. Only those unfortunate few with a genetic vulnerability will go on to develop schizophrenia (GxE again).

The mechanisms of the second hit are more speculative and more complex. One theory posits that infections acquired during gestation and associated with neuro-inflammatory processes lie dormant (or semi-dormant in cases where premorbid symptoms are in evidence) until puberty, when immune surveillance is weakened (Muller & Schwarz, 2006). The immune system can keep the latent problem in abeyance until puberty, when the thymus gland (an endocrine gland vital to the immune system) starts to undergo a major reduction in tissue volume and function (Kinney et al., 2010).[3] Through a tangle of intricate chemical activity, the processes initiated by the first hit combine with possible excess synapse losses in adolescence and the reduction in thymus structure and function to produce the symptoms of schizophrenia. This combination initiates or contributes to the dysregulation of the neurotransmitter systems (the second hit) that causes the aberrant S:N of schizophrenia. According to Kinney and colleagues (2010:555), the neurodevelopmental theory of abnormal immune system response "may help explain roles of prenatal hazards, post-pubertal onset, stress, genes, climate, infections, and brain dysfunction." In other words, we may finally have a unified theory of schizophrenia that ties all of its many correlates together in one (not quite yet neat) bundle.

Schizotypy: Subclinical Schizophrenia

Schizotypy is part of the schizophrenia spectrum, and is a subclinical manifestation of many of the same underlying factors that produce full-blown schizophrenia. Even while not displaying clinical-level signs of the disorder, we would expect close relatives—particularly MZ twins—of individuals with full-blown schizophrenia to harbor a greater genetic risk for schizophrenia than people in general, and they do. These individuals have a lifetime vulnerability to developing full-blown schizophrenia, with the odds of a first-degree relative being diagnosed with the disorder being ten times greater than the odds of someone in the general population being diagnosed (McDonald et al., 2009).

Because symptoms are not sufficient to seriously affect their lives, schizotypal individuals are usually identified by scores on the Schizotypal Personality Questionnaire (SPQ). High scorers on the SPQ evidence sub-psychotic signs identified by behavioral, psychometric, and neuroimaging techniques. For instance, recalling that schizophrenics are more than three times more likely to smoke than the general population, one study found that high scorers on the SPQ were twice as likely to smoke as control subjects (Stewart, Cohen & Copeland, 2010). Another study using the SPQ found that high schizotypy was related to reduced empathy, increased negative affect, and poorer social functioning (Henry, Bailey & Rendell, 2008).

---

3   The thymus gland is essential to the maintenance of the immune response. It increases rapidly in size from infancy to puberty, slowly building up the body's stock of T-cells (thymus lymphocytes), which are white blood cells originating in the bone marrow. There are several types of T-cells, all of which are vital to immunity. After reaching its maximum size at puberty, the thymus decreases by about 3% each year to become almost indistinguishable from surrounding tissue in old age (Barton et al., 2000).

On the other hand, Nettle and Clegg (2005) found individuals high on schizotypy to be more creative than controls, which is compatible with our earlier observations.[4]

Brain imaging studies also show schizotypal individuals to have neural profiles intermediate between full-blown schizophrenics and controls. A review of 20 fMRI studies of nonpsychotic relatives of schizophrenics matched with controls showed consistent activational differences (increases or decreases in activation) between the groups in the same brain areas associated with schizophrenia. The most consistent finding across the 20 studies was increased activity in the right ventral PFC, followed by increased activity in the right parietal cortex. In studies that included increases or decreases from either brain hemisphere as abnormalities, the most consistently findings were impairments of the cerebellum, dorsal prefrontal, lateral temporal and parietal cortices, and the thalamus. The authors concluded that the overall lesson of the 20 studies: "suggests a very broad impact of liability genes, consistent with findings in the illness itself" (McDonald et al., 2009:1,159).

A meta-analysis of 25 studies imaging brain volume (as opposed to brain activity) comparing 1,065 nonpsychotic first-degree relatives of schizophrenics with controls also found significant differences compared to controls (Boos et al., 2007). The largest effect found ($d = 0.31$) was reduction in hippocampal volume among the first-degree relatives, followed by smaller third ventricle ($d = 0.21$) and gray matter ($d = 0.18$) volume. Taken together, all lines of evidence indicate that nonpsychotic first-degree relatives share the genetic risk for developing full-blown schizophrenia, but have somehow managed to avoid clinical-level symptoms. However, they do manifest behavior, personality, and neural anatomy and physiology profiles that suggest they are mildly affected.

The Link between Schizophrenia and Crime

After decades of denying that there was any link between mental illness and crime, the psychiatric community has reversed its stance. It was true at one time that researchers found little or no link between mental illness and crime, but most of the studies that led to that conclusion were conducted during the period when individuals with serious mental illnesses were routinely institutionalized for very long periods, sometimes for life. The deinstitutionalization movement in the 1960s pushed many such persons back into the community, which resulted in greater visibility and higher arrest rates for the mentally ill.

Even with the new evidence that there is a consistent and robust link between mental illness and criminal behavior, there is some reluctance to affirm the link between crime and mental illness out of fear of further stigmatizing an already highly stigmatized group. However, the evidence cannot be dismissed or ignored. In one review of 86 studies that examined the relationship between mental illness and criminal/antisocial behavior, 79 (92%) found the relationship to be positive,

---

4   See note 1 in this chapter.

6 studies were non-significant, and only one study found that mental illness was associated with lower levels of criminal and antisocial behavior (Ellis and Walsh, 2000). Researchers in Denmark looking at more than 300,000 individuals followed to age 43 found that persons with histories of psychiatric hospitalization were 3–11 times more likely to have criminal convictions than people with no psychiatric history (Hodkins et al., 1996). A Swedish study reported that people with psychosis are about four times more likely to have a criminal record than members of the general population (Tuninger et al., 2001). Finally, a meta-analysis of 20 studies including over 18,000 subjects found that the LODs for risk of violence among schizophrenics compared to the general population ranged 1–7 for men and 4–29 for women (Fazel et al., 2009). When calculated for those comorbid for substance abuse disorders (no gender distinctions) the LODs increased to 3–25. In five studies represented in the meta-analysis that examined homicide and schizophrenia, the pooled odds ratio (LOD scores are quite different from odds ratios) comparing schizophrenics to the general population was 19.5. We can thus conclude that the risk for committing a violent crime for persons with schizophrenia is considerably greater than that of the population at large.

However, taken as a whole, schizophrenics are more likely to be sinned against than to sin. This has led to attempts to differentiate between antisocial and non-antisocial schizophrenics along a number of dimensions. Schug and Raine (2009) conducted a meta-analysis of 43 studies that compared neurophysiological performance (a total of 98 different neurological assessment tools were reported across the 43 studies) between antisocial and non-antisocial schizophrenics and antisocial individuals who were not mentally impaired. Antisocial schizophrenics demonstrated numerous deficits across many domains of cognitive functioning compared to non-schizophrenic antisocial individuals. However, in comparison to non-antisocial schizophrenics, they only demonstrated deficits in general intellectual functioning and memory dysfunction. The authors suggest that their findings imply that orbital frontal PFC functioning is a common denominator in schizophrenia and antisocial behavior, and that dorsolateral PFC functioning differentiates antisocial schizophrenics from non-schizophrenic antisocials.

To summarize the literature about the link between mental illness and violence, Marzuk concluded that:

> [W]e must recognize that the link is a real one and that it persists even after controlling for demographic … variables. The link appears strongest for the severe mental illnesses, particularly those involving psychosis …. It is likely that active symptoms, particularly distorted perceptions, faulty reasoning, and distorted modulation of affect are more important than the label of a specific diagnosis. (1996:484)

Nevertheless, the vast majority of the mentally ill are nonviolent, and they are more likely to be victims of violence than perpetrators. The mentally ill most at risk include the homeless, those who use alcohol and other drugs, and those who do not take their antipsychotic medication (Buckley, 2004). A meta-analysis of nine studies found that mentally ill individuals (all with schizophrenia or some other psychosis) were 2.3–140.4 times more likely to be victimized than the non-mentally ill in the general population. These large odds differences from the various studies were attributable to differences in the severity of symptoms, homelessness, engagement in criminal activity, and alcohol or drug abuse (Maniglio, 2009). The mentally ill are particularly likely to be victimized in jails or prisons by other inmates, who call them "bugs" and exploit them materially and sexually. Correctional personnel also have a number of occasions to "discipline" the mentally ill for things such as self-mutilation, excessive noise, refusing medication, and poor hygiene (Stohr, Walsh & Hemmens, 2009).

Culture Matters

We have mentioned a number of environmental factors associated with schizophrenia, but they have been related to geographic, ecological, and economic developmental factors rather than cultural factors. It has long been known that people with schizophrenia are disproportionately from the lower SES classes of society and from urban as opposed to rural areas. This can be interpreted in at least two ways. First, low-SES individuals are more likely to be exposed to many more stressors living in poor urban areas, and are more likely than higher-SES persons to have been exposed prenatally to noxious substances that can negatively affect the developing brain (see Chapter 3). Secondly, people in urban areas are exposed to more infectious diseases, pollutants, toxins, and psychosocial stressors than are people living in rural areas. But let us not fall into the trap of supposing that a person's SES per se causes his or her mental illness, since there is ample research showing that lower SES is most often a consequence, not a cause, of mental illness. That is, becoming mentally ill precipitates a downward spiral in the SES of mental health sufferers compared to the SES of their parents (Thaker, Adami & Gold, 2001).

Cultural arguments revolve around debating the reality of this or that construct and how that construct fits in with the whole culture. As social constructionists and cultural relativists are fond of reminding us, schizophrenia (and other mental illnesses) has been viewed very differently across time and culture. Thomas Szaszs's many works in the 1960s and 1970s made much of the different ways that schizophrenics have been responded to in history, and maintained that psychiatry's labels were mere bogus judgments of disdain used to support middle-class views of proper behavior and to guard the power of psychiatric community (Szasz was himself a psychiatrist). He made many arguments that on close inspection turn out to be non sequiturs, such as saying that if you talk to God, that's OK because you are praying, but if God talks to you, you are a schizophrenic. That argument makes a point about cultural relativism, because there are cultures where the notion of the gods speaking to privileged individuals is accepted, but it is hardly an argument against the objective existence or non-existence of schizophrenia.

At certain times and in certain places when the condition was viewed as demonic possession, schizophrenic-like behavior has been terribly punished by torture or death. On the other hand, such behavior has also been found to be valued in other cultures. For instance, Robert Sapolsky (1997) has pointed out that schizophrenic-like behavior may have been the origin of shamans in many different cultures, and that shamans are valued *because* the gods speak to them. Sapolsky (1997:243) explains that Shamans are:

> the forbidding, charismatic religious leaders in tribal life, the ones who sit and converse with the dead ancestors, who have solitary sojourns in the desert, who huts sit separate from everyone else's, who spend the night transformed into wolves, bears or hyenas, the ones who lead the trance dances and talk in tongues and bring word of the wishes of the gods.

Again, this is all very interesting, but it should not be used to dismiss the concept of schizophrenia (Sapolsky, a neuroscientist, does not dismiss its reality). Those individuals who engage in the kinds of behavior described by Sapolsky simply would not fit into modern societies where rational and predictable behavior is required. Yet there are still those who argue that schizophrenia is a social construct, and that because this is true, searching for causes is futile (Boyle, 1990). The value of social constructionism is that it gives us pause when we begin to believe that our concepts and practices are natural and inevitable, rather than contingent. But social constructionism is not a useful epistemology to guide us in our search for knowledge; it is a brake preventing us from going too far in our claims, not an engine moving us forward. In many ways, it is a dangerous relativism when it slams on the brake and diminishes the importance of science in searching for causes in the minds of those drawn to radical forms of social constructionism. Thankfully for those who suffer from mental illnesses (which are really diseases of brain circuitry), people in the "hard" sciences tend not to be seduced by the allure of such things as social constructionism, and have concentrated on finding ways to alleviate the suffering of people in the grip of mental illness.

Conclusion

Mental illnesses, especially schizophrenia, are associated with an elevated risk of committing criminal acts. Schizophrenics are also much more vulnerable that the average person to be victimized, especially those showing the most severe symptoms, the homeless, and those comorbid for drug and/or alcohol abuse. If we as a society can come to view schizophrenia as a disease of the brain circuitry that results in bizarre behavioral symptoms, rather than a "mental" disease or an eccentric abuse of free will, we should find less stigma attached to the condition.

We have long known that genes play a large role in the etiology of schizophrenia, but also that they were far from the whole story. If genes were the whole story, it would certainly make it easier to come to grips with dealing with the disease. With the emergence of the neurodevelopmental "one-two hit" model of schizophrenia, researchers have been about to tie together many correlates of the disease from the most proximate cause of positive symptoms (S:N) to the most distal (a possible type-2 immune response to embryonic/fetal exposure to viruses and other neurotoxins). This is a huge improvement over the "cold mother" notions prevalent not too long ago, when our only "solution" to schizophrenics in our midst was to lock them up in rubber rooms for life. We can now "see" schizophrenia in the very structure and function of the brain, thanks to advances in brain-imaging techniques. The more criminologists come to understand conditions such as schizophrenia, the more they will come to understand criminality as a multifaceted phenomenon rooted in the brain.

Chapter 9
Criminal Violence and the Brain

Violence and Aggression: Learned or Unlearned?

Violent crimes—murder, rape, robbery, and assault—are crimes that evoke the greatest fear and outrage in us all. Violent crime is the use of force exercised without excuse or justification to achieve a goal at the expense of a victim. Physically harming a victim may be the motive behind a violent crime, or harm may be secondary to achieving the perpetrator's goal, as in a robbery. We exclude from our consideration other kinds of violence such as state warfare, violence occurring in sports, justified use of force by law enforcement officers, or the use of violence in defending oneself from unprovoked attack.

Let us first distinguish between three terms that are often used interchangeably: aggressiveness, aggression, and violence. *Aggressiveness* is a trait, high levels of which imply a potential for aggressive behavior which may or may not be realized. *Aggression* is a behavior which may be prosocial, as in sports participation, justified, as in reactive or defensive aggression, or antisocial, as in bullying behavior. *Violence* is extreme aggression designed to hurt another person, and may be exercised defensively (reactive violence) or proactively (predatory or instrumental violence).

A large bone of contention is social science is whether we learn to be violent, or whether it is part of our evolutionary baggage that we must learn to control. The argument is caught up in two philosophical fallacies: the naturalistic and the moralistic fallacies. The naturalistic fallacy is the fallacy of confusing an empirical *is* with a moral *ought*. We commit the naturalistic fallacy if we believe that by admitting that violence is part of human nature we are saying that it is natural, and therefore it is good, or at least justifiable. The signatories of the famous (or infamous) Seville Statement on Violence commit this fallacy when they state that: "biological findings" have been used "to justify violence and war" (in Fox 1988:36). The statement does not provide an example of anyone's "biological findings" that have been used to "justify violence or war," probably because there are no such examples. Biological findings do point to violence as a natural part of the human behavioral repertoire, however, and that automatically means to some that those who advance such findings must think it a good thing.

The signatories to this document evidently see what they believe, rather than believe what they see: this is the moralistic fallacy. The less familiar moralistic fallacy is the opposite of the more familiar naturalistic fallacy, in that it confuses *ought* with *is*. It deduces a fact from a moral judgment. To commit this fallacy is to argue that if something is morally offensive, it is *a priori* false: violence is evil, therefore it cannot be part of human nature. The Seville Statement commits this fallacy when it says in capital letters and delivered *ex cathedra*: "IT IS SCIENTIFICALLY INCORRECT to say that in the course of human evolution there has been a selection for aggressive behavior any more than for other kinds of behavior" (in Fox, 1988:36). How the signatories to this document believe that the mechanisms of aggression and violence got into us is anyone's guess, and what could "any more than for other kinds of behavior" mean here? Perhaps it is an escape hatch for those who wanted a way out after their warm feelings of self-righteousness produced by penning their names on the document wore off. After all, the qualifying phrase "any more than any other kinds of behavior" implies that the signatories knew that it has been selected for like "other kinds of behavior."

The learned/natural debate is played out most familiarly in criminology among social learning and social control theorists. Social learning theorists believe that the default option for humans unsullied by malevolent families, peers, neighborhoods, and so on is to be good social animals, and so they ask: "What causes crime?" How the sum of inherently good individuals equals a bad society is never addressed by the adherents of these theories, who have probably never given the contradiction any serious thought. Social control theorists believe that the default option for humans not taught to behave well is to behave poorly, so they ask: "Why don't most of us commit crimes?" Gwynn Nettler (1984:313) said it most colorfully on behalf of the social control position: "If we grow up 'naturally,' without cultivation, like weeds, we grow up like weeds—rank."

Scientific questions are not settled by "official" dogmas so baldly stated in the Seville Statement, but by evidence. Longitudinal studies of children find that the frequency of hitting, biting, and kicking peak around 2 years of age, and decline by about 66% by age 12 (Tibbetts & Hemmens, 2010). A longitudinal study tracing the trajectory of physical aggressive behavior among children deemed low, moderate, and high on such behavior at age 6 showed that the trend was for aggressive behavior to diminish among the low and moderate groups. Among the highly aggressive children, after dropping to moderate levels by age 12, aggressive behaviors rose again during puberty before dropping off to levels observed at age 6 (Tremblay, 2008). Summing up the literature on this issue, Tremblay (2008:2619) states: "By monitoring the development of physical aggression from infancy onwards, recent longitudinal studies show that human infants spontaneously use physical aggression and that humans learn not to physically aggress rather than learn to aggress." There are no studies running counter to this—studies showing a childhood distaste for aggressive acts that slowly dissipates with age as they are exposed to a malevolent society. One might chuckle over a 2-year-old hitting, kicking or biting, but the same actions from a 22-year-old are no laughing matter. The evidence seems unequivocal that humans must learn to control behavior that evidently "comes naturally."

Researchers in different disciplines ask different questions about violence. Sociologists ask about the social structure or norms of a society that lead to different rates of violence in different societies, and psychologists ask what personality traits or developmental experiences increase the risk of violence for individuals. Geneticists ask about the mix of genetic and environmental factors associated with violence, neuroscientists ask about the neurotransmitters and brain structures associated with it, and evolutionary biologists ask about its adaptive function.

The bloody history of humanity attests to how easily we are moved to create situations that lead to violence, and that we do so with alarming frequency. The fact that we occasionally find cultures that are apparently nonviolent (in the sense that they do not make war on their neighbors) does not gainsay this, although there are those who think it does. Giorgi (2001:172) writes that: "If human beings are congenitally violent, the many non-violent cultures describes in the literature ... must be made of creatures that are not human beings." This is a red herring of the ripest kind, since Giorgi defines violence purely in terms of war. Supposedly nonviolent cultures are typically pre-state cultures isolated from potential war enemies and living in resource-poor environments in which strong norms of cooperation are imperative. But nonviolence rapidly changes to violence in the face of threat, and that is the evolutionary function of violence.

Giorgi (2001) correctly notes that peaceful cooperation defines our species more than violent conflict, but the presence of one does not imply the absence of the other. In *The Decent of Man*, Darwin wrote about cooperation three times more often than about competition (Levine, 2006), but criminologists, whose stock in trade is vice, not virtue, are more interested in conflict. The great majority of humans are not attracted to violence, want to avoid it, and generally strongly condemn it, but that does not mean that it is not a part of our evolutionary baggage. Most humans in modern Western societies probably go from cradle to grave without ever committing a serious act of violence (Collins, 2009), but they owe this to the fact that they inhabit societies in which law enforcement and the judiciary are largely respected and trusted.

Such trust is evolutionarily novel. Eisener's (2001) examination of the historical dynamics of European homicide rates showed that they dropped from a high average of 32 per 100,000 in the thirteenth and fourteenth centuries to 19, 11, 3.2, 2.6, and 1.4 per 100,000 in subsequent centuries. The notorious unreliability of crime statistics suggests that these figures are severely underestimated, and the unreliability doubtless becomes greater the farther back we go. Eisener (2001) concludes that such social control mechanisms as the state's monopoly of power, the expansion of universal schooling, the rise of religious reform movements, and the organized discipline of the manufacturing workplace largely accounted for this precipitous decline. Eisener's data show that sociocultural inputs can change behavioral strategies, but these strategies serve the same evolutionary ends of acquiring and protecting resources. Europeans have sensibly moved from high-risk violent strategies to low-risk strategies to acquire resources and defend their interests once they became available. Historical data thus strongly support the social control tradition in criminology. The relative rarity of violence in developed societies renders it imperative to root out explanations for the few among us who appear to relish it.

Evolutionary Considerations: What is Violence For?

When evolutionary biologists explore the behavioral repertoire of any species, their first question is: "What is the adaptive significance of this behavior?" With regard to violence, they want to know how violence was adaptive in evolutionary environments, what its function is, and what environmental circumstances are likely to evoke it. Evolutionary biologists assume that aggression and violence evolved to solve some adaptive problems, such as the acquisition of mates, resources, and territory. Why do humans carry the ability to explode into violent action and harm others when it is something the great majority of us abhor and seek to avoid?

Natural selection has not strongly favored violent battles over access to females in long-lived species such as ours. Males in long-lived species have time to move up status hierarchies and acquire mates via courtship, rather than risking their lives in desperate mating battles as short-lived species typically do (Alcock, 2005). The male–female body size ratio in a species is an indicator of its mating history. Selection for violent competition results in males becoming much larger than females as size and strength become the coinage of reproductive success. A high degree of sexual dimorphism reflects a polygynous mating history in which dominance is established by physical battles among males. The fossil record shows that early hominid males (*Australopithecines*) were 50–100% larger than females (Geary, 2000). The fairly low degree of sexual dimorphism for body size among modern *Homo sapiens* (males are only about 15% larger than females, on average) indicates an evolutionary shift from violent male competition for mates to a more monogamous mating system and an increase in paternal investment (Plavcan & Van Schaik, 1997).

It is a central tenet of evolutionary theory that the human brain evolved in the context of overwhelming concerns for resources and mate acquisition. When food, territory, and mates are plentiful, the use of violent tactics to obtain them is a risky and unnecessary waste of energy, but when resources are scarce, acquiring them any way one can, including the use of violence, may be worth the risk. Violence, and the ability to make credible threats of violence, is related to reproductive success in almost all animal species through its role in helping individuals to attain status and dominance in the group, and thus access to more resources and to more females. In evolutionary environments, you could not dial 911 to call the police to dissuade some scoundrel from stealing your resources. If you wished to keep them, it would be wise to respond aggressively. It would be even better if you cultivated a reputation for violence by demonstrating your willingness to become violent when challenged. Likewise, in modern environments where men are expected to take care of their own problems rather than involve the police, violence or the threat of violence lets any potential challenger know that it would be in his or her best interests to avoid you and your resources and look elsewhere. This is why a "badass" reputation is so valued in inner-city subcultures, why those with it are always looking for opportunities to validate it, and why it is craved to such an extent that: "Many inner city young men ... will risk their lives to attain it" (Anderson, 1994:89).

Having a reputation for being ever ready to use violence in defense of one's interests has long been considered virtuous for males. It has been enshrined in the cult of machismo and in the centuries-long practice of fighting duels over quite trivial matters of "honor." Status is not necessarily associated with aggressive and violent tactics (typically, quite the opposite is true today in most social contexts), but it almost certainly was more so in our ancestral environments (Wrangham & Peterson, 1996). Because status brought more copulation opportunities, genes inclining males to aggressively pursue their interests enjoyed greater representation in subsequent generations. From the evolutionary point of view, violence is something human males, as well as males in numerous other species, are designed by nature to exhibit under evolutionarily relevant circumstances. In cultures where polygyny and low paternal investment exist, we find homicide rates greatly exceeding those of any modern society, such as the Agta rate of 326 per 100,000 and the Yanomamo rate of 166 per 100,000 (Ellis & Walsh, 2000:71). Homicide translates directly into reproductive success among the Yanomamo, with males who have killed the most in inter-village warfare having, on average, three times as many wives and children as those who have killed least or not at all (Chagnon, 1988).

A violent reputation may be valued, but exercising it imposes a cost on those who use it because they could be killed or maimed in the process. This is why most of us seek to avoid it when there are alternative ways of resolving disputes. But anyone unprepared to match violence with violence may lose their life as well as their resources. Natural selection has provided us with the ability to switch to a violence mode quickly when we have reason to believe that things we value may be taken from us (Gaulin & McBurney, 2001). This propensity is most useful today in disorganized neighborhoods in which a tradition of settling one's own quarrels without involving the authorities is entrenched—that is, in neighborhoods in which social institutions that control, shape, and sublimate violent tendencies are absent or enfeebled.

Individuals living in more "respectable" areas who have faith in the fairness of the criminal justice system rarely, if ever, have to resort to violence to gain what they want or to protect what they have. Natural selection has favored flexibility over fixity of human behavior, which is why behaving violently is very much contingent on environmental instigation. The evolutionary point of view is that the major long-term factor in variation in the ease of violence instigation is how much violence a person has been exposed to in the past. When many acts of violence are observed: "there is a feedback effect; each violent act observed makes observers feel more at risk and therefore more likely to resort to preemptive violence themselves" (Gaulin & McBurney, 2001:83).

The Triple Imbalance Hypothesis

The most comprehensive account of antisocial aggression and violence at the neurohormonal level is the *triple imbalance hypothesis* (TIH) of Jack van Honk and colleagues (2010). The TIH brings together several lines of research on reactive aggression among non-humans and humans and avers that it is subconsciously motivated by an imbalance of three neurohormonal systems: the subcortical, cortical-subcortical, and cortical systems. The subcortical imbalance hypothesis maintains that aggression is motivated by imbalances of the steroid hormones cortisol (low) and testosterone (high). This hormonal imbalance also down-regulates cortical–subcortical communication; this is the cortical–subcortical imbalance hypothesis. The third imbalance—the cortical imbalance hypothesis—involves low serotonergic functioning and frontal lobe asymmetry.

We know that high levels of testosterone and low levels of cortisol are implicated in criminal behavior because T facilitates dominance striving, and both high T and low cortisol reduce fear and anxiety. Testosterone (an anabolic steroid) is the end product of the hypothalamic–pituitary–gonadal (HPG) axis, and cortisol (a catabolic steroid) is the end product of the hypothalamic–pituitary–adrenal axis. The two endocrine axes have mutually inhibitory effects on each other. Stress-induced activation of the HPA axis affects all body systems, including inhibition of the HPG axis, with high doses of cortisol resulting in the reduction of T. Conversely, high T inhibits the adrenal glands' responses to adrenocorticotropic hormone (ACTH) that stimulates the release of cortisol (Brownlee, Moore & Hackney, 2005). The T–cortisol interplay is part of a system influencing autonomic responses to threats, and thus modulates approach-avoidance behaviors. This balance between activation and inhibition at the "visceral" HPA–HPG level is analogous to the more "cerebral" BIS–BAS balancing system previously discussed, although the two balancing systems are integrated (Terburg, Morgan & Van Honk, 2009).

Using fMRI, Hermans, Ramsey & Van Honk (2008) showed that high T–cortisol ratios are associated with significantly increased activation of the hypothalamus and the amygdala, which are important components of the subcortical reactive stress circuit, in response to angry faces. High T enhances attention to angry faces, while low cortisol (low fear) facilitates an aggressive response to the angry signals of others. As Terburg, Morgan and Van Honk (2009:217) put it: "high testosterone/low cortisol ratios seem to predict approach motivation/reward sensitivity. In these motivational stances, individuals are more likely to confront threat, which could result in aggressive behavior. A high testosterone/cortisol ratio therefore predisposes for socially aggressive behaviors."

The cortical–subcortical imbalance hypothesis avers that high T tends to decrease the coupling of the cortical–subcortical regions, thus impeding information transfer between the orbitofronatal cortex (OFC) and the amygdala. There are dense connections between the OFC and the amygdala, underlining the critical role of the OFC in guiding and monitoring fear-generated aggressive responses. Amygdala–OFC communication depends on accurate mutual feedback.

That is, the OFC interprets amygdala activity, but the ability of the OFC to appropriately guide emotional behavior depends on balanced input from the amygdala. Communication deficits in either system can result in high levels of reactive (but not instrumental) aggression. It is apparently through this reduced activation of the circuitry of impulse control and self-regulation that T increases the propensity toward aggression (Mehta & Beer, 2009).

Numerous imaging studies have noted OFC–amygdala connectivity during emotion-regulation. Much of the evidence of OFC–amygdala disconnectedness comes from studies of individuals with intermittent explosive disorder (IED), defined as: "recurrent acts of impulsive, affectively-driven aggression that are disproportionate to any actual provocation" (Coccaro et al., 2007:168). Coccaro and colleagues (2007) found that IED patients exhibited exaggerated amygdala reactivity and diminished OFC activation compared to controls when presented with images of angry faces. Moreover, this amygdala–OFC activation pattern was differentially related to prior aggressive behavior in the real world.

The final imbalance in the TIH is the cortical imbalance hypothesis, which centers on left-side frontal cortex dominance and serotonergic activity. As with many other brain structures, the frontal cortices are bilaterally distributed. These asymmetries are naturally occurring and correlate with individual differences in approach–avoidance tendencies, with left-side dominance predictive of approach behavior, and the right with avoidance behavior (Schutter et al., 2008). A number of studies have shown that anger predicts increased left and decreased right frontal activity (Hewig et al., 2006). Using transcranial magnetic stimulation (TMS), researchers have been able to manipulate cortical excitability by electromagnetic stimulation (reducing or increasing left- or right-side activity of the frontal cortex), producing emotions indexed by the engagement of the sympathetic and parasympathetic branches of the ANS (Van Honk et al., 2002:86). These and numerous other studies lead Van Honk and colleagues to propose that extreme left-side imbalance indicates "a state of readiness to respond to social threat with anger and aggression rather than fear and submission."

Van Honk and colleagues (2010) further propose that low CNS serotonergic functioning promotes reactive aggressive behavior for individuals with a high T–cortisol ratio because low serotonin is associated with impulsiveness and aggression (Dolan, Anderson & Deakin, 2001). It is also fairly well established that T modulates serotonergic receptor activity in ways that can result in violence by influencing serotonin functioning in the OFC and by enhancing amygdala reactivity to cues of social threat (Birger et al., 2003; Mehta & Beer, 2009). Figure 9.1 presents the triple imbalance theory in schematic form.

Testosterone, Serotonin, and Violence

Nothing is ever as simple as high or low levels or ratios of this or that substance accounting for variance in human behavior. As we have emphasized before,

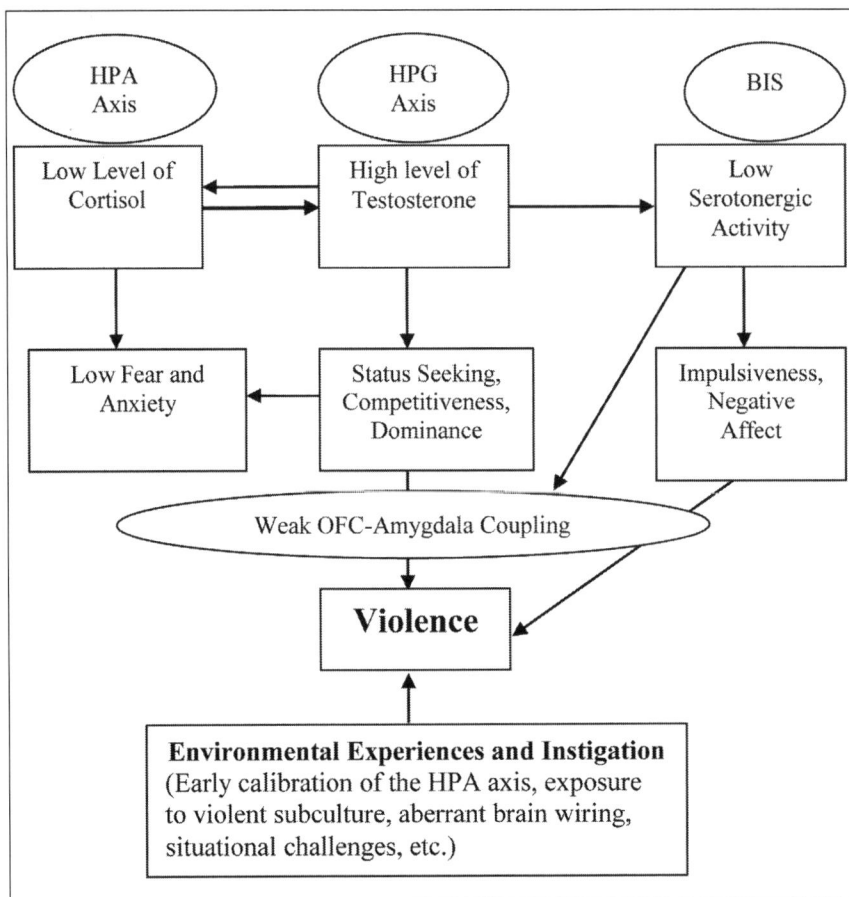

Figure 9.1   The neurohormonal basis of violence according to the triple imbalance hypothesis

T does not "turn on" aggression or violence by activating neurons in the amygdala, rather, it "turns up" the volume by making already excited amygdaloid neurons more excitable. In individuals with weak connections between the amygdala and the OFC, there is little to prevent the volume from becoming ear-shattering. Furthermore, as with other substances related to behavior, at the strictly chemical level (ignoring environmental effects for the moment) the effects of T do not depend simply on basal levels, but also on its receptors.

Androgen receptors are proteins specified by the androgen receptor gene (ARG). The ARG is a highly polymorphic gene with a tri-nucleotide C-A-G repeat within the normal range from 11 to 30 repeats. There are significant racial differences in the average number of repeats, with males of African descent having an average of 16.7–17.8 repeats, males of European descent 19.7, and males of Asian descent 20.1 (Manning, 2007). A review of 11 studies of the AR gene and race/ethnicity with a cut-point of ≤22 found that 76% of African Americans, 62% of Caucasian Americans, and 55% of Asian Americans had the short alleles (Nelson & Witte, 2002). Low repeats are associated with greater binding affinity for all androgens. This black > white > Asian pattern of short repeat polymorphism is another possible molecular piece of the puzzle explaining the ubiquitous black > white > Asian pattern in criminal activity.

Because male characteristics are developmentally controlled by androgens and because maleness is highly related to antisocial behavior, variation in androgen signaling is expected to be associated with antisocial behavior. Among a sample of violent Chinese criminals and controls, Cheng and colleagues (2006) found that the criminal group had a significantly greater number of short repeats (defined as ≤17) than did the control group, and that the short repeat criminals began their criminal careers earlier than the long repeat criminals. Similarly, Rajender and colleagues (2008) compared CAG repeats among 374 violent Indian criminals convicted of murder, rape, or rape/murder and 271 non-criminal control subjects matched for ethnicity. Among the murderers, 80% had the short repeat (defined as ≤21 in this study) allele, 75% of the rapists had it, but only 37% of the controls. Writing that shorter CAG repeats produce effects equivalent to high T levels, Rajender and colleagues (2008:371) write: "This may indicate that smaller CAG repeats may be associated with criminal behavior characterized by repeated crimes and sever offenses."

There is also a relationship between low levels of serotonin and violent behavior, probably reflecting the relationship between serotonin and impulsivity, which has been called "perhaps the most reliable findings in the history of psychiatry" (Fishbein, 2001:15). Serotonin levels are highly heritable, but most of the effects are attributable to the environment and may reflect social position in local status hierarchies. It has been shown that serotonin underlies primate status hierarchies, with the highest-ranking males having the highest levels of serotonin and the lowest ranking having the lowest (Wrangham & Peterson, 1996). In established hierarchies, low-status males defer with little fuss to the demands of higher-ranking males, suggesting that low serotonin levels for those at the bottom of the social heap may be nature's way of preventing them from challenging those at the top when a successful challenge is unlikely. When the hierarchy is disrupted, however, it is the impulsive low-serotonin males who become the most aggressive in the competition for available resources. Living on the ground floor of the status hierarchy is not at all pleasant, and natural selection has built into us a penchant for revolting when possibilities exist to reverse our fortunes. Males who succeed in rising up a new status hierarchy find that their serotonin rises to levels commensurate with their new position (Brammer, Raleigh & McGuire, 1994).

Experiments with rhesus monkeys have shown that peer-raised monkeys have lower concentrations of serotonin than parentally raised monkeys (Bennett et al., 2002; Kraeamer et al., 1998). In the case of humans, read this as "fatherless, gang-raised children." Children raised in this manner are especially prone to be abused and neglected and to be raised in poverty-stricken, violent subcultures. Low self-control and negative emotionality are affected by child abuse and neglect, and low serotonin underlies both traits (Caspi et al., 1994). Abused and neglected children raised in violent subcultures are thus likely to experience both elevated levels of testosterone *and* lowered levels of serotonin (as well as lower cortisol)—a combination especially likely to result in violence (Fox, 1998). High-testosterone/low-serotonin males in violent subcultures who "try their luck" in elevating their status do so against others with similar chemical profiles and status aspirations, which means that the potential for violent confrontation is always present (Bernhardt, 1997).

Culture Matters

We previously noted that long-lived species do not engage in desperate mating battles because they have plenty of time to move up status hierarchies and draw females to them. But what if individuals' perceptions and interpretations tell them that they do not have "plenty of time," and that they cannot advance in life through cooperative and peaceful means? In this case, might it make evolutionary sense for these individuals resort to the tactics associated with short-lived species—reproduce early, take risks, and discount the future? Criminologists frequently note that impulsivity and discounting the future are maladaptive. Wilson and Daly (1997:1271), however, suggest that discounting the future

> may be a "rational" response to information that indicates an uncertain or low probability of surviving to reap delayed benefits, for example, and "reckless" risk taking can be optimal when the expected profits from safer courses of action are negligible.

In other words, when people perceive little opportunity for legitimate success and when many people they know die at an early age, then living for the present and engaging in risky violence to obtain resources makes evolutionary sense. After all, we are designed to respond to our environmental contexts in a flexible algorithmic "if this, then do that" fashion. Males compete for status and resources by whatever means are available to them in the cultural environments in which they live.

Wilson and Daly (1997) tested their evolutionary hypothesis with data from 77 neighborhoods in Chicago for the years 1988–95. They hypothesized that neighborhoods with the lowest income levels and the shortest life expectancies (excluding homicides) would have the highest homicide rates. Life expectancy (effects of homicide mortality removed) ranged from 54.3 years in the poorest neighborhood to 77.4 years in the wealthiest, and the attending homicide rates ranged from 1.3 to 156 per 100,000, a huge 120-fold difference. Wilson and Daley interpreted the data as reflecting escalations of risky tactics that make sense from an evolutionary point of view given the conditions in which people in disorganized neighborhoods live. Natural selection has equipped humans to respond to extreme levels of inequality and short life expectancy by creating risky, high-stakes male–male competitions that too frequently result in homicide. From a moral point of view, this is something to be condemned, but to the extent that such contingent responses are the products of natural selection, they are not pathological from the point of view of evolutionary biology.

Thus, from an evolutionary perspective, violence is something we should expect to see in environments in which social control has largely broken down. According to Cao, Adams, and Jensen (1997:367), the "subculture of violence" thesis formulated by criminologists Wolfgang and Feracutti in 1967: "remains *the* definitive argument for society's role in creating violent criminal behavior." A subculture of violence is a subculture in which the norms, values, and attitudes of its members legitimize the use of violence to resolve conflicts. The thesis reminds us that violence is not evenly distributed among all groups and in all locations in society, and it is necessary to find out why it is more prevalent in some areas and among some groups than in others. Wolfgang and Feracutti reasoned that "by identifying the groups with the highest rates of homicide, we should find in the most intense degree a subculture of violence" (1967:153). They found such a culture in Philadelphia's black community in the mid-1950s, where the homicide rate for young males was 27 times higher than for young white males, and the female rate was 23 times greater than for white females (Wolfgang & Feracutti, 1967:152).

Violent subcultures are supported by a set of conduct norms that favor the use of violence to settle differences over other methods: "In the most impoverished pockets of the inner city, interpersonal relations are now governed by informal rules that emphasize the threat and use of violence rather than civility" (Ismaili, 2001:233). Violence is especially likely to be used in situations that threaten a male's status or reputation on the street. Violent subcultures are not limited to the United States or to African Americans within it. As the data on homicide around the world clearly show, they exist in many countries where the people living in them do not trust the legal system to protect them.

Subcultural practices cannot be properly examined or understood without reference to the structural factors present in the larger society that led to their formation. Wolfgang and Feracutti believed that such subcultures could have begun as a "negative reaction [to a mainstream culture] that turned into regularized, institutionalized patterns of prescription" (1967:162). A number of African American scholars have traced the subculture of violence to the odious institution of slavery (Frazier, 1939; Patterson, 1998; Wilson, 1987). Slavery can be likened to what has been called a *total institution* (Goffman, 1961) to describe prisons. A total institution is one in which a large group of people live together under the restricted and coercive control of others, and in which controllers and controlled are physically and psychologically isolated from one another by mutual distrust and hostility. To adjust to life in prison, inmates develop an *inmate code* that is contrary to the code of the prison staff to guide their behavior toward each other and toward their controllers. The inmate code includes prohibitions against cooperating with guards beyond the level necessary to avoid trouble, against showing subservience and friendliness toward staff unless you can use them for your own ends, and against ratting on other inmates ("Be a man and settle your own beefs"). Compliance with the code is necessary to become a good convict and to be accepted by other inmates.

Likewise, African Americans developed their subculture in response to slavery without much reference to what whites considered acceptable. Although slavery has long gone, the subculture born of it remains, just as the inmate code remains a part of the psychology of the long-term convict long after release. Slaves did everything in their power to deceive their masters, which evolved into cultural norms that lauded thievery and deception and which warned about treacherous whites (Clarke, 1998).

Black lawlessness was reinforced by white indifference to black-on-black crime. Blacks who committed crimes against other blacks were granted leniency and protection from prosecution, particularly if powerful whites employed the perpetrators. Valuable and submissive blacks secured immunity from punishments for a variety of serious offenses, which led to many blacks having "extraordinary liberty to do violent things to other Negroes" (Dollard, 1988:201). This situation generated a tradition of settling differences without involving the authorities. A 1930s commentator wrote that because blacks had no faith in the police to protect them, they resorted to "the ready use of firearms in trivial matters. Many Southern leaders, white and Negro feel strongly that the inadequate police protection provided within Negro communities virtually breeds crime" (in Clarke, 1998:212). A particularly noteworthy example of this powerful cultural tradition is that as long as the FBI has been collating statistics (since 1930), black females have had a higher homicide rate than white males (Barak, 1998). Most of these homicides involve women killing intimate partners in self-defense situations. Intimate personal violence is two to three times more prevalent and more deadly among African American males than among males of other races (Hampton, Oliver & Macgarian, 2003).

Being left to their own devices and building on a tradition of rule-challenging, blacks did not look to white standards to determine their worth. Like convicts, African Americans were expected by their cultural code to settle matters "like a man," and to take care of their own beefs. "Taking care of business" often involves violence in a subculture where it is not viewed as illicit. It is part of the street code that "emerges where the influence of the police ends and where personal responsibility for one's safety is felt to begin" (Anderson, 1999:33). The successful application of aggression as a manifestation of subcultural values *and* as a disavowal of mainstream cultural values is a source of pride (Anderson, 1999). Kenneth Stampp's classical work on slavery similarly concluded that in the black community, "Success, respectability, and morality were measured by *other* standards, and prestige was won in *other* ways" (1956:334).

Other social scientists may attribute the extraordinary level of violence in the inner cities to a culture of poverty rather than a culture of violence per se. They may point out that while white poverty is dispersed across many different neighborhoods, black poverty is highly concentrated in racially segregated single neighborhoods. This concentration has been called hyper-ghettoization (Sampson & Wilson, 2000:152). In other words, the problem is one of social class rather than race.

The class/poverty argument implies that violent subcultures only exist among the poor, and implies that the "subculture of violence" thesis is about race. Neither implication is correct. Wolfgang & Feracutti used black neighborhoods in Philadelphia to illustrate their theory because that is where they found the best contemporary example of their thesis. Subcultures of violence have always existed, and have also been referred to as "honor subcultures." Honor subcultures are communities where males are hypersensitive to insult, and will defend their reputation in dominance contests such as dueling (Mazur & Booth, 1998). Cultural norms that allowed duels over trivial matters of "honor" were common among the most polished and cultivated gentlemen of Europe and the American South in bygone days. Such "honor" duels enhanced the duelists' reputations and provided them with public validation of their self-worth (Baumeister, Smart & Boden, 1996). Only with the establishment of modern law was dueling as a way to settle disputes brought into disrepute. Far from acting in pathological ways, males in modern honor subcultures are acting in historically and evolutionarily normative ways. Although this does not make such behavior morally acceptable, it makes it understandable.

Because the brain physically captures our experiences by molding and shaping neuronal circuitry in ways that make our behavior adaptive in the environments in which we find ourselves, we have further insight into how violence begets violence. Impulsiveness is the proximate behavioral expression of a brain wired by consistent exposure to violence (Niehoff, 2003). If our brains develop in violent environments, we expect hostility from others and behave accordingly ("Do onto others before they do it to you"). By doing so, we invite the very hostility we are on guard for, thus confirming our belief that the world is a hostile place and setting in motion a vicious circle of negative expectations and confirmations.

Chronic vicarious exposure to violence through violent video games has been shown to desensitize viewers to it and make them callous and indifferent to the suffering of others (Cooley-Quille et al., 2001). Frequent players of these games show lower physiological responses when exposed to depictions of violence than do non-players (Carnagey, Anderson & Bushman, 2007). Studies of frequent viewers show decreased activity in brain areas that regulate aggression, and increased activity in areas associated with increased aggression (Murray et al., 2006). Experimental studies such as these are conducted with subjects exposed to chronic *vicarious* violence, not real violence aimed at themselves or at loved ones. Children raised in poor, socially disorganized areas certainly witness an incredible amount of real violence. A study of Chicago schoolchildren found that 33% had witnessed a homicide and 66% had witnessed a serious assault (Osofsky, 1995). Another study found that 32% of Washington, DC children and 51% of New Orleans children had been victims of violence, and 72% of Washington, DC and 91% of New Orleans children had witnessed violence (Osofsky, 1995). Witnessing and experiencing violence "upfront and personal" is presumably captured on the neural circuitry of children more strongly, and plants a warning sign there that the world is a dangerous place in which they must be prepared to protect their interests by violent means if necessary.

Conclusion

Aggression and violence, while sometimes adaptive, are a major source of concern in modern societies. It is clear that all humans, particularly males, have an unlearned propensity to react aggressively and violently in evolutionarily relevant situations—when resources (including one's "honor") are in danger of being appropriated by others. Having said that, however, we again emphasize that violence is only a functional potentiality in humans, the expression of which, for the vast majority, depends on evolutionarily relevant cues. The great majority of individuals in modern society do not have to engage in violence in any form since they can acquire resources peacefully by working, and they can rely on the trusted criminal justice system to protect what they have. In socially disorganized areas where inhabitants perceive themselves to have few opportunities to gain resources legitimately and are less trustful of the law to protect them, many individuals resort to a more ancient evolutionary script to look after their interests.

Van Honk and colleagues' (2010) triple imbalance hypothesis is the most comprehensive theory of reactive aggression and violence currently available to us. It integrates a number of lines of evidence into a neat package. However, we cannot lose sight of the fact that environment and culture have the major part to play in explaining the prevalence and incidence of violence in modern societies. The experiences that individuals have growing up in what has been termed honor subcultures are literally captured in the brain's circuitry. These experiences calibrate the brain to respond aggressively and violently to challenges, however trivial they may be. Understanding the neurobiology of violence leads us to embrace liberal recommendations that we do what we can to strengthen families and various other informal social control mechanisms that serve generally to keep violence in abeyance.

Chapter 10

Gender, Crime, and the Brain

Feminist Criminology and the Gender Ratio Problem

The two great issues in feminist criminology are: (1) whether traditional male-centered theories of crime apply to women, and (2) what explains the universal fact that women are far less likely than men to involve themselves in criminal activity (Price & Sokoloff, 1995). The first issue need not concern us, but the second one—the gender ratio problem—is our focus in this chapter. The fact of huge gender differences in criminal behavior is not in dispute by feminists or anyone else: "[W]omen have had lower rates of crime in *all nations*, in *all communities* within nations, for *all age groups*, for *all periods in recorded history*, and for practically *all crimes*" (Leonard, 1995:55). The arrests for the FBI's index crimes (rape omitted) in 2008 broken down by gender in Figure 10.1 illustrate the difference in the modern American context. The issue of why males commit more criminal acts than females has been called the "single most important fact that criminology theories must be able to explain" (Bernard, Snipes & Gerould, 2010: 299). This may or may not be so, but Gottfredson and Hirschi (1990:149) have concluded that such an explanation is "beyond the scope of any available set of empirical data."

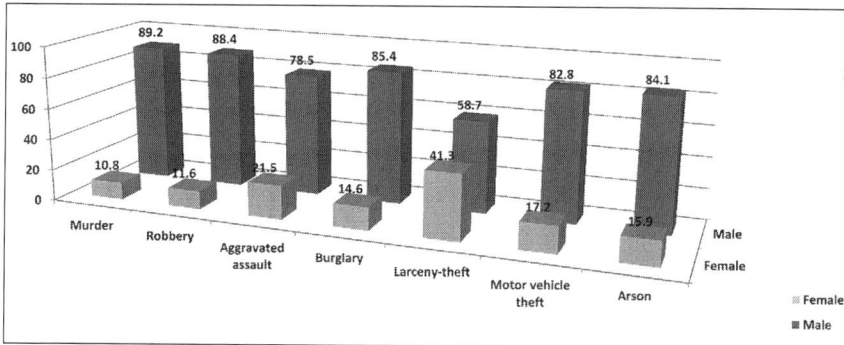

Figure 10.1   Percentage of male/female arrests for FBI Part 1 crimes

Source: FBI (2009) Crime in the United States: 2008. Washington, DC: U.S. Government Printing Office

It is beyond the scope of traditional sociological criminology because sociology tends to view gender differences in traits and behavior (indeed, any differences across any classifications of individuals) solely as products of differential socialization. It is reasoned that males are socialized to be aggressive, dominant, and tough, which are traits conducive to criminal behavior, and females are socialized to be nurturing, empathetic, and conforming, which are traits conducive to prosocial behavior. This suggests that if females were socialized in the same way as males (or vice versa), they would respond to environmental inducements to criminal behavior in like manner and their rates of offending would be roughly the same. This also further suggests that gender socialization is arbitrary. However, this is not the case. If socialization patterns were arbitrary, simple probability tells us one-third would have opted to socialize boys to masculinity and girls to femininity, one-third would have chosen the opposite route, and one-third would have opted for androgyny, yet every known culture socializes boys to masculinity and girls to femininity.[1] Parents in all cultures socialize males and females differently because they *are* different. Socialization patterns "simply represent social confirmation of a basic biological reality that is easily recognized by people in all societies" (Sanderson, 2001:198).

Socialization influences extend beyond parental influences into the larger society and the roles it deems appropriate for categories of people. The roles people occupy are said to influence their global personalities and behaviors, thus

---

1   Margaret Mead's *Sex and Temperament in Three Primitive Societies* (1935) purported to show precisely such an arbitrary socialization among the Arapesh, Mundugumor, and Tchambuli peoples of New Guinea. According to Mead, the Arapesh were a gentle, cooperative people who believed what Westerners define as a feminine temperament to be ideal for both sexes. The violent, warlike Mundugumor considered proper for both sexes what Westerners define as a masculine temperament. Strangest of all were the Tchambuli, who turned things on their head by favoring a feminine temperament for males and a masculine temperament for females. Mead's work became iconic for feminists and social constructionists, but subsequent research found that sex-based temperament and behavior among these peoples were not too different from what they are in other cultures around the world. Among the "gentle" Arapesh: "Violence and war were very much a part of their established tradition" (Roscoe, 2003:589). The "masculine" Mundugumor women expressed their "aggression" mainly by striving to please their men in ways that upstaged their co-wives, and the supposedly sex-reversed Tchambuli turned out to be a thoroughly male-dominated society where "aggressive" behavior on the part of women earned them a beating from their "feminine" husbands (Gewertz & Errington, 1991). The mature Mead acknowledged her youthful blunders in *Sex and Temperament* in her later work *Male and Female* (1949): "If any human society—larger or small, simple or complex—is to survive, it must have a pattern of social life that comes to terms with the differences between the sexes" (1949:173). Like all budding biosocial scientists, she even traced these differences to "sex differentiated reproductive strategies" (1949:160). As for her youthful claims about the Tchambuli, she remarked: "All the claims so glibly made about societies ruled by women are nonsense. We have no reason to believe that they ever existed. Men everywhere have been in charge of running the show" (in Goldberg, 1986:31).

social role theory predicts that gender differences in personality and behavior will diminish as the sexes come to occupy similar social roles in more egalitarian, less patriarchal, cultures (Wood & Eagly, 2002). Social role theory would also predict that gender differences would be strongest in traditional and patriarchal cultures where sex roles are most distinct, but this is the opposite of what we actually find. A study of personality across 26 cultures (n = 23,031) showed that gender differences were most pronounced in modern *egalitarian* cultures in which traditional sex roles are minimized (Costa, Terracciano & McCrae, 2001). Another study (McCrae & Terracciano, 2005) using different measures in 50 cultures (n = 11,985) found the same thing. A study by Schmitt and colleagues (2008) of the "big five" personality traits in 55 cultures (n = 17,637) once again found that the biggest gender differences were found in cultures where sex role differences are minimized. In other words, in the cultures of North America and Western Europe, individuals are freer to live, act, and construct their environments in ways consistent with their innate proclivities. The increased sexual dimorphism in personality in developed societies is a function of the natural tendency of males and females to develop different personalities. Schmitt and colleagues (2008) argue that traditional agrarian cultures with their typically extreme levels of gender and other inequalities represent the largest departure from the egalitarian hunter-gatherer cultures that characterized our species for 99.9% of our history, and that Western post-agrarian cultures are closer to egalitarian hunter-gatherer psychology.

The Neurohormonal Basis of Gender

Biosocial explanations of gender differences in criminality rest on a firm foundation of differential neurological organization shaped by a complicated mélange of prenatal genetic and hormonal processes. Most gender differences in behavior are small and inconsequential, but the differences at the center of one's identity as male or female are very large (Hines, 2004). Not surprisingly, these core gender differences are precisely the traits that are most strongly and positively related to criminal behavior (aggression, callousness, impulsiveness, and so forth) or negatively related (empathy, altruism, nurturance), all of which are underlain by differential neurobiology.

Doreen Kimura informs us that males and females arrive in this world with "differently wired brains," and these brain differences "make it almost impossible to evaluate the effects of experience [the socialization process] independent of physiological predisposition" (1992:119). Bennett, Farrington, and Huesman (2005:273) concur, and explain the pathways from sex-differentiated brain organization to antisocial behavior:

> Males and females vary on a number of perceptual and cognitive information-processing domains that are difficult to ascribe to sex-role socialization. The

human brain is either masculinized or feminized structurally and chemically before birth. Genetics and the biological environment in utero provide the foundation of gender differences in early brain morphology, physiology, chemistry, and nervous system development. It would be surprising if these differences did not contribute to gender differences in cognitive abilities, temperament, and ultimately, normal or antisocial behavior.

Sexing the Brain

Male vulnerability to antisocial behavior is largely a function of exposure to androgens in utero that "sex" the brain. Male and female brains can be distinguished on the basis of structural organization at the gross, cellular, and molecular levels: "Thousands of studies have documented sex differences in the brain in practically any parameter imaginable" (De Vries & Sodersten, 2009:589). These differences are encoded in the genes present on the sex chromosomes that specify either a XX female or XY male: "These genes are differentially represented in the cells of males and females, and have been selected for sex-specific roles. The brain is a sexually dimorphic organ and is also shaped by sex-specific [evolutionary] selection pressures" (Arnold, 2004:1).

Sex differentiation begins with the male-specific Y chromosome that contains only 27 genes coding for proteins, as opposed to the X, shared by both males and females, that encodes about 1,500 (Arnold et al., 2009). Many Y genes have homologous genes on the X chromosome, which reduces the functional differences in XY and XX cells. This leaves few genes that are male-specific, and perhaps only one that really is, and that is the SRY (sex-determining region of the Y chromosome) gene. In all mammalian species, maleness is induced from an intrinsically female form by processes initiated by the SRY gene. All XY individuals would develop as females without the SRY gene, and XX individuals have all the material needed to make a male except this one gene.

The major function of the SRY gene, and its downstream genetic cohorts such as the autosomal SOX9 gene, is to induce the development of the testes from the undifferentiated gonads, rather than the ovaries that would otherwise develop in its absence. The testes then produce androgens, the major one being testosterone, which, when transformed by the enzyme aromatase into estradiol, will masculinize the brain by saturating neurons with the appropriate T receptors, and as a result the structure and functioning of these regions become altered, as are the behaviors they control (Yang, Baskin & DiSandro, 2010). The testes also produce Mullerian inhibiting substance (MIS), which causes the atrophy of internal female sex organs.

Once prenatal androgens have sensitized receptors in the male brain to their effects, there is a second surge from about the second week of life to about the sixth month of life that further "imprints" the male brain, and then a third surge at puberty that activates the brain to engage in male-typical behavior (Sisk & Zehr, 2005; see Figure 5.2). The additional steps required to switch the male brain from its "default" female form is the reason that significantly more males than females suffer from all kinds of neurological problems, because things can go awry when perfectly good systems are meddled with.

Sexual Selection, Human Nature, and Gender Nature

Given the sexually dimorphic brain, the issue becomes what evolutionary pressures selected for them. We expect natural selection to explain most of the characteristics of any organism as functional adaptations—as the result of genes that have survived the evolutionary sieve because of the fitness benefits they confer. However, Darwin himself noted that there are many male traits that are so energy-demanding and so inimical to survival that natural selection should have culled them long ago (Vandermassen, 2004). For instance, natural selection cannot explain the bright colors and elaborate morphology of peacocks' tails in terms of some survival advantage because there is none. The peacock's bright plumage attracts females by indicating "good genes," but it is costly and attracts predators. So why is it there, and why does it survive?

The simple answer is that it survives because peahens like it. Darwin posited his theory of sexual selection to account for many conspicuous physical and behavioral traits in males in a variety of species that have negative survival value. Fitness is about the number of copies an animal contributes to future generations, not how long it survives. Sexual selection involves competition for mating partners, and favors traits that lead to reproductive success regardless of their survival value. Thus, sexual selection, like natural selection, causes changes in the relative frequency of alleles in populations based on the demands of the environment, but it operates on the demands of sex-specific mating challenges rather than general sex-neutral challenges (Qvarnstrom, Brommer & Gustafsson, 2006). This has led to a suite of traits and characteristics in human males and females that render them differentially responsive to criminal opportunities.

Staying Alive and Status Striving

According to Ann Campbell's (1999) "staying alive" hypothesis, unlike males, females are limited in the number of children they can have, so one of the biggest fitness problems facing our ancestral mothers was how to stay alive to care for and protect their offspring to reproductive age. Because female obligatory parental investment is enormously greater than that of males, and because of the infant's dependence on its mother, a mother's presence is more critical to offspring survival, and hence to the mother's reproductive success, than is a father's. Throughout human history: "Desertion of one's mother means almost certain death, whereas desertion by one's father means only a reduction in resources" (Mealey, 2000:341). Each child represents an enormous personal investment for women that they will not relinquish without the most compelling reasons to do so. Female reproductive success thus lies primarily in parenting rather than mating effort, and this requires "staying alive."

The practice of keeping nursing children in close proximity in ancestral environments posed risks to both mother and child if the mother placed herself in risky situations. To avoid doing so, females have evolved a greater propensity to experience more situations as fearful than do males. After all, in reproductive terms, women have less to gain and more to lose by engaging in risky behavior. Fear of injury accounts for the greater tendency of females to avoid or remove themselves from potentially violent situations, and to employ indirect and low-risk strategies in competition and dispute-resolution compared to males. Fear is a basic affective state that signals danger in all animals. It is an unpleasant state of arousal, most immediately experienced as a rapid increase in heart rate, which motivates those experiencing it to escape the immediate threat and to avoid being in similar positions in the future (Steimer, 2002). While unpleasant, it is an adaptively functional experience that facilitates the emergence of escape/avoidance behaviors that enhance an organism's chances of survival.

Females experience fear more readily and more strongly than males, whether assessed in early childhood (Kochanska & Knaack, 2003), the middle-school years (Terranova, Morris & Boxer, 2008), or among adults in a variety of cultures (Brebner, 2003). A meta-analysis of 150 risk experiment studies found that sex differences were greater when the risk involved meant actually carrying out a behavioral response rather than simply responding to hypothetical scenarios requiring only cognitive appraisals of possible risk (Byrnes, Miller & Schafer, 1999). Despite being objectively less at risk for criminal victimization, fear of crime studies consistently find that females are more fearful than males, and that they assess their chances of victimization as higher (Fetchenhauer & Buunk, 2005).

The amygdala is crucially involved with processing fear, which implies that there should be sex differences in amygdala functioning. Neuroimaging studies of the amygdala strongly suggest that females have evolved a more sensitive and more persistent system for detecting danger signals (Williams et al., 2005). Gur and colleagues (2002) found a significantly greater ratio of orbital frontal cortex to amygdala volume in females compared to males. Because the frontal cortices play the major cognitive role in modulating behavior, this suggests that females would be less likely to express anger in aggressive ways by cortical dampening of limbic system activity.

Campbell (1999) asserts that when females engage in crime, they almost always do so for instrumental reasons, and the crimes rarely involve risk of physical injury. Both robbery and larceny/theft involve expropriating resources from others, but as seen in Figure 10.1, females constitute about 41% of arrests for larceny/theft and only about 12% of arrests for robbery (almost always with and at the instigation of male partners; Miller, 1998), a crime carrying a relatively high risk of personal injury. There is no mention in the literature that female robbers crave the additional payoffs of dominance that male robbers do, or a "badass" reputation. Aggressive females are not particularly desirable as mates, and a woman with a reputation as a "badass" would be most unattractive. Campbell (1999:210) notes that while women do aggress and steal, "they rarely do both at the same time because the equation of resources and status reflects a particularly masculine logic."

This observation leads us to the second component of Campbell's "staying alive" hypothesis—status competition. Because males have greater variance in reproductive success than females but less parental certainty, they have more to gain and less to lose by engaging in competition for mating opportunities (Campbell, 2009). That competition is more for social dominance and status than directly for access to females. Status is so valued by males around the world because females are drawn to high-status males and their resources. Because dominance and status are less reproductively consequential for females, there has been less evolutionary pressure for the selection of mechanisms useful in that endeavor for females than for males.

Although females engage in intrasexual competition for mates, the competition is rarely violent. Most of it is low-key, low-risk, and chronic, as opposed to high-key, high-risk, and acute, as it is in male competition. A study of 20 different populations around the world found that only 2.5% of all homicides involved females killing females (Daly & Wilson, 2001), and we have seen that when females kill, they typically kill intimate partners in self-defense situations. We do not see violent competition for mates among women because the female assets men seek are youth and beauty, things that cannot be won in competition; one either has them or one does not. Male assets that females desire for their reproductive success are resources, which can be won in competition with other males. Thus, males are willing to incur high risks to achieve the status that bring them resources and thus access to more females.

Tending and Befriending

Another evolutionary hypothesis that augments Campbell's risk-aversion model and which can also be fruitful in explaining gender differences in criminal behavior is the "tending and befriending" hypothesis (Taylor et al., 2000; Taylor, 2006). This hypothesis is a stress response model associated with the female parenting role. Taylor and colleagues' survey of the rodent, primate, and human literature on coping strategies in response to threats of danger found a robust sex difference; females typically "tend and befriend," as opposed to the more male-typical "fight or flight" response. Tending and befriending is the tendency to respond to stressors by drawing closer to offspring and intensifying their care, and by drawing closer to social support networks of other females. Males also tend and befriend in response to threat, but not in the same ways, to the same degree, or in response to the same threats as females. Likewise, females will fight or flee when conditions demand it, but in different ways and to different degrees. This tendency among females apparently arose to protect themselves and their children in situations in which fighting or fleeing were not viable options. Of course, when there are no other options, females will flee with their young and fight fiercely to protect them.

The female inclination to tend and befriend is assumed to have coevolved from the more primitive attachment and nurturing systems chemically organized and sustained by oxytocin, a vitally important peptide for mammalian attachment often referred to as "the cuddle chemical" because it "calms and connects." Oxytocin operates in both sexes, but is especially relevant for females because it and its receptors are regulated by estrogen (Campbell, 2008). Interestingly, the nucleus accumbens is a major target for OT, stressing again that natural selection provides us with reward systems for behaving in ways that lead to the proliferation of our DNA (MacDonald & MacDonald, 2010).

Most stress encountered by males in evolutionary environments came from other males in the competition for status and access to females, or from predators during food acquisition. It was "fight or forfeit mating" in the first case, or "take risks or starve" in the second. Male-typical responses to stress are driven by T, which works antagonistically to OT (Taylor, 2006). When men befriend in the face of threat, T tends to rise in anticipation of aggressive responses (Geary & Flinn, 2002).

In most threat situations faced by females in evolutionary environments, the fight or flight response would not have been be viable. A woman was unlikely to outfight or outrun an aggressive male, and if the threat came from a non-human predator, fleeing would mean abandoning her offspring to their fate. A more adaptive response in both cases was to hunker down and tend to her offspring and to turn to her social network of other females to help with her defense. The initial physiological stress response is identical in males and females—arousal of the ANS—but the response is downregulated in females by OT, which reduces amygdala activity and increases parasympathetic ANS activity (MacDonald & MacDonald, 2010).

As the "tend and befriend" hypothesis would lead us to suspect, a number of studies show that there are fundamental sex differences in the organization of ANS functioning (Sax, 2006). The sympathetic branch dominates in males, with the primary neurotransmitter being norepinephrine and the primary hormone being epinephrine. In females, the parasympathetic branch is dominant, with acetylcholine being the primary neurotransmitter and OT the major hormonal factor. According to Sax (2006), the activation of the ANS in females tends to result in slowing or freezing, and is experienced as unpleasant and stressful. In males, on the other hand, it typically results in sharpened senses, and is often subjectively experienced as thrilling. The "tend and befriend" hypothesis is thus useful to us in understanding the ultimate evolutionary and proximate neurohormonal mechanisms that underlie the tendency for women to be less physically aggressive when threatened. Although there are no sex differences in the frequency or intensity of anger, men are more likely to express it via confrontation and verbal and/or physical aggression. The female tendency is to discuss the situation (venting) with a friend or other uninvolved individual, or to cry and seek solace (Campbell, 2006).

Empathy and Altruism

Being strongly selected for parenting effort, we would expect that selection pressures for empathy would have operated more strongly in females than in males. Empathy is the cognitive and emotional ability to understand the feelings and emotions of others as if they were our own. The cognitive component allows us to understand why others are feeling distress, and the emotional component allows us to "feel" it with them. The basis of empathy is our own distress when witnessing the distress of others, and if we can alleviate their distress, we thereby alleviate our own. Empathy thus has a selfish component, but it is a good thing that it does, because we call people who lack emotional connectedness to others psychopaths, and such people are callously indifferent to the needs and suffering of others.

Empathy is an ancient phylogenic capacity pre-dating the emergence of *Homo sapiens* which evolved rapidly in the context of mammalian parental care (De Waal, 2008). Empathy is an integral component of offspring nurturing because caregivers must quickly and automatically relate to the distress signals of their offspring. Parents who were not alerted to or were unaffected by their offspring's distress signals or by their smiles and cooing are surely not among our ancestors. Like the diffusion of adaptive love and nurturance of genetic offspring to the non-adaptive love and nurturance of the children of others and to pets, the capacity for empathetic responses, once locked into the human repertoire, diffused to a wider network of social relationships.

Neuroscientists have located the ability to "read" the minds of others in so-called mirror neurons. Mirror neurons are cells that fire (respond) equally whether an actor performs an action or witnesses someone else performing the action. It is not simply a matter of being cognitively aware of the actor ("Jane is upset"); it is the actual firing of *identical* neurons in the observer's brain that are firing in the brain of the person being observed. It is assumed that this unconscious communication between neurons of one person and another reflects a correspondence between self and other that turns an observation into empathy. The human mirror neuron system (hMNS) is distributed throughout motor areas of the brain and the sub-cortices of the PFC. It has been shown in fMRI studies that mirror neuron mechanisms are selectively recruited when attributing feelings to the self or to others in response to viewing a variety of emotional facial expressions (angry, fearful, sad, and so forth). It is also found that subjects with higher empathy scores on a variety of empathy scales show stronger brain activation, particularly in the various frontal cortices (Schulte-Rüther et al., 2007).

Females are found to more empathetic than males regardless of the methods used to assess it (Campbell, 2006). Part of this sex difference may be traced at the proximate level to the effects of fetal T on males (Knickmeyer et al., 2006), and/or to higher OT effects on females (Taylor, 2006). A study of 20 healthy females who received either a single sublingual dose of T or a placebo found that the T-administered group showed a significant reduction in empathetic responses to experimental stimuli (Hermans, Putman & Van Honk, 2006). Conversely, a study of 30 healthy males by Domes and colleagues (2007) showed that a single intranasal dose of OT significantly enhanced their ability to infer the mental states of others compared to a placebo control group. An fMRI double-bind study of 15 healthy males (Kirsch et al., 2005) showed that a single intranasal dose of OT significantly reduced amygdala activity in response to angry faces and threatening scenarios compared to subjects receiving a placebo. Thus, males become more empathetic with the administration of OT, and females become less so with the administration of T. These responses take place outside conscious awareness because the target sites for both T and OT are located in the limbic system. Another fMRI study comparing neural correlates of empathy found that females recruit far more emotion-related brain areas than males when processing empathy-related stimuli (Derntl et al., 2010).

Empathy is a feeling or emotion, but emotions or feelings per se cannot enhance fitness. There has to be a behavior associated with the internal state to give it selective potency, because it is the consequences of behavior on which natural selection passes judgment. Empathy provides impetus for us to perform some altruistic behavior to alleviate the distress of others. Altruism, the active regard for the well-being of another, is the polar opposite of criminality, which is an active disregard for the well-being of others. As an active regard for others, altruism is a socially valued trait because it serves as a buffer against antisocial behavior. While humans are necessarily born with a central concern for their own well-being, we are also born with altruistic tendencies that curb excesses and direct our self-concern in prosocial directions. Warneken and Tomasello (2009) show that altruistic tendencies emerging before socialization can have major effects, and that later socialization is only effective if it meshes with a disposition to be altruistic.

Given its importance in social life in blunting antisocial impulses, it makes sense that altruism would exert pressure for selection. Altruism entails providing a benefit to others at some expense to one's self, but we gladly impose that expense upon ourselves because we are rewarded when we do. A number of fMRI studies have shown that the same reward areas in the brain are activated whether giving or receiving something of value, but areas associated with social attachments and affiliation only "light up" when giving. The authors of one such study wrote in their conclusion that:

> Taken together, these lines of evidence indicate that human altruism draws on general mammalian neural systems of reward, social attachment, and aversion. In the context of intertwined social and motivational contingencies, however, altruism tied to abstract moral beliefs relies on the uniquely developed human anterior prefrontal cortex. (Moll et al., 2006:15,626)

Although individual organisms are adapted to act in fitness-enhancing ways, not to behave for the good of the group, unconscious fitness goals are best realized by adhering to the rules of cooperation, and that is "for the good of the group."

The conscious intentions of altruists are other-oriented, but actions are judged good or bad by natural selection according to their consequences, not by their intentions, That is, although altruism is ultimately (but unconsciously) self-serving, this does not diminish its value to its beneficiaries one bit. Selfishness, as understood by biologists, is both individually and socially desirable. It is by cooperating with others and being actively concerned with their well-being (and others also behaving that way) that we are able to simultaneously serve our own best interests and the best interests of our communities. This is quite different from selfishness as understood in the vernacular—the crabbed egotism of the antisocial individual shorn of any concern for others (Walsh, 2009a). This form of selfishness is ultimately self-defeating.

Evidence of gender differences in altruism comes from self-report, observational, experimental, and neuroimaging studies, and shows, almost without exception, that females are more altruistic than males. Andreoni and Vesterlund (2001) found that when altruism was cheap, men were more altruistic, but when it was more costly, women were. Piper and Schnepf's (2008) analysis of charitable giving revealed that after controlling for personal income and marital status, women donated significantly more money than men. Women's giving was focused more on nurture-related charities such as animal, children, and elderly welfare, while men's giving was more focused on religious organizations. Yamasue and colleagues' (2008:2,337) fMRI study of 155 Japanese subjects showed that the higher measured cooperativeness of females compared to males was tightly coupled with gray matter volume in the various frontal cortices. These authors concluded that: "The present findings suggest that genetic factors coding development of the social brain influence altruistic cooperativeness more directly in females." This is exactly what Darwinists would predict, and it would be one of the factors they would offer to explain gender differences in criminal behavior.

Gender Differences in Other Prosocial Traits

Guilt-proneness, conscientiousness and agreeableness are three other traits that help to explain gender differences in criminality. Guilt is an important self-regulatory emotion that involves anxiety, remorse, and concern about how one's actions have negatively impacted others. It is a socially adaptive because it motivates both avoidance and approach behavior. Because guilt is psychologically punitive, it motivates one not to repeat the transgression (avoidance), and because it also moves one toward reparative behavior (apologies, restitution), it motivates approach behavior. As we might expect, guilt is positively related to empathy, since persons are not likely to feel bad about offending others if they are indifferent to them (Silfver & Klaus, 2007). Females show higher overall levels of guilt-proneness than males, whether assessed via self-reports (Silfver et al., 2008), or PFC activity recorded by EEGs (Amodio, Devine & Harmon-Jones, 2007). In short, guilt focuses a person's thoughts on recognizing the rights of others and one's duty to respect that. This inner voice (conscience) is conspicuously absent or greatly attenuated in criminals, and less developed in males in general. Thus, we have yet another reason for suspecting *a priori* that women would offend less than men.

Conscientiousness and agreeableness are two other prosocial traits in which numerous studies show the genders to be significantly different, and which are conspicuously absent in criminals. We would expect people who are more fearful, guilt-prone, and empathetic to be both more conscientious and agreeable in their associations with others lest they offend. In the Costa, Terracciano and McCrae (2001) and Schmitt and colleagues (2008) studies of personality in cultures around the world discussed earlier, higher levels of both agreeableness and conscientiousness were reported by females compared to males in almost all of them. Again, the biggest gender differences in conscientiousness and agreeableness were found in the most egalitarian and economically developed societies in both studies.

Gender and Antisocial Traits

The traits we have examined so far are prosocial traits on which females score significantly higher than males. Space limitations allow us only to briefly mention antisocial traits on which females score significantly lower than males.

Low Self-control

Impulsiveness, low constraint, and low self-control are different constructs, but they are similar enough to be treated as one because all three involve disinhibited behavior in which actors are unable or unwilling to consider the long-term consequences of their behavior. We learn to control our behavior via two routes, the first of which is entirely visceral in nature (sympathetic ANS arousal), called *reactive inhibition*. Reactive inhibition is fear-based, and automatically impels attention to threats and initiates avoidance/withdrawal behavior in response. The second system is *effortful control*. Effortful control allows for reflection on the long-term negative consequences of a contemplated behavior. Behavioral inhibition is thus more a function of visceral fear (harm avoidance) than other more cognitive components of inhibition such as guilt and embarrassment (Driscoll et al., 2006). Because females are less vulnerable to brain insults than males, and because reactive inhibition has more valence for them because of higher levels of fear, they are better able to exercise effortful control (Bennett, Farrington & Huesmann, 2005). Whether it be a function of reactive or effortful control (these mechanisms are not mutually exclusive), females have, *without exception*, shown greater levels of constraint/self-control across numerous studies regardless of differences in data, methods, culture, or ages of subjects (Chapple & Johnson, 2007).

ADHD/CD

Males are significantly more likely to be diagnosed with ADHD than females. The male–female ratio is largest for the combined type (7.3:1), the type most associated with antisocial behavior, followed by the hyperactive-impulsive type (4:1), and lowest for the inattentive type (2.7:1). As opposed to the typical male ADHD+CD comorbidity, females with ADHD tend to be comorbid for internalizing disorders such as depression and anxiety rather than CD (Sasi, 2010).

Sex differences in the serotonergic system help us to understand gender differences in ADHD behaviors that involve disinhibition. Neuroimaging studies report significant sex differences in serotonin receptor and transporter binding sites in the brain (for example, Jovanovic et al., 2008), and estrogen is known to increase certain serotonin receptor and transporter sites (Verona & Vitale, 2006). We have frequently noted the strong relationship between low serotonin and impulsive behavior, but a good deal of research has shown that males and females react differently to serotonin reduction. One study, using a biochemical manipulator process that rapidly decreases brain serotonin levels called "acute tryptophan depletion," found that men became more impulsive and women became more cautious with lowered serotonin (Walderhaug et al., 2007). These opposite outcomes tell us a lot about gender differences in criminal propensity.

Alcoholism

Males (10.5%) are about twice as likely as females (5.1%) to meet the criteria for alcohol dependence or abuse in the general population (Morse & Flavin, 1992). As we noted in Chapter 6, criminally related Type II alcoholism is almost exclusively a male type. Different patterns of comorbidity with alcoholism are also frequently found between males and females. As Prescott (2002:269) explains: "Male and female alcoholics differ in their patterns of comorbidity, with women having higher rates of comorbid anxiety and affective disorders and males having higher rates of comorbid use of other drugs, conduct disorder, and antisocial personality disorder." These different patterns of alcohol comorbidity have obvious different risk levels for criminal behavior attached to them.

Psychopathy

Cale and Lilienfeld (2002) describe self-report studies of psychopathic traits based on the Psychopathic Personality Inventory (PPI), which contains subscales measuring Machiavellian egocentricity, coldheartedness, fearlessness, impulsiveness, and stress immunity. A Cohen's *d* of 0.97 was found for sex differences in PPI scores averaged across all subscales, with males scoring significantly higher on all subscales. As is the case with ADHD and alcoholism, female psychopaths display different comorbidity and symptom patterns than males. Among female criminals, psychopathy scores tend to be correlated with crimes typically associated with women, such as property crimes and prostitution, and not with crimes of violence, as they are with males (Warren et al., 2005). Similarly, Verona and Vitale's (2006) review of the literature found that disorders most commonly diagnosed in females, such as borderline personality disorder and histrionic personality disorder, tend to represent female expressions of psychopathy, as opposed to such things as sadism and violent aggression that often represent male psychopathy. In terms of externalized behaviors of female psychopaths, Verona and Vitale list prostitution, abuse and neglect of offspring, intimate partner violence, and "relational forms of aggression such as friendship betrayal and 'backbiting'" (2006:431). Thus, even when clinically diagnosed with the label that represents the quintessential criminal, female psychopaths exhibit less serious forms of criminal behavior than their male counterparts.

Conclusion

Cross-cultural, evolutionary, hormonal, genetic, and neurological data all converge on the conclusion that we should strongly *expect* to see the low rate of criminal offending among females in comparison to males. There is no mystery about it; the gender ratio problem is only a problem for those who refuse to look beyond traditional sociological factors for explanation of human behavior. A profound mystery would exist if we actually found a culture in which we *did not* find large sex differences in antisocial behavior. If there were no deep biological differences between the sexes, and if socialization practices alone accounted for gendered behavior, we would see some cultures in which female rates were close to or even surpassed male rates. No such culture has ever existed, thus it is a fool's errand to continue to explore gender differences in criminal behavior in terms of such things as socialization and sex roles

If forced to boil down the proximate foundational reasons for the universal sex difference in criminal behavior to their bare minimum, it would have to be differences in empathy and fear. Empathy and fear are the natural enemies of crime. Empathy is other-oriented and prevents one from committing acts injurious to others because one has an emotional and cognitive investment in the well-being of others. Fear is self-oriented and prevents one from committing acts injurious to others out of fear of the consequences to oneself. Many other prosocial tendencies flow from these two basic foundations, such as a strong conscience, altruism, self-control, and agreeableness. These sex-differentiated levels of empathy and fear have evolved in response to sex-differentiated reproductive roles of males and females. Empathy assured the rapid identification and provision of infant needs, and nourished social relationships. Fear kept both mother and child out of harm's way and provided a sturdy scaffold around which to build a conscience.

Chapter 11
The Psychopath:
The Quintessential Criminal

What is a Psychopath?

The psychopath is the consummate instance of the criminal who "mirrors the elemental nature and embodies the pejorative essence of antisocial behavior" (DeLisi, 2009:257). The psychopath is defined by a laundry list of affective and behavioral characteristics, such as narcissism, deception, irresponsibility, impulsiveness, sensation-seeking, and shallow affect (Muller, 2010). Although the term "psychopath" is relatively new, those whom the term denotes have preyed on us since the dawn of time. Those who commented on the trademark behavior of such people in classical, biblical, and medieval works recognized the same characteristics in them as we do today (Hare, 1996). In the *Nicomachean Ethics*, Aristotle (384–322 BC) wrote of individuals with a "brutish nature," which arises from three sources: "by reason of injuries to the system, by reason of acquired habits, and by reason of originally bad nature" (McKeon, 1947:453). Even preliterate cultures, such as the Eskimos (Inuit), recognize a class of psychopathic individuals they call *kunlangeta*, who repeatedly lie, steal, freeload, and who, when the other men are out hunting, "take advantage of many women" (Murphy, 1976:1026).

Philippe Pinel provided the first clinical term for extreme antisocial individuals in 1806, calling the syndrome *manie sans delire* ("insanity without delirium"), implying that while psychopaths were "insane," they could function normally, if not morally, in society. The first person to use the term "psychopath" was the German psychiatrist Emil Kraepelin in the early twentieth century (Millon, Simonsen & Birket-Smith, 2002). Several other clinical terms have been used to refer to people who exhibit serious antisocial behavior but do not show signs of mental illness, including "moral insanity," "moral imbecility," "sociopathy" and "antisocial personality disorder." It was probably the psychopath who Cesare Lombroso had in mind with his "morally insane" category of born criminals—those "who appear normal in physique and intelligence but cannot distinguish good from evil" (in Gibson, 2002:25).

Depending on whom you ask, psychopathy, sociopathy, and antisocial personality disorder (APD) are synonymous terms describing the same constellation of traits, or they are separate concepts with fuzzy boundaries. The weight of the current evidence appears to favor the distinction between psychopathy and sociopathy, each with their own causal mechanisms (Walsh & Wu, 2008). Many leading researchers in this area believe that the psychopath is almost purely a product of biology with no significant environmental input, and that the sociopath is the product of adverse environmental conditions interacting with genetic traits (Hare et al., 2000; Pitchford, 2001). Psychopaths constitute a small group of individuals whose numbers appear to remain stable across cultures and periods, and can come from any social class, family type, or racial group. It is estimated that 1–3% of the male population are psychopaths (Pitchford, 2001). The number of sociopaths, on the other hand, fluctuates with environmental conditions, and they tend to come from the lower social classes and from dysfunctional families (Lykken, 1995).

Antisocial personality disorder is a clinical diagnostic term applicable to both psychopaths and sociopaths that psychiatrists apply to persons who consistently display a range of antisocial attitudes and behaviors after reaching the age of 15, such as deceitfulness, impulsivity, aggressiveness, irritability, irresponsibility, and lack of remorse. Candidates for the APD label must also be at least 18 years old, must have been diagnosed with conduct disorder prior to their fifteenth birthday, and their antisocial behavior must not occur solely during schizophrenic or manic episodes (American Psychiatric Association, 1994).

Although behavior-based criteria may be useful for guiding decision-making for legal and correctional personnel, criminologists want to define individuals according to criteria that are independent of their behavior, and then to determine in what ways those so defined differ from individuals not so defined. The "gold standard" for accomplishing this for the psychopathy concept is the Psychopathy Checklist-Revised (PCL-R) developed by Robert Hare, a pioneer in scientific psychopathy research. The PCL-R has been validated in forensic populations around the world by a wide variety of independent research teams (Williams & Paulhus, 2004). For PLC-R diagnosis, the diagnostician must be a doctoral-level clinician with special training with the instrument. Using case histories and semi-structured interviews that may last up to two hours, clinicians rate subjects on each of the 20 traits or behaviors listed below on a three-point scale ranging from 0 to 2. Individuals receiving a score of 30 or higher out of a possible 40 are considered psychopaths (Hare, 1996).[1] To put this number in perspective, offenders in general have a mean PCL-R score of 22, and non-offenders a score of 5 (Hare, 1996). Only about 15–25% of offenders diagnosed with APD fit PCL-R criteria for psychopathy (Hare, 2000).

Factor analyses of the PCL-R reveal that psychopathy is comprised of two major factors (three- and four-factor models have also been proposed for finer

---

1   This number is somewhat arbitrary. Clinicians and researchers in other countries use different PCL-R cut-off scores, such as 25 in the UK and 28 in German-speaking countries (Weber et al., 2008). We also see many American studies using lower cut-points to define psychopaths, probably due to the paucity of individuals who score 30 or higher. Self-report measures of psychopathy are also available, but they cannot be seen as having the same reliability and validity as the expertly administered PCL-R.

discrimination). Factor 1 describes a constellation of personality traits that indicate insensitivity to the feelings of others, and Factor 2 reflects an impulsive and deviant lifestyle (see factor list in Table 11.1). While these two factors can exist independently, they are consistently found to be correlated at around 0.50 (Patrick, 2006). The biological anomalies associated with psychopathy typically correlate highly with scores on Factor 1 (personality traits), but not necessarily with Factor 2 (unstable and antisocial lifestyle), and low IQ correlates with high scores on Factor 2, but not on Factor 1 (Harris, Skilling & Rice, 2001; Patrick, 2006). Individuals who score high on Factor 1 are less likely than those who score high on Factor 2 to improve with age (Meadows & Kuehnel, 2005).

Table 11.1　Personality and behavioral traits measured by Hare's PCL-R

Factor 1	Factor 2
Glibness/superficial charm Grandiose sense of self-worth Pathological lying Cunning/manipulative Lack of remorse or guilt Emotionally shallow Callous/lack of empathy Failure to accept responsibility for actions	Need for stimulation/proneness to boredom Parasitic lifestyle Poor behavioral control Promiscuous sexual behavior Lack of realistic, long-term goals Impulsiveness Irresponsibility Juvenile delinquency Early behavioral problems Revocation of conditional release

What Causes Psychopathy: Evolutionary Explanations

The stability of the prevalence of psychopaths over time and place has led to the virtual dismissal of environmental causes of psychopathy by those most engaged in this line of research (Blair, 2008; Kinner, 2003). As Hare (1993:170) remarks: "I can find no convincing evidence that psychopathy is the direct result of early social or environmental factors." If psychopaths are "born" that way, we have to appeal to evolutionary explanations of why these individuals exist. Psychopathy researchers working within a Darwinian framework do not view psychopaths as Lombrosian pathological atavists, but as individuals behaving exactly as they were designed to—to seek their goals unburdened by the normative constraints of society (Harris, Skilling & Rice, 2001; Quinsey, 2002). Unlike the distress and impairments of schizophrenia, psychopaths are famously undisturbed by their condition. If psychopaths suffer at all, their suffering is not intrinsic to their condition, but rather imposed by society in response to their behavior. However, even if psychopathy is not pathological from a Darwinian perspective, society must consider their behavior *morally* pathological, and punish it accordingly.

Linda Mealey's (1995) two-path evolutionary model of primary and secondary sociopaths posits that they are products of two different causal mechanisms. Mealey renamed her primary sociopaths "psychopaths" and her secondary sociopaths as "sociopaths" after reflecting on comments on her model made by 42 other scientists. This renaming has resulted in greater terminological consistency and is warranted by the empirical evidence—psychopaths are individuals scoring high on Factor 1, but not necessarily high on Factor 2, and sociopaths are those scoring high on Factor 2, but not necessarily high on Factor 1.

Both psychopaths and sociopaths engage in high levels of cheating behavior (a general term used by animal biologists to describe an organism's exploitation of conspecifics for its own advantage). According to Mealey, traits conducive to cheating are normally distributed in populations of any social species, but there is a small but stable percentage of individuals at one extreme of the distribution for whom cheating is an *obligate* (genetically mandated) strategy. This obligate strategy is said to result from "frequency-dependent, genetically-based individual differences in the use of a single (antisocial) strategy" (Mealey, 1995:526). According to this model, individuals whose cheating is supposedly obligatory would be psychopaths, and contingent cheaters would be sociopaths.

A frequency-dependent strategy refers to a balancing evolutionary selection mechanism in which the fitness payoff accompanying a particular behavioral strategy depends on the number of organisms in a population practicing that strategy. Frequency-dependent strategies genetically maintain more than one type of individual in species: a predominant type whose average fitness is superior in the long term, and an alternative type whose average fitness is superior when there are relatively few organisms of that type. The alternative strategy is a mating strategy involving cheating behavior to gain short-term mating opportunities and mate-poaching (Buss, 2009). Cheater males avoid the time and energy used in normal courting processes, therefore they enjoy a disproportionate degree of reproductive success, thus passing on the genes underlying the deceptive strategy. Frequency-dependent strategies eventually result in organisms that are taxonomically discrete.

After a few generations, the process reverses itself because a cheating strategy enhances the fitness of those who practice it only up to a point—cheating is a useful strategy for getting what you want when only a few members of the population practice it. As cheater phenotypes increase in a population, the fitness advantage of the strategy decreases. The fluctuating levels of reproductive success attending a frequency-dependent strategy combined with the evolution of counter-pressures against cheating in the population assure that obligate cheaters are rare (2–10%) in any species (Moore & Rose, 1995). When there are too many cheats, there is no advantage, as cheaters come more and more in contact with each other, usually resulting in a net loss to both. Once the cheater genotype is in a population, it becomes an evolutionarily stable strategy not likely to be eliminated. It is stable because as non-cheats become more numerous compared to cheats, the remaining cheats have rich pickings again and the evolutionary game repeats itself.

This line of thought posits that psychopaths are the human equivalent of cheater males found in other animal species. Researchers who claim that psychopathy constitutes a discrete taxonomic subclass base their arguments on statistical analyses of psychopathy scores that tend to be strongly bimodal (Skilling, Quinsey & Craig, 2001). However, strong taxonomical arguments are difficult to support. Taxonomists in biology argue about what belongs in a taxon and what the criteria for inclusion should be (witness the brouhaha over human racial classification, for instance). The argument boils down for us in terms of just how "distinct" a group of organisms must be to describe a taxon. The male–female taxa in a species are not controversial because they are clearly qualitative rather than quantitative in nature, unlike many other classifications. Most researchers favor a dimensional over a categorical approach to psychopathy (Muller, 2010). That is, even though diagnostic thresholds that place individuals into non-overlapping discrete categories are useful for clinical or research purposes, psychopathy is best viewed as a continuous trait rather than something one either is or is not (Hare & Neumann, 2008). This is much like the stance toward schizophrenia as a spectrum disorder held by most clinicians and researchers in that area, as discussed in Chapter 8.

Behavior genetic research has shown that the various components of psychopathy have strong genetic underpinnings, suggesting that psychopaths are situated at the extremes of a number of trait and behavioral continua (Viding et al., 2005), and that makes them distinct in some ways. Cohort studies tend to support the claim that psychopaths constitute a fairly stable proportion of any population, in that they consistently report roughly similar percentages of chronic offenders. The 1945 Philadelphia birth cohort studies of boys born in 1945 (Wolfgang, Figlio & Selin, 1972) and 1958 (Tracy, Wolfgang & Figlio, 1987) showed that a very few boys (6% in the first cohort and 7.5% in the second) committed the vast majority of the crimes in the cohort: 6% (18% of the subset of delinquents) in the 1945 cohort committed 71% of the homicides, 73% of the rapes, 82% of the robberies, and 69% of the aggravated assaults. The corresponding percentages in the 1958 cohort were 61, 75, 73, and 65. Similar cohort studies in other US cities and in other Western countries have found almost identical figures (Moffitt & Walsh, 2003). The fact that most of the chronic offenders were poor minority youths in these cohort studies suggests sociopathy rather than psychopathy, although of course that does not preclude the presence of psychopaths in these cohorts.

Psychopathy and the Social Emotions

If psychopathy is an alternate reproductive strategy forged by natural selection, or even if psychopaths are individuals with extreme genetic and neurobiological signatures for antisocial behavior, there must be a number of identifiable biological markers that distinguish them from non-psychopaths. The greatly reduced ability to experience the social emotions of shame, embarrassment, guilt, empathy, and love has marked psychopaths across time and cultures, and these inabilities have biological underpinnings (Patrick, 2006).

The social emotions are distinguished from the primary emotions such as anger and fear. The social emotions have evolved as integral parts of our social lives that serve to provide clues about the kinds of relationships that we are likely to have with others (cooperative versus uncooperative), and serve as "commitment devices" and "guarantors of threats and promises" (Mealey, 1995:525). Barkow (1989:121) describes them as involuntary "limbic system overrides" that serve to adjust our behavior in social situations. Social emotions focus and modify brain activity in ways that lead us to choose certain responses over others. They move us to behave in ways that enhanced our distant ancestors' reproductive success by overriding decisions suggesting alternatives to cooperation (cheating) that may have been more rational in the short term, but fitness-reducing in the long term (Walsh, 2006). The feelings of guilt, shame, and embarrassment arising in the limbic system that undergird our consciences prevent us from doing things that might be to our immediate advantage (steal, lie, cheat), but would cost us in reputation and future positive relationships if discovered. Thus, the positive and negative feelings we experience when we survey the possible consequences of our actions keep most of us on the straight and narrow most of the time. The weaker we feel them, the more likely we are to exploit others; the stronger we feel them, the less likely we are to exploit others.

The social emotions are vital evolved mechanisms that regulate self-interest and promote group interests. They also serve the function of detecting cheats, thus helping us to avoid being exploited by them. But as our ancestors got better at detecting and punishing cheats, cheats evolved mechanisms to become better cheaters. This process is an "arms race" similar to the co-evolution of predator and prey, in which the adaptations of one species are molded by the adaptations of the other. As cooperators underwent evolutionary emotional tuning for detecting cheats, cheats evolved mechanisms that served to hide their true intentions (Buss, 2009). One obvious candidate for such an adaptation is the dampening of the neurohormonal mechanisms that regulate the social emotions, such as some decoupling of the cortical-subcortical pathways. One of the most consistent physiological findings about psychopaths is their inability to "tie" the brain's cognitive and emotional networks together (Patrick, 2006; Scarpa & Raine, 2003). Richard Wiebe (2004:33) explains how this reduced ability would be useful for psychopaths in following their antisocial strategy:

> Unlike non-psychopaths, psychopaths tend not to react autonomically to either faces or words that convey emotions. Further, they do not recognize fear and disgust as readily, although they can identify other basic emotions. These features allow the psychopath to cold-bloodedly pursue selfish interests, without being distracted by emotional signals, especially the fear and disgust of another person.

Wiebe reminds us that the defining traits of chronic offenders evolved for successful mating effort, not for the purposes of carjacking, stock market fraud, arson, drug dealing, robbery, or any other act we call criminal. Because of this, cads and crooks are woven from the same evolutionary cloth, and the traits useful to such individuals must involve the social emotions. Chronic cheats operate "below the emotional poverty line" (Hare, 1993:134), and thus do not reveal physical clues, such as blushing, looking away, or other signs of nervousness that would allow others to judge their intentions. Lacking an emotional basis for self-regulation, chronic cheats make social decisions exclusively on the basis of rational calculations of immediate costs or benefits (Walsh, 2006; Weibe, 2004). David Rowe (2002:62–3) provides us with an excellent thumbnail sketch of the traits useful in supporting the "cad" mating strategy—traits that can clearly be co-opted to support criminal behavior:

> A strong sexual drive and attraction to novelty of new sexual partners is clearly one component of mating effort. An ability to appear charming and superficially interested in women while courting them would be useful. The emotional attachment, however, must be an insincere one, to prevent emotional bonding to a girlfriend or spouse. The cad may be aggressive, to coerce sex from partly willing partners and to deter rival men. He feels little remorse about lying or cheating. Impulsivity could be advantageous in a cad because mating decisions must be make quickly and without prolonged deliberation; the unconscious aim is many partners, not a high-quality partner.

There is strong empirical evidence supporting the link between an excessive concentration on mating effort and criminal behavior. A review of 51 studies examining the relationship between number of sex partners and criminal behavior found 50 of them to be positive, and also that age of onset of sexual behavior was negatively related to criminal behavior (the earlier the age of onset, the greater the criminal activity) in all 31 studies (Ellis & Walsh, 2000). A cohort study of over 1,100 British twin pairs found that the most antisocial 10% of males in the cohort fathered 27% of the children (Jaffee et al., 2003), and studies of gang members find that members have more sex partners than non-gang members in the same neighborhoods, and that gang leaders have more sex partners than other gang members (Padilla, 1992; Palmer & Tilley, 1995). Recall the studies examined in Chapter 2 relating to the DAT1 polymorphism. The studies of Beaver, Wright, and Walsh (2008) and Guo, Tong, and Cai (2008) both found that individuals homozygous for the 10 repeat version of the DAT1 allele had a significantly greater number of sex partners (80–100% more, depending on age) and were significantly more antisocial than individuals who were heterozygous (10/9) or homozygous for the 9 repeat allele.

Cortical-subcortical Decoupling

As is the case with schizophrenia, there are a number of models seeking to explain psychopathy at the proximal level. Also as with schizophrenia research, these models mostly complement one another, differing only in where they place their emphasis. All agree that there is a decoupling of the cortical and subcortical structures that tie the rational and the emotional together in coherent ways, with emphasis on the amygdala and the prefrontal cortices, the most studied brain areas relating to psychopathy. We know that the amygdala is a crucial area for aversive conditioning and for making appropriate emotional responses to cues from others in our social worlds, and that the PFC is critical to guiding the amygdala in these endeavors. R.J. Blair (2008:2,562) briefly explains the roles of the amygdala and the ventromedial PFC (vmPFC) in understanding psychopathy:

> [T]he amygdala is crucial for stimulus-reinforcement learning and responding to emotional expressions, particularly fearful expressions that, as reinforcers, are important initiators of stimulus-reinforcement learning … [and is] involved in the formation of both stimulus-punishment and stimulus-reward associations. Individuals with psychopathy show impairment in stimulus-reinforcement learning … and responding to fearful and sad expressions. It is argued that this impairment drives much of the syndrome of psychopathy.
>
> VmPFC is considered critical for the representation of reinforcement Information by other structures to implement behavior. Impairments in vmPFC functioning means that psychopaths will show impaired decision making.

Psychopathy research has moved somewhat away from considering whether the problem lies in impairments of the amygdala (for example, hyporeactivity) or impairments of the PFC subareas (for example, reduced gray matter), although both are empirically well supported, to consider dysfunctions in the pathways linking these systems. For instance, a landmark study by Craig and colleagues (2009) using diffusion tensor imaging involving nine British violent criminals with PCL-R scores ranging from 25 to 34 and nine healthy controls matched for IQ found remarkably strong results. They examined the uncinate fasciculus (UF), which is the white matter tract connecting the anterior temporal lobe (where the amygdala resides) with the frontal lobes, to analyze its volume and structural integrity. The researchers found significant correlations between PCL-R Factor 2 scores and tract volume in both the left and right UF ($r = -0.88$, $p = 0.004$). Psychopaths also had a significantly reduced fractional anisotropy ($p = 0.003$) in the right, but not left UF.[2] Craig and colleagues (2009) concluded that: "Taken

---

2   Fractional anisotropy (FA) is a mathematical measure that provides information about the shape of water diffusion along white matter fibers (myelinated axons). The measure ranges from 0 (isotropy) to 1 (anisotropy). Isotropy implies random movement in all directions, much like an ink drip spreading out on blotting paper in all directions.

together, our findings suggest that abnormal connectivity in the amygdala–OFC limbic network may contribute to the neurobiological mechanisms underpinning the impulsive, antisocial behaviour and emotional detachment associated with psychopathy." These findings support at the micro-architectural level what researchers have long discovered using grosser measures such as EEG and fMRI (Weber et al., 2008).

Fear, Empathy, and Psychopathy

In Chapter 10, we noted that empathy (a social emotion) and fear (a primary emotion) are the natural enemies of crime, thus it follows that the lack (or relative lack) of empathy and fear are its natural allies. If the social emotions are foreign to psychopaths, it is not surprising that they cannot vicariously experience the emotions of others. If the fine-tuning of the social emotions is realized through fear of punishment, it is again not surprising that psychopaths have very little appreciation of them. Psychopaths are thus granted permission to prey on others by their lack of concern for the feelings of others, and by the lack of fear about the possible punitive consequences to themselves for doing so.

According to Lykken's low-fear hypothesis, psychopathy is rooted in and nourished by low fear. Lykken writes: "Like the ability to experience pain, the fear mechanism is especially useful early in life before the individual's judgment and reason are sufficiently dependable guides to behavior" (1995:144). Fear and anxiety are emotional components of the conscience, the strength of which has a lot to do with the amygdala and ANS's arousal levels (the amygdala is an important component of ANS arousal). Lykken's premise is that psychopaths are difficult to condition because they are relatively fearless, and that they are relatively fearless because they have hypoarousable ANSs.

Fearlessness makes it difficult to visualize the negative aspects of impending events, much of which relies on emotional processing. This gives rise to the tendency to take risks that most of us would rather avoid because of the negative consequences associated with them. In other words, low fear would foster a tendency to favor approach over avoidance behavior in most situations. Because approach/avoidance aspects of behavior are regulated by the BAS and the BIS of reinforcement dominance theory, the neurotransmitters associated with approach/avoidance behavior are expected to be strongly involved in psychopathy. In a

---

Anisotropy is directional and non-random, much like rainwater running one way in rain gutters. The white matter fibers are the brain's rain gutters, acting as barriers to free diffusion and guiding the diffusion in one direction—parallel to them. Thus, the greater the FA value, the better the integrity of the axonal connection between brain areas, indexed by the ability of the white matter to maintain anisotropy. Because psychopaths had significantly reduced FA in the right UF, there is less efficient coupling between the OFC and the amygdala (see Mori & Zhang, 2006).

study of 28 seriously violent Swedish offenders, Soderstrom and colleagues (2003) assessed the relationship between PCL-R scores and cerebral spinal fluid measures of homovanillic acid (HVA) and 5-hydroxyindoleactic acid (5-HIAA), metabolites of dopamine and serotonin, respectively. They found that the ratio of HVA to 5-HIAA was strongly related to PCL-R personality traits ($r = 0.50$, $p < 0.01$) and to PCL-R behavioral aspects ($r = 0.523$, $p < 0.004$). A high HVA to 5-HIAA ratio implies high dopamine turnover and/or deficient serotonergic regulation of the dopamine system: in short, a reward-dominant brain with poor behavioral controls.

The empathy dimension in psychopathy goes beyond low empathy to imply a high level of callousness. The lack of empathy by itself need not lead to the exploitation of others, because the lack of empathy is a deficiency of the "social brain" present in the autism spectrum disorders such as Asperger syndrome. People who suffer from these disorders simply cannot "read" the mind of others, but do not seek to exploit them. Callousness is not a dismissal of the distress of others—the lack of an empathetic response—but rather a hostile reaction to that distress, and even the sadistic enjoyment of it (Shirtcliff et al., 2009). To be callous is to know at a cognitive level that a person is suffering, but not at the emotional level. The psychopath knows the words to the song, but not the music. This again highlights the fact that psychopathy involves reduced connectivity between limbic and higher cortical regions.

Because low empathy is a strong marker of psychopathy, and given the well-established relationship between oxytocin (positive) and testosterone (negative) and empathy, surprisingly few studies have examined the relationship between these hormones and psychopathy. One early study (Stålenheim et al., 1998) found that high T was significantly positively related to PCL-R scores (Factor 2 only) and to Type II alcoholism among criminal undergoing forensic investigation in Sweden. There is a large literature supporting the notion that the oxytocin receptor gene OXTR relates strongly to the lack of empathy in persons with autism spectrum disorders (for example, Gurrieri & Neri, 2009). A recent Swedish community study showed some modest significant relationships between psychopathic traits (not measured by the PCL-R) such as callousness and certain OT polymorphisms (Kollberg, 2010).

Given that hormone systems are highly interconnected, hormone systems should be studied simultaneously and ratios examined in order to gain a clearer picture of their effects on psychopathy. A community study by Glenn and colleagues (2010) examined the relationship between psychopathy scores (again, not PCL-R), testosterone, and cortisol. Psychopathy scores were not related to either hormone independently, but were related to an increased ratio of testosterone to cortisol. Although community samples are rather poor proxies for the real thing, and although they necessitate self-report measures rather than expert assessment, even weakly significant findings in the hypothesized directions are useful in helping to elucidate the defining traits of psychopathy.

Culture Matters: The Sociopath

Like Robert Hare, R. James Blair asserts that: "Currently, there are no known environmental factors (including trauma and neglect) that can give rise to the pathophysiology seen in psychopathy" (2008:2,557). Even if environmental factors do not cause psychopathy, it does not mean that they are irrelevant to understanding how psychopathic *behavior* is expressed. Psychopaths exist on the Wall Streets of the world as well as its Mean Streets. They can be successful entrepreneurs, CEOs, lawyers, cult leaders, or politicians who, while they may exploit and manipulate others, might never commit any violation of the penal code (or at least, may never be caught or convicted of such a violation). Babiak, Neumann, and Hare (2010), for instance, assessed 203 corporate professionals participating in management development programs using the PCL-R in conjunction with copious other data supplied by their parent companies. It was found that 3% of participants had PCL-R scores at or above the 30 cut-point for psychopathy, compared to 0.2% in a large community sample, and 5.9% had scores indicative of potential or possible psychopathy, compared to 1.2% in the community sample.

On the basis of their biographies, a number of historical figures have also been considered psychopathic. Although this is a dangerous practice lacking formal evaluation, few would dispute that the likes of Hitler, Stalin, or Mao Zedong were psychopaths. More controversial are the heroic figures Lykken lists among his possible "good guy" psychopaths. He includes astronaut Chuck Yeager, Lyndon Johnson, Winston Churchill, and Sir Richard Burton, and states that: "the hero and the psychopath may be twigs of the same genetic branch" (1995:116–18). The nineteenth-century British explorer Sir Richard Burton has been described as an "Adventurer, linguist, scholar, swordsman, rogue, deviant, genius—he possessed wild, monstrous talents and was burdened by defects almost as grave" (Spalding, 2004:1). If Burton had been the son of a laborer instead of an army colonel, his "monstrous talents" may have been utilized for criminal purposes instead of those to which he actually put them, and he may have ended up with a rope around his neck rather than the sash of knighthood.

When an individual's behavior mirrors that of the stereotypical psychopath (chronic and callous criminal behavior) but does not score high on Factor 1 of the PCL-R, the person is typically labeled a sociopath. Unlike psychopaths, all sociopaths are criminals by definition, and have been colorfully described as: "feral creatures, undomesticated predators, stowaways on our communal voyage who have never signed the Social Contract" (Lykken, 1995:22). Mealey (1995:539) sees sociopaths as individuals who employ a "cheating strategy not as clearly tied to genotype (as is that of the psychopath)." Similarly, Lykken (1995:23) states that sociopaths: "possess impulse peculiarities or habit patterns that are traceable to deviant learning histories interacting, perhaps, with deviant genetic predilections." For these researchers, sociopaths acquire the kind of emotional calluses through inadequate socialization and hostile childhood experiences that psychopaths are supposedly born with. Sociopaths are also viewed as more of a threat to society than psychopaths because they are just as dangerous, but more numerous. Their numbers are essentially a function of poor parenting, which is increasing in many societies due to the increase in the number of children being raised in fatherless homes, due to increasing divorce rates and/or illegitimacy rates (Barber, 2007; Walsh, 2003b).

Illegitimacy drives numerous problems (drug abuse, poverty, illiteracy, homelessness, and so forth) other than crime. A great deal of cross-cultural evidence supports the contention that being raised in a fatherless home substantially increases children's risk of antisocial behavior. A Finnish cohort study found that living in a single-parent home roughly doubles a child's probability of becoming criminal, controlling for many other risk factors (Rasanen et al., 1999), and two British longitudinal studies found that boys born out of wedlock were involved in delinquent and other behavioral problems at a much higher level than children born in wedlock and matched for socioeconomic status (Maughan & Pickles, 1990; West & Farrington, 1977). A study of 264 rural counties in four states in the US found that "a 10 percent increase in female-headed households was associated with a 73- to 100-percent higher rates of arrest for all offenses except homicide [a 10% increase was associated with a 33% increase in homicide]" (Osgood & Chambers, 2003:6). At an international level, Barber (2004) found that illegitimacy ratios (the ratio of married to unmarried births) were the strongest predictors of violent crime rates in 39 nations from Argentina to Zimbabwe, independently explaining 27, 38, and 36% of the variance in murder, rape, and assaults, respectively.

According to a behavior genetic study of 1,524 sibling pairs from different family structures taken from the National Longitudinal Survey of Youth, Cleveland and colleagues (2000) found that heritable traits associated with antisocial behavior select individuals into different family structures. Cleveland and colleagues assert that, on average, unmarried mothers have a tendency to follow an impulsive and risky lifestyle, to be more promiscuous, and to have a below-average IQ. The family type that put offspring most at risk for antisocial behavior were families headed by single mothers with children fathered by different men—a family structure suggesting high mating effort. Two-parent families with full siblings, which suggests high parenting effort, was the family type that placed offspring at lowest risk for antisocial behavior. Cleveland and colleagues found that genetics accounted for 94% of the variance on an antisocial subscale between the most at-risk group (single parent, half-siblings) and the least at-risk group (two parents, full siblings). Similar findings and conclusions from a large-scale British behavior genetic study have been reported (Moffitt & the E-Risk Study Team, 2002).

David Rowe does not want to lay the entire burden on mothers, and instead emphasizes the traits of the "feckless boyfriends" who abandon their pregnant girlfriends. These traits, including "strong hypermasculinity, early sexuality, absence of pair bonding capacity, and ... other hallmarks of 'psychopaths' ... are all passed on genetically to offspring" (1997:257). Thus, according to Rowe, the important factor in understanding the relationship between out-of-wedlock birth and criminal behavior is not anything intrinsic to single parenting (some single parents make excellent caregivers), but rather the genetically transmitted traits of fathers. Studies of fathers of illegitimate children have found that they are more than twice as likely to be involved in delinquent and criminal behavior as non-fathers in the same neighborhoods (Thornberry et al., 2000; Stouthamer-Loeber & Wei, 1998).

It takes two to tango, and most of us tend to tango with mates who are like us, and when both mother and father are antisocial, a father in residence is worse than an absentee father. Assortative mating is non-random mating based on couple resemblance, and assortative mating for antisocial behavior is troubling in terms of increasing the probability of inter-generational transmission of criminal traits. A British sample found a correlation of 0.50 between husbands' and wives' criminal convictions (Rowe & Farrington, 1997); a New Zealand study found an average correlation of 0.54 between mates for a variety of antisocial attitudes and traits (Krueger et al., 1998), and an American study found positive correlations between partners/mates for general and serious offending, delinquent peers and beliefs, and problem drinking (Knight, 2008). Offspring with two antisocial parents receive both paternal and maternal alleles for traits that increase the probability of criminality as well as a home environment modeling such behavior. Children caught in this situation suffer the double whammy of gene–environment correlation (Jaffee et al., 2003).

Can Environmental Experiences Lead to Psychopathy-like Neurological Signatures?

With all due respect to the superior expertise and reputations of scientists such as Robert Hare and R. James Blair, at least some of the neurological signatures that identify psychopaths can be environmentally written. In Chapter 3 we explored the wealth of findings on the neurobiological consequences of maltreatment during childhood. It was shown that teratogenic substances interfere with brain development prenatally, as does the lack of affectionate bonding postnatally. We also saw that chronic stress can result in allostatic changes in the hypothalamic–pituitary–adrenal axis such as hypocortisolism, which in turn interferes with fear conditioning. It is also incontrovertible that severe abuse and neglect can lead to the blunting of the social emotions via the blunting of ANS and HPA axis reaction (Daversa, 2010). Abuse and neglect, combined with prenatal insults to normal brain development, both of which are more common in lower-SES environments, lead to early predisposition to antisocial behavior which, with the right genetic profile, may reach psychopathic/sociopathic proportions.

The Romanian orphanage children studies mentioned in Chapter 3 showed that early deprivation of affection/bonding lead to aberrant OT functioning difficulties and in forming such bonds later in life. Chugani and colleagues (2001) conducted a PET scan study with ten of these children after they had resided in their foster home for an average of 5 years and 7 months. Compared with control subjects, these children showed significantly decreased metabolism in precisely the areas most related to psychopathy—the PFC and the amygdala. Another study of Romanian orphanage children with matched controls using DTI conducted by Eluvathingal and colleagues (2006) examined the uncinate fasciculus (among other brain areas). Fractional anisotropy values were significantly smaller (p = 0.003) in the left uncinate, but not the right uncinate, in the post-institutionalized orphans compared with controls. Thus, this study, along with many others that have looked at the neurobiological consequences of abuse and neglect, shows that children who suffer early socioemotional deprivation *can* indeed develop a number of the neurobiological abnormalities seen in psychopathy. When individuals who are seriously criminally involved manifest these abnormalities, does it really matter whether we call their condition psychopathy, acquired psychopathy, or sociopathy?

Conclusion

This chapter has surveyed evidence for the neurobiological underpinnings of psychopathy. We have shown the emerging consensus that psychopathy, sociopathy, and APD are three different but overlapping constructs. There also appears to be an emerging consensus that psychopathy is a stable phenotype that evidences a fairly constant prevalence across time, culture, and socioeconomic status. This constancy has led psychopathy researchers to posit that the construct is an evolutionarily stable trait forged by frequency-dependent selection. The principal mechanism apparently forged by this process is the muting of the social emotions made possible by the damping of the reactivity of the ANS and the HPA axis, endowing psychopaths with reduced fear and empathy, which is very useful when pursuing a cheater mating strategy. Once in place, the traits associated with a cheater strategy also prove useful for cheating behavior in all social domains.

The neurophysiological features that differentiate psychopaths from non-psychopaths appear to be congenital, but they may be acquired by experience. These experiences are those that we explored in some detail in Chapter 3, and include anything that interferes with experience-expected and/or experience-dependent neurological development. Whether we call individuals who acquire neurological signatures of psychopaths "sociopaths" or "acquired psychopaths" is of no real consequence, but the fact that they continue to be made certainly is.

If sociopaths are made by environmental conditions that can often lead to allostatic changes in physiology, it would be a good idea to see what we as a society can do to prevent making them. Given the many and severe deficits faced by most children born out of wedlock, the gist of such a preventative policy should probably be focused on preventing illegitimacy. The criminologists Gottfredson and Hirschi (1997:33) have concluded that reducing illegitimacy is *the* policy recommendation deducible from their self-control theory: "Delaying pregnancy among unmarried girls would probably do more to affect the long-term crime rates than all the criminal justice programs combined." This is not a statement of moral condemnation, but one that recognizes that the circumstances in which most children born out of wedlock find themselves constitute fertile soil for growing future sociopaths. It is fertile ground because the human brain captures all the toxicity of such circumstances, and will inevitably spew it back on society at some time in the future.

Bibliography

Adams, B. & B. Moghaddam (2000). Tactile stimulation activates dopamine release in the lateral septum. *Brain Research*, 858:177–80.

Agnew, R. (1992). Foundations for a general strain theory of crime and delinquency. *Criminology*, 30:47–87.

—— (2005). *Why do criminals offend? A general theory of crime and delinquency.* Los Angeles, CA: Roxbury.

Ahmed, S., M. Graupner & B. Gutkin (2009). Computational; approaches to the neurobiology of drug addiction. *Pharmacopychiatry*, 42:S144–S152.

Akers, R. (1998). *Social learning and social structure: A general theory of crime and deviance.* Boston, MA: Northeastern University Press.

Alcock, J. (2005). *Animal behavior: An evolutionary approach.* Sunderland, MA: Sinauer Associates.

Allman, J., A. Hakeem, J. Erwin, E. Nimchinsky & P. Hop (2001). The anterior cingulate cortex, the evolution of an interface between emotion and cognition. *Annals of New York Academy of Sciences.* 935:107–17.

Almeida, R., P. Ferrari, S. Parmigiani & K. Miczek (2005). Escalated aggressive behavior: Dopamine, serotonin and GABA. *European Journal of Pharmacology*, 526:51–64.

Altukhov, Y. & E. Salmenkova (2002). DNA polymorphisms in population genetics. *Russian Journal of Genetics*, 38:1,173–95.

American Psychiatric Association (1994). *Diagnostic and statistical manual of mental disorder* (4th ed.). Washington, DC: American Psychiatric Association.

Amodio, D., P. Devine & E. Harmon-Jones (2007). A dynamic model of guilt: Implications for motivation and self-regulation in the context of prejudice. *Psychological Science*, 18:524–30.

Anderson, E. (1994). The code of the streets. *The Atlantic Monthly*, 5:81–94.

—— (1999). *Code of the street: Decency, violence, and the moral life of the inner city.* New York: W.W. Norton.

Andreoni, J. & L. Vesterlund (2001). Which is the fair sex? Gender differences in altruism. *The Quarterly Journal of Economics*, 115:293–312.

Applebaum, K. (2009). Attention-deficit hyperactivity disorder in prison: A treatment protocol. *The Journal of the American Academy of Psychiatry and Law*, 37:45–9.

Arcos-Burgos, M. & M. Acosta (2007). Tuning major gene variants condition human behavior: The anachronism of ADHD. *Current Opinion in Genetics and Development*, 17: 234–8.

Arnold, A. (2004). Sex chromosomes and brain gender. *Nature Reviews: Neuroscience*, 5:1–8.

——, J. Xu, W. Grisham, X. Chen & Y. Kim (2009). Minireview: Sex chromosomes and brain differentiation. *Endocrinology*, 145:1,057–62.

Arnsten, A. (2009). The emerging neurobiology of attention deficit hyperactivity disorder: The key role of the prefrontal cortex. *The Journal of Pediatrics*, 154:S22–S28.

Ash, J. & G. Gallup (2007). Paleoclimatic variation and brain expansion during human evolution. *Human Nature*, 18:109–24.

Babiak, P., C. Neumann & R. Hare (2010). Corporate psychopathy: Talking the walk. *Behavioral Sciences and the Law*, 28:174–93.

Badawy, A. (2003). Alcohol and violence and the possible role of serotonin. *Criminal Behaviour and Mental Health*, 13:31–44.

Badcock, C. (2000). *Evolutionary psychology: A critical introduction*. Cambridge: Polity Press.

Bailey, D. & D. Geary (2009). Hominid brain evolution: Testing climactic, ecological, and social competition models. *Human Nature*, 20:67–79.

Barak, G. (1998). *Integrating criminologies*. Boston, MA: Allyn and Bacon.

Barber, N. (2004). Single parenthood as a predictor of cross-national variation in violent crime. *Cross-Cultural Research*, 38:343–58.

—— (2007). Evolutionary explanations for societal differences and historical change in violent crime and single parenthood. *Cross-Cultural Research*, 41:123–48.

Barkow, J. (1989). *Darwin, sex and status: Biological approaches to mind and culture*. Toronto: University of Toronto Press.

Barnett, R., L. Zimmer & J. McCormack (1989). P>V sign and personality profiles. *Journal of Correctional and Social Psychiatry*, 35:18–20.

Barton, F., M. Haynes, M. Lousie, G. Sempowski, S. Patel & L. Hale (2000). The role of the thymus in immune reconstitution in aging, bone marrow transplantation, and HIV-1 Infection, *Annual Review of Immunology*, 18:529–60.

Bauer, C., J. Lange, S. Shankaran, H. Bada, B. Lester, L. Wright, H. Krause-Steinrauf, V. Smeriglio, L. Finnegan, P. Maza & J. Verter (2005). Acute neonatal effects of cocaine exposure during pregnancy. *Archives of Pediatric and Adolescent Medicine*, 159:824–34.

Baumeister, R., L. Smart & J. Boden (1996). Relation of threatened egoism to violence and aggression: The dark side of self-esteem. *Psychological Review*, 103:5–33.

Beaver, K. (2009). Molecular genetics and crime. In A. Walsh & K. Beaver. *Biosocial Criminology: New directions in theory and research*, pp. 50–72. New York: Routledge.

——, J. Wright, M. DeLisi, A. Walsh, M. Vaughn, D. Boisvert & J. Vaske (2007). A gene X gene interaction between DRD2 and DRD4 in the etiology of conduct disorder and antisocial behavior. *Behavioral and Brain Functions*, 30:1–8.

———, J. Wright & A. Walsh (2008). A gene-based evolutionary explanation for the association between criminal involvement and number of sex partners. *Biodemography and Social Biology*, 54:47–55.

Beckman, M. (2004). Crime, culpability, and the adolescent brain. *Science,* 305:596–9.

Bellinger, D. (2008). Neurological and behavioral consequences of childhood lead exposure. *PLoS Medicine*, 5:690–92.

Benes, F. (2009). Neural circuitry models of schizophrenia: Is it dopamine, GABA, Glutamate, or something else? *Biological Psychiatry*, 65:1,003–5.

Bennett, A., K. Lesch, A. Heills, J. Long, J. Lorenz, S. Shoaf, M. Champoux, S. Suomi, M. Linnoila & J. Higley (2002). Early experience and serotonin transporter gene variation interact to influence primate CNS functioning. *Molecular Psychiatry*, 7:118–22.

Bennett, S., D. Farrington & L. Huesmann (2005). Explaining gender differences in crime and violence: The importance of social cognitive skills. *Aggression and Violent Behavior*, 10:263–88.

Bernard, T., J. Snipes & A. Gerould (2010). *Vold's theoretical criminology*. New York: Oxford University Press.

Bernhardt, P. (1997). Influences of serotonin and testosterone in aggression and dominance: Convergence with social psychology. *Current Directions in Psychological Science*, 6:44–8.

Betjemann, R., E. Johnson, H. Barnard, R. Boada, C. Filley, P. Filipek, E. Willcutt, J. DeFries & B. Pennington (2010). Genetic covariation between brain volumes and IQ, reading performance, and processing speed. *Behavior Genetics*, 40:135–45.

Bevilacqua, L. & D. Goldman (2009). Genes and addictions. *Clinical and Pharmacological Therapy*, 85:359–61.

Bierut, L., A. Agrawal, K. Bucholz, K. Doheny, C. Laurie, E. Pugh, S. Fisher, L. Fox, W. Howells, S. Bertelsen, A. Hinrichs, L. Almasy, N. Breslau, R. Culverhouse, D. Dick, H. Edenberg, T. Foroud, R. Grucza, D. Hatsukami, V. Hesselbrock, E. Johnson, J. Kramer, R. Krueger, S. Kuperman, M. Lynskey, K. Mann, R. Neuman, M. Nöthen, J. Nurnberger, B. Porjesz, M. Ridinger, N. Saccone, S. Saccone, M. Schuckit, J. Tischfield, J. Wang, M. Rietschel, A. Goate & J. Rice (2010). A genome-wide association study of alcohol dependence. *Proceedings of the National Academy of Sciences*, 107:5,082–7.

Biglan, A. & C. Cody (2003). Preventing multiple problem behaviors in adolescence. In D. Romer (ed.). *Reducing adolescent risk: Toward an integrated approach*, pp. 125–31. Thousand Oaks, CA: Sage.

Bing, L. (1991). *Do or die*. New York: HarperCollins.

Birger, M., M. Swartz, D. Cohen, Y. Alesh, C. Grishpan & M. Kotelr (2003). Aggression: the testosterone–serotonin link. *Israeli Medical Association Journal*, 5:653–8.

Bjorklund, D. & A. Pellegrini (2000). Child development and evolutionary psychology. *Child Development*, 71:1,687–708.

Blair, R.J. (2008). The amygdala and ventromedial prefrontal cortex: Functional contributions and dysfunctions in psychopathy. *Philosophical Transactions of the Royal Society: Biological Sciences*, 363:2,557–65.

Blomgren, K., M. Leist & L. Groe (2007). Pathological apoptosis in the developing brain. *Apoptosis*, 12:993–1,010.

Blonigen, D. (2010). Explaining the relationship between age and crime: Contributions from the developmental literature on personality. *Clinical Psychology Review*, 30:89–100.

Bobb, A., F. Castellanos, A. Addington & J. Rapoport (2005). Molecular genetic studies of ADHD: 1991 to 2004, *American Journal of Medical Genetics: Neuropsychiatric Genetics,* 132:109–25.

Bond, R. & P. Saunders (1999). Routes of Success: Influences on the occupational attainment of young British males. *British Journal of Sociology*, 50:217–40.

Boos, H., A. Aleman, W. Cahn, H. Hullshoff Poll & R. Kahn (2007). Brain volumes in relatives of patients with schizophrenia. *Archives of General Psychiatry*, 64:297–304.

Booth, A., D. Granger, A. Mazur & K. Kivligan (2006). Testosterone and social behavior. *Social Forces*, 85:167–91.

Bouchard, T. (1998). Genetic and environmental influences on adult intelligence and special mental abilities. *Human Biology*, 70:275–9.

—— & M. McGue (1981). Familial studies of intelligence: A review. *Science*, 212:1,055–9.

——, N. Segal, A. Tellegen, M. McGue, M. Keyes & R. Krueger (2003). Evidence for the construct validity and heritability of the Wilson-Patterson conservatism scale: A reared-apart twins study of social attitudes. *Personality and Individual Differences*, 34:959–69.

Boyle, M. (1990). *Schizophrenia: A scientific delusion*. London: Routledge.

Brammer, G., M. Raleigh & M. McGuire (1994). Neurotransmitters and social status. In L. Ellis (ed.). *Social stratification and socioeconomic inequality, volume 2: Reproductive and interpersonal aspects of dominance and status*, pp. 75–91. Westport, CT: Praeger.

Brebner, J. (2003). Gender and emotions. *Personality and individual differences*, 34:387–94.

Brennan, P., E. Grekin & M. Sarnoff (1999). Maternal smoking during pregnancy and adult male criminal outcomes. *Archives of General Psychiatry*, 56:215–19.

Brookman, F. (2005). *Understanding homicide*. Thousand Oaks, CA: Sage.

Brown, A. (2006). Prenatal infection as a risk factor for schizophrenia. *Schizophrenia Bulletin,* 32(2):200–202.

Brownlee, K., A. Moore & A. Hackney (2005). Relationship between circulating cortisol and testosterone: Influences of physical exercise. *Journal of Sports Science and Medicine*, 4:76–83.

Bubar, M.J. & K.A. Cunningham (2006). Serotonin 5-HT 2A and 5-HT 2C receptors as potential targets for modulation of psychoactive stimulant use and dependence. *Current Topics in Medicinal Chemistry*, 6(18):1,971–85.

Buckley, P. (2004). Pharmacological options for treating schizophrenia with violent behavior. *Psychiatric Times* (supplement), October:1–8.

Bukowski, W., L. Sippola & A. Newcomb (2000). Variations in patterns of attraction to same- and other-sex peers during early adolescence. *Developmental Psychology*, 36: 147–54.

Burns, K. (2009). Commentary: The top ten reasons to limit prescription of controlled substances in prison. *The Journal of the American Academy of Psychiatry and Law*, 37:50–52.

Buschkuebl, M. & S. Jaeggi (2010). Improving intelligence: A literature review. *Swiss Medical Weekly*, 140:266–72.

Buss, D. (2005). *The murderer next door: Why the mind is designed to kill*. New York: Penguin.

—— (2009). How can evolutionary psychology successfully explain personality and individual differences? *Perspectives on Psychological Science*, 4:359–66.

Butcher, L., E. Meaburn, L. Liu, C. Fernandes, L. Hill, A. Al-Chalabi, R. Plomin, L. Schalkwyk & I. Craig (2004). Genotyping pooled DNA on microarrays: A systematic genome screen of thousands of SNPs in large sample to detect QTLs for complex traits. *Behavior Genetics*, 34:549–55.

Byrnes, J., D. Miller & W. Schafer (1999). Gender differences in risk taking: A meta-analysis. *Psychological Bulletin*, 125:367–83.

Cale, E. & S. Lilienfeld (2002). Sex differences in psychopathy and antisocial personality disorder: A review and integration. *Clinical Psychology Review*, 22:1,179–207.

Campbell, A. (1999). Staying alive: Evolution, culture, and women's intrasexual aggression. *Behavioral and Brian Sciences*, 22:203–14.

—— (2006). Sex differences in direct aggression: What are the psychological mediators? *Aggression and Violent Behavior*, 6:481–497.

—— (2008). Attachment, aggression and affiliation: The role of oxytocin in female social behavior. *Biological Psychology*, 77:1–10.

—— (2009). Gender and crime: An evolutionary perspective. In A. Walsh & K. Beaver (eds.). *Criminology and Biology: New directions in theory and research*, pp. 117–36. New York: Routledge.

Cannon, T. (2009). What is the role of theories in the study of schizophrenia? *Schizophrenia Bulletin*, 35:563–7.

Cao, L., A. Adams & V. Jensen (1997). A test of the black subculture of violence thesis: A research note. *Criminology*, 35:367–9.

Capron, C. & M. Duyme (1989). Assessment of effects of socioeconomic status on IQ in a full cross fostering study. *Nature*, 340:552–4.

Carnagey, N., C. Anderson & B. Bushman (2007). The effect of video game violence on physiological desensitization to real violence. *Journal of Experimental Social Psychology*, 43:489–96.

Carrasco, X., P. Rothhammer, M. Moraga, H. Henríquez, R. Chakraborty, F. Aboitiz & F. Rothhammer (2006). Genotypic interaction between DRD4 and DAT1 loci is a high risk factor for attention-deficit/hyperactivity disorder in

Chilean families. *American Journal of Medical Genetics: Neuropsychiatric Genetics*, 141B:51–4.

Casey, B., R. Jones, L. Levita, V. Libby, S. Pattwell, E. Ruberry, F. Soliman & L. Somerville (2010). The storm and stress of adolescence: Insights from human imaging and mouse. *Developmental Psychobiology*, 52:225–35.

Caspi, A., T. Moffitt, P. Silva, M. Stouthamer-Loeber, R. Krueger & P. Schmutte (1994). Are some people crime-prone? Replications of the personality–crime relationship across countries, genders, races, and methods. *Criminology*, 32:163–94.

——, J. McClay, T.E. Moffitt, J. Mill, J. Martin, I.W. Craig, A. Taylor & R. Poulton (2002). Role of genotype in the cycle of violence in maltreated children. *Science*, 297:851–4.

——, K. Sugden, T. Moffitt, A. Taylor, I. Craig, H. Harrington, J. McClay, J. Mill, J. Martin, A. Braithwaite & R. Poulton (2003). Influence of life stress on depression: Moderation by a polymorphism in the 5-HTT gene. *Science*, 301:386–9.

——, B. Williams, J. Kim-Cohen, I. Craig, B. Milne, R. Poulton, L. Schalkwyk, A. Taylor, H. Werts & T. Moffitt (2007). Moderation of breastfeeding effects on the IQ by genetic variation in fatty acid metabolism, *Proceedings of the National Academy of Sciences*, 104:1–6.

Cauffman, E., L. Steinberg & A. Piquero (2005). Psychological, neuropsychological, and psychophysiological correlates of serious antisocial behavior in adolescence. *Criminology*, 43:133–76.

Cecil, K., C. Brubaker, C. Adler, K. Dietrich, M. Altaye, J. Egelhoff, S. Wessel, I. Elangovan, R. Hornung, K. Jarvis & B. Lanphear (2008). Decreased brain volume in adults with childhood lead exposure. *PLoS Medicine*, 5:742–50.

Chagnon, N. (1988). Life histories, blood revenge, and warfare in a tribal population, *Science*, 239:985–92.

Chakraborty, B., H. Lee, M. Wolujewicz, J. Mallik, G. Sun, K. Dietrich, A. Bhattacharya, R. Deka & R. Chakraborty (2008). Low dose effect of chronic lead exposure on neuromotor response impairment in children is moderated by genetic polymorphisms. *Journal of Human Ecology*, 23:183–94.

Chao, J. & E. Nestler (2004) Molecular neurobiology of drug addiction. *Annual Review of Medicine*. 55:113–32.

Chapple, C. & K. Johnson (2007). Gender differences in impulsivity. *Youth Violence and Juvenile Justice*, 5:221–34.

Chen, C. & S. Farruggia (2002). Culture and adolescent development. *Online Readings in Psychology and Culture*, Unit 11, Chapter 2. Bellingham, WA: Center for Cross-Cultural Research, Western Washington University.

Cheng, D., C. Hong, D. Liao & S. Tsai (2006). Association study of androgen receptor CAG repeat polymorphism and male violent criminal activity. *Psychoneuroendocrinology*, 31:548–52.

Chiang, M.-C., M. Barysheva, D. Shattuck, A. Lee, S. Madsen, C. Avedissian, A. Klunder, A. Toga, K. McMahon, G. de Zubicaray, M. Wright, A. Srivastava,

N. Balov & P. Thompson (2009). Genetics of brain fiber architecture and intellectual performance. *The Journal of Neuroscience*, 29:2,212–24.

Chiao, J. & N. Ambady (2007). Cultural neuroscience: Parsing universality and diversity across levels of analysis. In D. Cohen (ed.). *Handbook of cultural psychology*, pp. 237–54. New York: Guilford Press.

—— & K. Blizinsky (2010). Culture–gene coevolution of individualism–collectivism and the serotonin transporter gene. *Proceedings of the Royal Society of London B: Biological Sciences*, 277:529–37.

Chong, B., Sanders, J. & Jones, G (2000). Functional magnetic resonance imaging. In W. W. Orrison (Eds.), *Neuroimaging* Vol 1. (60–87). Philadelphia: Saunders.

Chou, S. (2009). Critique in the notion of model minority: An alternative racism to Asian American? *Research Express*, <http://research.ncku.edu.tw/re/articles/e/20090619/3.html>.

Choudhury, S. (2009). Culturing the adolescent brain: What can neuroscience learn from anthropology? *Social Cognitive and Affective Neuroscience*, doi: 10.1093/scan/nsp030.

Chugani, H., M. Behen, O. Muzik, C. Juhasz, F. Nagy & D. Chugani (2001). Local brain functional activity following early deprivation: A study of postinstitutionalized Romanian orphans. *Neuroimage*, 14:1,290–301.

Cirulli, F., A. Berry & E. Alleva (2003). Early disruption of the mother–infant relationship: Effects on brain plasticity and implications for psychopathology. *Neuroscience and Biobehavioral Reviews*, 27:73–82.

Clarke, J. (1998). *The lineaments of wrath: Race, violent crime, and American culture*. New Brunswick, NJ: Transaction Publishers.

Cleveland, H., R. Wiebe, E. van den Oord & D. Rowe (2000). Behavior problems among children from different family structures: The influence of genetic self-selection. *Child Development*, 71:733–51.

——, R. Wiebe & D. Rowe (2005). Sources of exposure to smoking and drinking friends among adolescents. *The Journal of Genetic Psychology*, 166:153–69.

Coccaro, E., M. McCloskey, D. Fitzgerald & K. Phan (2007). Amygdala and orbitofrontal reactivity to social threat in individuals with impulsive aggression. *Biological Psychiatry*, 15:168–78.

Collins, R. (2004). Onset and desistence in criminal careers: Neurobiology and the age–crime relationship. *Journal of Offender Rehabilitation*, 39:1–19.

—— (2009). The micro-sociology of violence. *British Journal of Sociology*, 60:566–76.

Comings, D., T. Chen, K. Blum, J. Mengucci, S. Blum & B. Meshkin (2005). Neurogenic interactions and aberrant behavioral co-morbidity of attention deficit hyperactivity disorder (ADHD): Dispelling myths. *Theoretical Biology & Medical Modeling*, 2:50–65.

Cooley-Quille, M., R. Boyd, E. Frantz & J. Walsh (2001). Emotional and behavioral impact of exposure to community violence in inner-city adolescents. *Journal of Clinical Child Psychology*, 30:199–206.

Coolidge, F., L. Thede & S. Young (2000). Heritability and the comorbidity of attention deficit hyperactivity disorder with behavioral disorders and executive function deficits: A preliminary investigation. *Developmental Neuropsychology*, 17:273–87.

Cooney, C.A. (2007). Epigenetics-DNA-based mirror of our environment? *Disease Markers*, 23(1–2):121–37.

Cooper, J., A. Walsh & L. Ellis (2010). Is criminology ripe for a paradigm shift? Evidence from a survey of American criminologists. *Journal of Criminal Justice Education*, 21:332–47.

Corr, P. (2004). Reinforcement sensitivity theory and personality. *Neuroscience and Biobehavioral Reviews*, 28:317–32.

Corwin, E. (2004). The concept of epigenetics and its role in the development of cardiovascular disease. *Biological Research for Nurses*, 6:11–16.

Costa, P., A. Terracciano & R. McCrae (2001). Gender differences in personality traits across cultures: Robust and surprising findings. *Journal of Personality and Social Psychology*, 81: 322–31.

Cota-Robles, S., M. Neiss & D. Rowe (2002). The role of puberty in violent and nonviolent delinquency among Anglo American, Mexican American, and African American boys. *Journal of Adolescent Research*, 17:364–76.

Crabbe, J. (2002). Genetic contributions to addiction. *Annual Review of Psychology*, 53:435–62.

Craig, I. & R. Plomin (2006). Quantitative trait loci for IQ and other complex traits: Single-nucleotide polymorphism genotyping using pooled DNA and microarrays. *Genes, Brain and Behavior*, 5:32–7.

Craig, M., M. Catani, Q. Deeley, R. Latham, E. Daly, R. Kanaan, M. Picchioni, P. McGuire, T. Fahy & D. Murphy (2009). Altered connections on the road to psychopathy. *Molecular Psychiatry*, 14:946–53.

Crowell, S., T. Beauchaine, L. Gatzke-Kopp, P. Sylvers, H. Mead & J. Chipman-Chacon (2006). Autonomic correlates of attention-deficit/hyperactivity disorder and oppositional defiant disorder in preschool children. *Journal of Abnormal Psychology*, 115:174–8.

Cullen, F. (2009). Foreword to A. Walsh & K. Beaver. *Biosocial Criminology: New directions in theory and research*. New York: Routledge.

Curatolo, P., C. Paloscia, E. D'Agati, R. Moavero & A. Pasini (2009). The neurology of attention deficit/hyperactivity disorder. *European Journal of Paediatric Neurology*, 13:299–304.

Daly, M. (1996). Evolutionary adaptationism: Another biological approach to criminal and antisocial behavior. In G. Bock & J. Goode (eds.). *Genetics of criminal and antisocial behaviour*, pp. 183–95. Chichester: Wiley.

—— & M. Wilson (2001). Risk-taking, intersexual competition, and homicide. *Nebraska Symposium on Motivation*, 47:1–36.

Darwin, C. (1871). *The descent of man, and selection in relation to sex*. London: J. Murray.

Daversa, M. (2010). Early environmental predictors of the affective and interpersonal constructs of psychopathy. *International Journal of Offender Therapy and Comparative Criminology*, 54:6–21.

Davidson, R., K. Putman & C. Larson (2000). Dysfunction in the neural circuitry of emotion regulation—a possible prelude to violence. *Science*, 289:591–4.

Day, J. & R. Carelli (2007). The nucleus accumbens and Pavlovian reward learning. *The Neuroscientist*, 13:148–59.

De Vries, G. & P. Sodersten (2009). Sex differences in the brain: The relation between structure and function. *Hormones and Behavior*, 55:589–96.

De Waal, F. (2008). Putting the altruism back into altruism: The evolution of empathy. *Annual Review of Psychology*, 59:279–300.

Deary, I. (2003). Reaction time and psychometric intelligence: Jensen's contributions. In H. Nyborg (ed.). *The scientific study of general intelligence: Tribute to Arthur R. Jensen*, pp. 53–75. Oxford: Elsevier.

——, L. Whalley, H. Lemmon, J. Crawford & J. Starr (2000). The stability of individual differences in mental ability from childhood to old age: Follow-up of the 1932 Scottish mental survey. *Intelligence*, 28:49–55.

——, F. Spinath & T. Bates (2006). Genetics of intelligence. *European Journal of Human Genetics*, 14:690–700.

——, W. Johnson & L. Houlihan (2009). Genetic foundations of human intelligence. *Human Genetics*, 126:215–32.

Decety, J. & P. Jackson (2006). A social-neuroscience perspective on empathy. *Current Directions in Psychological Science*, 15:54–8.

DeLisi, M. (2008). The etiology of criminal onset: The enduring salience of nature and nurture. *Journal of Criminal Justice*, 36(3):217.

—— (2009). Psychopathy is the unified theory of crime. *Youth Violence and Juvenile Justice*, 7:256–72.

——, K. Beaver, M. Vaughn & J. Wright (2009). All in the family: Gene x environment interaction between DRD2 and criminal father is associated with five antisocial phenotypes. *Criminal Justice and Behavior*, 36:1,187–97.

Department of Health and Human Services (2004). *Breastfeeding practices: Results from the National Immunization Survey*, <http://www.cdc.gov/breastfeeding/data/NIS_2004.htm>.

Depino, A. (2006). Maternal infection and offspring brain. *The Journal of Neuroscience*, 26:7,777–8.

Depue, R. & P. Collins (1999). Neurobiology of the structure of personality: Dopamine, facilitation of incentive motivation, and extraversion. *Behavioral and Brain Sciences*, 22:491–569.

Derntl, B., A. Finkelmayer, S. Eickhoff, T. Kellerman, D. Falkenberg, F. Schnieder & U. Habel (2010). Multidimensional assessment of empathetic abilities: Neural correlates and gender differences. *Psychoneuroendocrinology*, 35:67–82.

Dick, D., F. Aliev, J. Kramer, J. Wang, A. Hinricks, S. Bertlesen, S. Kuperman, M. Schuckit, J. Nurnberger, H. Edenburg, P. Porjesz, H. Begleiter, V. Hasselbrock,

A. Goate & L. Bierut (2007). Association of CHRM2 with IQ: Converging evidence for a gene influencing intelligence. *Behavior Genetics*, 37:265–72.

Dickens, W. & J. Flynn (2001). Heritability estimates versus large environmental effects: The IQ Paradox resolved. *Psychological Review*, 108: 346–9.

Ding, Y., H. Chi, D. Grady, A. Morishima, J. Kidd, K. Kidd, P. Flodman, M. Spence, S. Schuck, J. Swanson, Y. Zhang & R. Moyziz (2002). Evidence of positive selection acting at the human dopamine receptor D4 gene locus. *Proceedings of the National Academy of Science*, 99:309–14.

DiRago, A. & G. Vaillant (2007). Resilience in inner city youth: Childhood predictors of occupational status across the lifespan. *Journal of Youth Adolescence*, 36:61–70.

Ditton, P.M. (1999) *Mental health and treatment of inmates and probationers.* Bureau of Justice Statistics Special Report NCJ 174463. Washington, DC: US Department of Justice.

Dixon, P. (2005). An extension of Freud and Jung's theory of the relation of dream states to schizophrenia. *Current Psychological Research and Reviews*, 24:4–23.

Dolan, M., I. Anderson & J. Deakin (2001). Relationship between 5-HT function and impulsivity and aggression in male offenders with personality disorders. *British Journal of Psychiatry*, 178:352–9.

Dollard, J. (1988). *Caste and class in a southern town*. Madison, WI: University of Wisconsin Press.

Domes, G., M. Heinrichs, A. Michel, C. Berger & S. Herpertz (2007). Oxytocin improves "mind-reading" in humans. *Biological Psychiatry*, 61:731–3.

Drigotas, S. & J. Udry (1993). Biosocial models of adolescent problem behavior: Extensions to panel design. *Social Biology*, 40:1–7.

Driscoll, H., A. Zinkivskay, K. Evans & A. Campbell (2006). Gender differences in social representations of aggression: The phenomenological experience of differences in inhibitory control. *British Journal of Psychology*, 97:139–53.

Drug Enforcement Administration (2003). *Drugs of abuse*. Arlington, VA: US Department of Justice.

DrugWarFacts (2008). *Annual causes of death in the United States*, <http://drugwarfacts.org/cms/?q=node/30>.

Dunbar, R. & S. Shultz (2007). Evolution of the social brain. *Science*, 317:1,344–7.

Durston, S. (2003). A review of the biological bases of ADHD: What have we learned from imaging studies? *Mental Retardation and Developmental Disabilities*, 9:184–95.

Edelman, G. (1992). *Bright air, brilliant fire*. New York: Basic Books.

Egbert, S.C., W.T. Church & E.C. Byrnes (2006). Justice and treatment collaboration: A process evaluation of a drug court. *Best Practices in Mental Health*, 2(1):74–91.

Eisenberg, D., J. Mackillop, M. Modi, J. Beauchemin, D. Dang, S. Lisman, J. Lum & D. Wilson (2007). Examining impulsivity as an endophenotype using a behavioral approach: A DRD2 TaqI A and DRD4 48-bp VNTR association study. *Behavior and Brain Functions*, 3:2.

——, B. Campbell, P. Gray & M. Sorenson (2008). Dopamine receptor genetic polymorphisms and body composition in undernourished pastoralists: An exploration of nutrition indices among nomadic and recently settled Ariaal men of northern Kenya. *BMC Evolutionary Biology*, 8:6–12.

Eisener, M. (2001). Modernization, self-control, and lethal violence: The long-term dynamics of European homicide rates in theoretical perspective. *British Journal of Criminology*, 41:618–38.

Ellis, L. (2003). Genes, criminality, and the evolutionary neuroandrogenic theory. In Walsh, A. & L. Ellis (eds) *Biosocial criminology: Challenging environmentalism's supremacy*, pp. 15–34. Huntington, NY: Nova Science.

—— (2005). A theory explaining biological correlates of criminality. *European Journal of Criminology*, 2:287–315.

—— & A. Walsh (2000). *Criminology: A global perspective*. Boston, MA: Allyn and Bacon.

—— & J. McDonald (2001). Crime, delinquency, and social status: A reconsideration. *Journal of Offender Rehabilitation*, 32:23–52.

—— & A. Walsh (2003). Crime, delinquency and intelligence: A review of the worldwide literature. In H. Nyborg (ed.). *The scientific study of general intelligence: A tribute to Arthur R. Jensen*, pp. 343–65. Amsterdam: Pergamon.

——, S. Hershberger, E. Field, S. Wersinger, S. Pellis, D. Geary, C. Palmer, K. Hoyenga, A. Hetsroni & K. Karadi (2008). *Sex differences: Summarizing more than a century of scientific research*. New York: Psychology Press.

Eluvathingal, T., H. Chugani, M. Behen, C. Juhasz, O. Muzik, M. Maqbool, D. Chugani & M. Makki (2006). Abnormal brain connectivity in children after early severe socioemotional deprivation: A diffusion tensor imaging study. *Pediatrics*, 117:2,093–100.

Enoch, M. (2006). Genetic and environmental influences on the development of alcoholism: Resilience vs. risk. *Annals of the New York Academy of Sciences*, 1,094:193–201.

Ernst, M., D. Pine & M. Hardin (2006). Triadic model of the neurobiology of motivated behavior in adolescence. *Psychiatric Medicine*, 36:299–312.

Esch, T. & G. Stefano (2005). Love promotes health. *Neuroendocrinology Letters*, 3:264–7.

Eshel, N., E. Nelson, R. Blair, D. Pine & M. Ernst (2007). Neural substrates of choice selection in adults and adolescents: Development of the ventrolateral prefrontal and anterior cingulated cortices. *Neuropsychologia*, 45:1,270–79.

Evans, P., S. Gilbert, N. Mekel-Bobrov, E. Vallender, J. Anderson, L. Vaez-Azizi, S. Tishkoff, R. Hudson & B. Lahn (2005). Microcephalin, a gene regulating brain size, continues to evolve adaptively in humans. *Science*, 309:1,717–20.

Eysenck, H. & G. Gudjonsson (1989). *The causes and cures of criminality*. New York: Plenum.

Farrington, D. (1996). The explanation and prevention of youthful offending. In J. Hawkins (ed.). *Delinquency and crime: Current theories*, pp 68–148. Cambridge: Cambridge University Press.

Fatemi, S. & T. Folsom (2009). The neurodevelopmental hypothesis of schizophrenia revisited. *Schizophrenia Bulletin*, 35:528–54.

Fazel, D., G. Gulati, L. Linsell, J. Geddes & M. Grann (2009). Schizophrenia and violence: Systematic review and meta-analysis. *PLoS Medicine*, 6(8):e1000120.

FBI (2009). Crime in the United States: 2008. Washington, DC: U.S. Government Printing Office.

Feinberg, A. & R. Irizarry (2010). Stochastic epigenetic variation as a driving force of development, evolutionary adaptation, and disease. *Proceedings of the National Academy of Sciences,* 107:1,757–64.

Felson, R. & D. Haynie (2002). Pubertal development, social factors, and delinquency among adolescent boys. *Criminology*, 40:967–88.

Feng, Y. (2008). Convergence and divergence in the etiology of myelin impairment in psychiatric disorders and drug addiction. *Neurochemical Research*, 33(10):1,940–49.

Ferguson, C. (2010). Genetic contributions to antisocial personality and behavior: A meta-analytic review from an evolutionary perspective. *The Journal of Social Psychology*, 150:160–80.

Fetchenhauer, D. & B. Buunk (2005). How to explain gender differences in fear of crime: Towards an evolutionary approach. *Sexualities, Evolution and Gender*, 7:95–113.

Ficks, C. & I. Waldman (2009). Gene–environment interactions in attention-deficit/hyperactivity disorder. *Current Psychiatry Reports*, 11:387–92.

Fields, R. (2005). Myelination: An overlooked mechanism of synaptic plasticity. *The Neuroscientist*, 11:528–31.

Fincher, C., R. Thornhill, D. Murray & M. Schaller (2008). Pathology prevalence predicts human cross-cultural variability in individualism/collectivism. *Proceedings of the Royal Society of London B: Biological Sciences*, 275:1,279–85.

Fincher, J. (1982). *The human brain: Mystery of matter and mind.* Washington, DC: US News Books.

Fishbein, D. (1998). Differential susceptibility to comorbid drug abuse and violence. *Journal of Drug Issues*, 28:859–91.

—— (2003). Neuropsychological and emotional regulatory processes in antisocial behavior. In A. Walsh & L. Ellis (eds.) Biosocial criminology: Challenging environmentalism's supremacy, pp. 185–208. Hauppauge, NY: Nova Science.

—— (2001). *Biobehavioral perspectives in criminology.* Belmont, CA: Wadsworth.

Fisher, G. & T. Harrison (2005) *Substance abuse: Information for school counselors, social workers, therapists, and counselors.* Boston, MA: Pearson Education.

Fitzgerald, P., S. Fountain & J. Daskalakis (2006). A comprehensive review of the effects of rTMS on motor cortical excitability and inhibition. *Clinical Neurophysiology*, 117:2,584–96.

Flynn, J. (2007). *What is intelligence? Beyond the Flynn effect.* Cambridge: Cambridge University Press.

Fox, R. (1988). The Seville Declaration: Anthropology's auto-da-fe. *Academic Questions*, 1:35–47.

—— (1998). Testosterone is not alone: Internal secretions and external behavior. *Behavioral and Brain Sciences*, 21:375–6.

Fraga, M.F., E. Ballestar, M.F. Paz, S. Ropero, F. Setien, M.L. Ballestar, D. Heine-Suñer, J.C. Cigudosa, M. Urioste, J. Benitez, M. Boix-Chornet, A. Sanchez-Aguilera, C. Ling, E. Carlsson, P. Poulsen, A. Vaag, Z. Stephan, T.D. Spector, Y.Z. Wu, C. Plass & M. Esteller (2005). Epigenetic differences arise during the lifetime of monozygotic twins. *Proceedings of the National Academy of Sciences*, 102:10,604–9.

Frazier, E. (1939). *The Negro family in the United States*. Chicago, IL: University of Chicago Press.

Friedman, M., N. Chhabildas, N. Budhiraja, E. Willcutt & B.F. Pennington (2003). Etiology of the comorbidity between reading disability and ADHD: Exploration of the non-random mating hypothesis. *American Journal of Medical Genetics Part B: Neuropsychiatric Genetics*, 120b:109–15.

Fukuda, H., N. Sano, S. Muto & M. Horikoshi (2006). Simple histone acetylation plays a complex role in the regulation of gene expression. *Briefings in Functional Genomics and Proteomics*, 5(3):190–208.

Furmark, T., L. Appel, S. Henningsson, F. Åhs, V. Faria, C. Linnman, A. Pissiota, Ö. Frans, M. Bani, P. Bettica, E. Pich, E. Jacobsson, K. Wahlstedt, L. Oreland, B. Långström, E. Eriksson & M. Fredrikson (2008). A link between serotonin-related gene polymorphisms, amygdala activity, and placebo-induced relief from social anxiety. *The Journal of Neuroscience*, 28:13,066–74.

Galvan, A., T. Hare, C. Parra, J. Penn, H. Voss, G. Glover & B. Casey (2006). Earlier development of the accumbens relative to orbitofrontal cortex might underlie risk-taking behavior in adolescents. *The Journal of Neuroscience*, 26:6,885–92.

Garlick, D. (2002). Understanding the nature of the general factor of intelligence: The role of individual differences in neural plasticity as an explanatory mechanism. *Psychological Review*, 109:116–36.

—— (2003). Integrating brain science research with intelligence research. *Current Directions in Psychological Science*, 12:185–92.

Garrett, B. (2009). *Brain and behavior: Introduction to biological psychology*. Los Angeles, CA: Sage.

Gatzke-Kopp, L., A. Raine, R. Loeber, M. Stouthamer-Loeber & S. Steinhauer (2002). Serious delinquent behavior, sensation seeking, and electrodermal arousal. *Journal of Abnormal Child Psychology*, 30:477–86.

Gaulin, S. & D. McBurney (2001). *Psychology: An evolutionary approach*. Upper Saddle River, NJ: Prentice-Hall.

Gavin, D. & R. Sharma (2010). Histone modifications, DNA methylation, and schizophrenia. *Neuroscience and Biobehavioral Reviews*, 34:882–8.

Geary, D. (2000). Evolution and proximate expression of human paternal investment. *Psychological Bulletin*, 126:55–77.

—— (2005). *The origin of mind: Evolution of brain, cognition, and general intelligence*. Washington, DC: American Psychological Association.

—— & M. Flinn (2002). Sex differences in behavioral and hormonal response to social threat: Commentary on Taylor et al. (2000). *Psychological Review*, 109:745–50.

Gewertz, D. & F. Errington (1991). *Twisted histories, altered contexts: Representing the Chambuli in a world system*. Cambridge: Cambridge University Press.

Giancola, P., R. Josephs, D. Parrott & A. Duke (2010). Alcohol myopia revisited: Clarifying aggression and other acts of disinhibition through a distorted lens. *Perspectives on Psychological Science*, 5:265–78.

Gibson, M. (2002). *Born to crime: Cesare Lombroso and the origins of biological criminology*. Westport, CT: Praeger.

Giedd, J. (2004). Structural magnetic resonance imaging of the adolescent brain. *Annals of the New York Academy of Science*, 1,021:77–85.

Gilbert, D., K. Ridel, F. Sallee, J. Zhang, T. Lipps & E. Wassermann (2006). Comparison of the inhibitory and excitatory effects of ADHD medications methylphenidate and atomoxetine on motor cortex. *Neuropsychopharmacology*, 31: 442–9.

Giorgi, P. (2001). *The origins of violence by cultural evolution*. Brisbane: Minerva E. & S.

Gizer, I., C. Ficks & I. Waldman (2009). Candidate gene studies of ADHD: A meta-analytic review. *Human Genetics*, 126:51–90.

Glahn, D., P. Thompson & J. Blangero (2002). Neuroimaging endophenotypes: Strategies for finding genes influencing brain structure and function. *Human Brain Mapping*, 28:488–501.

Glaser, D. (2000). Child abuse and neglect and the brain: A review. *Journal of Child Psychology and Psychiatry*, 41:97–116.

Glenn, A., A. Raine, R. Schug, Y. Gao & D. Granger (2010). Increased testosterone-to-cortisol ratio in psychopathy. *Journal of Abnormal Psychology*, 120:389–99.

Goffman, E. (1961). *Asylums*. Garden City, NY: Anchor.

Goldberg, E. (2001). *The executive brain: Frontal lobes and the civilized mind*. New York: Oxford University Press.

Goldberg, S. (1986). Utopian yearning versus scientific curiosity. *Society*, 23:29–39.

Gluckman, P. & M. Hanson (2006). Changing times: The evolution of puberty. *Molecular and Cellular Endocrinology*, 255:26–31.

Goeders, N. (2002). Stress and cocaine addiction. *Perspectives in Pharmacology*, 301:885–9.

Goldberg, E. (2001). *The executive brain: Frontal lobes and the civilized mind*. New York: Oxford University Press.

Goldsmith, H. & R. Davidson (2004). Disambiguating the components of emotion regulation. *Child Development*, 75:361–5.

Goldstein, D. & I. Kopin (2007). Evolution of the concept of stress. *Stress*, 10:109–20.

Goodlett, C., K. Horn & F. Zhou (2005). Alcohol teratogenesis: Mechanisms of damage and strategies for intervention. *Developmental Biology and Medicine*, 230:394–406.

Gordon, J. & P. Moore (2005). ADHD among incarcerated youth: An investigation of the congruency with ADHD prevalence and correlates among the general population. *American Journal of Criminal Justice*, 30:87–97.

Gornick, M., A. Addington, P. Shaw, A. Bobb, W. Sharp, D. Greenstein, S. Arepalli, F. Castellanos & J.L. Rapoport (2007). Association of the dopamine receptor D4 (DRD4) gene 7-repeat allele with children with attention-deficit/ hyperactivity disorder (ADHD): An update. *American Journal of Medical Genetics*, 144:379–83.

Gottesman, I. & D. Hanson (2005). Human development: biological and genetic processes. *Annual Review of Psychology*, 56:263–86.

Gottfredson, L. (1986). Social consequences of the g factor in employment. *Journal of Vocational Behavior*, 29:379–410.

Gottfredson, M. & T. Hirschi (1990). *A general theory of crime*. Stanford, CA: Stanford University Press.

—— & T. Hirschi (1997). National crime control policies. In M. Fisch (ed.). *Criminology 97/98*, pp. 27–33. Guilford, CT: Dushkin Publishing.

Gottlieb, G. (2007). Probabilistic epigenesis. *Developmental Science*, 10(1):1–11.

Gray, J. & N. McNaughton (2000). *The neuropsychology of anxiety: An enquiry into the functions of the septo-hippocampal system*. Oxford: Oxford University Press.

—— & P. Thompson (2004). Neurobiology of intelligence: Science and ethics. *Nature Reviews: Neuroscience*, 5:471–82.

Greenberg, D. (1985). Age, crime, and social explanation. *American Journal of Sociology*, 91:1–21.

Gua, G. & D. Adkins (2008). How is a statistical link established between a human outcome and a genetic variant? *Sociological Methods and Research*, 37:201–26 (no citation).

Gudjonsson, G., J. Sigurddsson, S. Young, A. Newton & M. Peersen (2009). Attention deficit hyperactivity disorder (ADHD). How do ADHD symptoms relate to personality among prisoners? *Personality and Individual Differences*, 47:64–8.

Gunnar, M. & K. Quevedo (2007). The neurobiology of stress and development. *Annual Review of Psychology*, 58:145–73.

Guo, G., M. Roettger & J. Shih (2007a). Contributions of the DAT1 and DRD2 genes to Serious and violent delinquency among adolescents and young adults. *Human Genetics*, 121:125–36.

——, Y. Tong, C.-W. Xie & L. Lange (2007b). Dopamine transporter, gender, and number of sexual partners among young adults. *European Journal of Human Genetics*, 15:279–87.

——, Y. Tong & T. Cai (2008). Gene by social context interactions for number of sexual partners among white male youths: Genetics-informed sociology. *American Journal of Sociology*, 114:S36–S66

——, T. Cai, R. Guo, H. Wang & K. Mullen-Harris (2010). The dopamine transporter gene, a spectrum of most common risky behaviors, and the legal status of the behaviors. *PLoS ONE*, 5:1–11.

Gur, R.C., F. Gunning-Dixon, W. Bilker & R.E. Gur (2002). Sex differences in temporo-limbic and frontal brain volumes of healthy adults. *Cerebral Cortex*, 12:998–1,003.

Gurrieri, F. & G. Neri (2009). Defective oxytocin function: A clue to understanding the cause of autism? *BMC Medicine*, 7:63–7.

Hall, W. (2006). Avoiding potential misuses of addiction brain science. *Addiction*, 101(1):1,529–32.

Hampton, R., W. Oliver & L. Macgarian (2003). Domestic violence in the African American community: An analysis of social and structural factors. *Violence Against Women*, 9:533–57.

Hare, R. (1993). *Without conscience: The disturbing world of the psychopaths among us*. New York: Pocket Books.

—— (1996). Psychopathy: A clinical construct whose time has come. *Criminal Justice and Behavior*, 23:25–54.

—— (2000). Assessing psychopathy with the PCL-R. Paper presented at Sinclair Seminars, San Diego, CA, January 2000.

—— & C. Neumann (2008). Psychopathy as a clinical and empirical construct. *Annual Review of Clinical Psychology*, 4:217–46.

—— & C. Neumann. (2009). Psychopathy: Assessment and forensic implications. *Canadian Journal of Psychiatry*, 54:791–802.

——, D. Clark, M. Grann & D. Thornton (2000). Psychopathy and the predictive validity of the PCL-R: An international perspective. *Behavioral Sciences and the Law*, 18(5):623–45.

Hariri, A.R., V.S. Mattay, A. Tessitore, B. Kolachana, F. Fera, D. Goldman, M.F. Egan & D.R. Weinberger (2002). Serotonin transporter gene variation and the response of the human amygdala. *Science*, 297:400–403.

Harpending, H. & G. Cochran (2002). In our genes. *Proceedings of the National Academy of Science*, 99:10–12.

Hartshorne, M. (2000). Positron emission tomography. In W. W. Orrison (eds), Neuroimaging Vol 1. (87–122). Philadelphia: Saunders.

Harris, G., T. Skilling & M. Rice (2001). The construct of psychopathy. In M. Tonry (ed.). *Crime and justice: A review of research*, pp. 197–264. Chicago, IL: University of Chicago Press.

Hartman, T. (2000). *Thom Hartmann's complete guide to ADD*. Nevada City, CA: Underwood.

Hawks, J., E. Wang, G. Cochran, H. Harpending & R. Moyzis (2007). Recent acceleration of human adaptive evolution. *Proceedings of the National Academy of Science*, 104:20,753–8.

Haynes, E., H. Kalkwarf, R. Hornung, R. Wenstrup, K. Dietrich & P. Lanphear (2003). Vitamin receptor Fok1 polymorphism and blood lead concentration in children. *Environmental Health Perspectives*, 111:1,665–9.

Haynie, D. (2003). Contexts of risk? Explaining the link between girls' pubertal development and their delinquent involvement. *Social Forces*, 82:355–97.

Heck, K., P. Braveman, C. Cubbin, G. Chavez & J. Kelly (2006). Socioeconomic status and breastfeeding initiation among California mothers. *Public Health Reports*, 121:51–9.

Heinz, A. (2006). Staying sober: Better understanding of how alcohol alters brain chemistry reveals the mechanisms for beating dependency. *Scientific American*, April/May:57–61.

Henry, J., P. Bailey & P. Rendell (2008). Empathy, social functioning and schizotypy. *Psychiatry Research*, 160:15–22.

Hepburn, J.R. (2005). Recidivism among drug offenders following exposure to treatment. *Criminal Justice Policy Review*, 16(2):237–59.

Hepper, P. (2005). Unravelling our beginnings. *The Psychologists*, 18:474–7.

Hermans, E., P. Putnam & J. van Honk (2006). Testosterone administration reduces empathetic behavior: A facial mimicry study. *Psychoneuroendocrinology*, 31:859–66.

——, N. Ramsey & J. van Honk (2008). Exogenous testosterone enhances responsiveness to social threat in the neural circuitry of social aggression in humans. *Biological Psychiatry*, 63:263–70.

Heron, M. (2010). *Deaths: Leading causes in 2006*. Washington, DC: US Department of Health and Human Services, Centers for Disease Control.

Herrnstein, R. & C. Murray (1994). *The Bell Curve: Intelligence and class structure in American Society*. New York: Free Press.

Hewig, J., D. Hagemann, J. Seifert, E. Naumann & D. Bartussek (2006). The relation of cortical activity and BIS/BAS on the trait level. *Biological Psychology*, 71:42–53.

Hiller, J. (2004). Speculations on the links between feelings, emotions and sexual behaviour: Are vasopressin and oxytocin involved? *Sexual and Relationship Therapy*, 19:1,468–79.

Hines, M. (2004). *Brain gender*. Oxford: Oxford University Press.

—— (2006). Prenatal testosterone and gender-related behavior. *European Journal of Endocrinology*, 155:115–21.

—— & G. Alexander (2008). Monkeys, girls, boys and toys: A confirmation letter regarding "Sex differences in toy preferences: striking parallels between monkeys and humans." *Hormones and Behavior*, 54:359–64.

Hirschi, T. & M. Gottfredson (1983). Age and the explanation of crime. *American Journal of Sociology*, 89:552–84.

Hirvonen, M., A. Laakso, K. Nagren, J. Rinner, T. Pohjalainen & J. Hietala (2004). C957T polymorphism of the dopamine D2 receptor (DRD2) gene affects striatal DRD2 availability in vivo. *Molecular Psychiatry*, 9:1,060–61.

Hodkins, S., S. Mednick, P. Brennan, F. Schulsinger & M. Engberg (1996). Mental disorder and crime: Evidence from a Danish birth cohort. *Archives of General Psychiatry*, 53:489–96.

Huber, J. (2008). Reproductive biology, technology, and gender inequality: An autobiographical essay. *Annual Review of Sociology*, 34:1–13.

Hundt, N., N. Kimbrel, J. Mitchell & R. Nelson-Gray (2008). High BAS, but not low BIS, predicts externalizing symptoms in adults. *Personality and Individual Differences*, 44:565–75.

Hyman, S. (2007). The neurobiology of addiction: Implications for voluntary control of behavior. *The American Journal of Bioethics*, 7:8–11.

Ismaili, K. (2001). Code of the street: Decency, violence, and the moral life of the inner city/dealing crack: The social world of streetcorner selling. *Justice Quarterly*, 18:233–8.

Jacobson, J. & S. Jacobson (2002). Effects of prenatal alcohol exposure on child development. *Alcohol Research & Health*, 26:282–6.

Jaffee, S., T. Moffitt, A. Caspi & A. Taylor (2003). Life with (or without) father: The benefits of living with two biological parents depend on the father's antisocial behavior. *Child Development*, 74:109–26.

Jain, M., L. Palacio, F. Castellanos, J. Palacio, D. Pineda, M. Restrepo, J. Muñoz, F. Lopera, D. Wallis, K. Berg, J. Bailey-Wilson, M. Arcos-Burgos & M. Muenke (2007). Attention- deficit/hyperactivity disorder and comorbid disruptive behavior disorders: Evidence of pleiotropy and new susceptibility loci. *Biological Psychiatry*, 61:1,329–39.

James, D.J. & L.E. Glaze (2006). *Mental health problems of prison and jail inmates*. US Department of Justice Document NCJ 213600.

Jang, K., R. McCrae, A. Angleitner, R. Riemann & W. Livesley (1998). Heritability of facet-level traits in a cross-cultural twin sample: Support for a hierarchical model of personality. *Journal of Personality and Social Psychology*, 74:1,556–65.

Jausovec, N. & K. Jausovec (2008). Spatial rotation and recognizing emotions: Gender related differences in brain activity. *Intelligence*, 36:383–93.

Javitt, D. & J. Coyle (2004) Decoding schizophrenia. *Scientific American*, 290:48–55.

——, K. Spencer, G. Thaker, G. Winterer & M. Hajós (2008). Neurophysiological biomarkers for drug development in schizophrenia. *Nature Reviews: Drug Discovery*, 7:68–83.

Johansen, E., P. Killeen, V. Russell, G. Tripp, J. Wickens, R. Tannock, J. Williams & T. Sagvolden (2009). Origins of altered reinforcement effects in ADHD. *Behavioral and Brain Functions*, 1–15.

Johnson, B. & S. Betsinger (2009). Punishing the "model minority": Asian-American criminal sentencing outcomes in federal district courts. *Criminology*, 47:1,045–90.

Johnson, L., P. O'Malley & J. Bachman (2000). *Monitoring the future National Survey Results on drug use, 1975–1999*. Bethesda, MD: National Institute of Drug Abuse.

Johnson, W. (2010). Understanding the genetics of intelligence: Can height help? Can corn oil? *Current Directions in Psychological Science*, 19:177–82.

Jovanovic, H., J. Lundberg, P. Karlsson, Å. Cerin, T. Saijo, A. Varrone, C. Halldin & A. Nordström (2008). Sex differences in the serotonin 1A receptor and serotonin transporter binding in the human brain measured by PET. *NeuroImage*, 39:1,408–19.

Judge, T., C. Higgins, C. Thoresen & M. Barrick (1999). The big five personality traits, general mental ability, and career success across the lifespan. *Personnel Psychology*, 52:621–52.

Jung, R. & R. Haier (2007). The parieto-frontal integration theory (P-FIT) of intelligence: Converging neuroimaging evidence. *Behavioral and Brain Sciences*, 30:135–87.

Kalich, D.M. & R.D. Evans (2006). Drug court: An effective alternative to incarceration. *Deviant Behavior*, 27(1):569–90.

Kalivas, P. & C. O'Brien (2008). Drug addiction as a pathology of staged neuroplasticity. *Neuropsychopharmacology*, 33:166–80.

Kaminsky, Z., T. Tang, S.-C. Wang, C. Ptak, G. Oh, A. Wong, L. Feldcamp, C. Virtanen, J. Halfvarson, C. Tysk, A. McRae, P. Visscher, G. Montgomery, I. Gottesman, N. Martin & A. Petronis (2009). DNA methylation profiles in monozygotic and dizygotic twins. *Nature Genetics*, 41:240–45.

Kanazawa, S. (2008). Temperature and evolutionary novelty as forces behind the evolution of general intelligence. *Intelligence*, 36:99–108.

Kaufman, A. (1976). Verbal-performance IQ discrepancies on the WISC-R. *Journal of Counseling and Clinical Psychology*, 44:739–44.

Keltikangas-Jarvinen, L. & J. Salo (2009). Dopamine and serotonin systems modify environmental effects on human behavior: A review. *Scandinavian Journal of Psychology*, 50:574–82.

Kendler, K., C. Prescott, J. Myers & M. Neale (2003). The Structure of genetic and environmental risk factors for common psychiatric and substance use disorders in men and women. *Archives of General Psychiatry*, 60:929–37.

——, K. Jacobson, C. Gardner, N. Gillespie, S. Aggen & C. Prescott (2007). Creating a social world: A developmental twin study of peer group deviance. *Archives of General Psychiatry*, 64:958–65.

Kim-Cohen, J., A. Caspi, A. Taylor, B. Williams, R. Newcombe, I. Craig & T. Moffitt (2006). MAOA, maltreatment, and gene–environment interaction predicting children's mental health: New evidence and a meta-analysis. *Molecular Psychiatry*, 11:903–13.

Kimura, D. (1992). Sex differences in the brain. *Scientific American*, 267:119–25.

Kingston, P. (2006). How meritocratic is the United States? *Research in Social Stratification and Mobility*, 24:11–130.

Kinner, S. (2003). Psychopathy as an adaptation: Implications for society and social Policy. In R. Bloom & N. Dass (eds.). *Evolutionary psychology and violence*, pp. 57–81. Westport, CT: Praeger.

Kinney, D., K. Hintz, E. Shearer, D. Barch, C. Riffin, K. Whitley & R. Butler (2010). A unifying hypothesis of schizophrenia: Abnormal immune system development may help explain roles of prenatal hazards, post-pubertal onset, stress, genes, climate, infections, and brain dysfunction, *Medical Hypotheses*, 74:555–63.

Kirsch, P., C. Esslinger, Q. Chen, D. Mier, S. Lis, S. Siddhanti, H. Gruppe, V. Mattay, B. Gallhofer & A. Meyer-Lindenberg (2005). Oxytocin modulates neural circuitry for social cognition and fear in humans, *Journal of Neuroscience*, 25:11,489–93.

Kish, S., J. Lerch, Y. Furukawa, J. Tong, T. McCluskey, D. Wilkins, S. Houle, J. Meyer, E. Mundo, A. Wilson, P. Rusjan, J. Saint-Cyr, M. Guttman, D. Collins, C. Shapiro, J. Warsh & I. Boileau (2010). Decreased cerebral cortical serotonin transporter binding in ecstasy users: A positron emission tomography/[^{11}C] DASB and structural brain imaging study. *Brain*, 133(6):1,779–97.

Knickmeyer, R., S. Baron-Cohen, P. Raggatt, K. Taylor & G. Hackett (2006). Fetal testosterone and empathy. *Hormones and Behavior*, 49:282–92.

Knight, K. (2008). Assortative mating for antisocial behavior: A comparison of mates and partners. Paper presented at the American Sociological Association Annual Meeting, Boston, MA.

Kobak, R., K. Zajac & S. Levine (2009). Cortisol and antisocial behavior in early adolescence: The role of gender in an economically disadvantaged sample. *Development and Psychopathology*, 21:579–91.

Kochanska, G. & A. Knaack (2003). Effortful control as a personality characteristic of young children: Antecedents, correlates, and consequences. *Journal of Personality*, 71:1,087–112.

Kollberg, L. (2010). *Variation in the oxytocin receptor gene and the relation to psychopathic traits in young adults*. Stockholm: Institutionen för Klinisk Neurovetenskap, Karolinska Institutet.

Koller, K., T. Brown, A. Spurfeon & L. Levy (2004). Recent developments in low-level lead exposure and intellectual impairment in children. *Environmental Health Perspectives*, 112:987–94.

Koob, G. & M.J. Kreek (2007). Stress, dysregulation of drug reward pathways, and the transition to drug dependence. *American Journal of Psychiatry*, 164(8):1,149–59.

—— & M. Le Moal (2008). Addiction and the brain antireward system. *Annual Review of Psychology*, 59:29–53.

Koukkou, M. & D. Lehmann (2006). Experience dependent brain plasticity: A key concept for studying nonconscious decisions. *International Congress Series*, 1,286:45–52.

Kraeamer, G., M. Ebert, D. Schmidt & W. McKinney (1998). A longitudinal study of the effect of different social rearing conditions on cerebrospinal fluid norepinephrine and biogenic amine metabolites in rhesus monkeys. *Neuropsychopharmacology*, 2:175–89.

Kramer, M., F. Aboud, E. Mironova, I. Vanilovich, R. Platt, L. Matush, S. Igumnov, E. Fombonne, N. Bogdanovich, T. Ducruet, J.P. Collet, B. Chalmers, E. Hodnett, S. Davidovsky, O. Skugarevsky, O. Trofimovich, L. Kozlova & S. Shapiro, for the Promotion of Breastfeeding Intervention Trial (PROBIT) Study Group (2008). Breastfeeding and child cognitive development: New evidence from a large randomized trial. *Archives of General Psychiatry*, 65:578–84.

Krause, D., J. Matz, E. Weidinger, J. Wagner, A. Wildenauer, M. Obermeier, M. Riedel & N. Müller (2010). The association of infectious agents and schizophrenia. *World Journal of Biological Psychiatry*, 11:739–43.

Krueger, R., T. Moffitt, A. Caspi, A. Bleske & P. Silva (1998). Assortative mating for antisocial behavior: Developmental and methodological implications. *Behavior Genetics*, 28:173–85.

Kubota T., K. Miyake, T. Hirasawa, K. Nagai & T. Koide (2010). Novel etiological and therapeutic strategies for neurodiseases: Epigenetic understanding of gene–environment interactions. *Journal of Pharmacological Sciences*, 113:3–8.

Kuhn, T. (1970). *The structure of scientific revolutions*. Chicago: University of Chicago Press.

Lahey, B. & R. Loeber (1994). Framework for a developmental model of oppositional defiant disorder and conduct disorder. In D. Routh (ed.). *Disruptive behavior disorders in childhood*, pp. 139–80. New York: Plenum.

Laland, K., J. Odling-Smee & S. Myles (2010). How culture shaped the human genome: Bringing genetics and the human sciences together. *Nature Reviews: Genetics*, 11:137–48.

Lamb, H.R., L.E. Weinberger & B.H. Gross (2004) Mentally ill persons in the criminal justice system: Some perspectives. *Psychiatric Quarterly*, 75:107–26.

Le, Y., Y. Zhou, P. Iribarren & J. Wang (2004). Chemokines and chemokinase receptors: Their manifold roles in homeostasis and disease. *Cellular & Molecular Immunology*, 95–104.

Lee, V. & P. Hoaken (2007). Cognition, emotion, and neurobiological development: Mediating the relation between maltreatment and aggression. *Child Maltreatment*, 12:281–98.

Leonard, E. (1995). Theoretical criminology and gender. In B. Price & N. Sokoloff (eds.). *The criminal justice system and women: Offenders, victims, and workers*, pp. 54–70. New York: McGraw-Hill.

Levine, A.A., Z. Guan, A. Barco, S. Xu, E.R. Kandel & J.H. Schwartz (2005). CREB-binding protein controls response to cocaine by acetylating histones at the fosB promoter in the mouse striatum. *Proceedings of the National Academy of Sciences of the United States of America*, 102(52):19,186–91.

Levine, D. (2006). Neural modeling of the dual motive theory of economics. *The Journal of Socio-Economics*, 35:613–25.

Levy, F. (2004). Synaptic gating and ADHD: A biological theory of comorbidity of ADHD and anxiety. *Neuropsychopharmacology*, 29:1,589–96.

Lewandowski, K. (2007). Relationship of catechol-O-methyltransferase to schizophrenia and its correlates: Evidence for associations and complex interactions. *Harvard Review of Psychiatry*, 15:233–44.

Li, C., X. Mao & L. Wei (2008). Genes and (common) pathways underlying drug addiction. *PLoS Computational Biology*, 4:28–34.

Lilly, J., F. Cullen & R. Ball (2007). *Criminological theory: Context and consequences*. Thousand Oaks, CA: Sage.

Linden, D. (2006). How psychotherapy changes the brain: The contribution of functional neuroimaging. *Molecular Psychiatry*, 11:528–38.

Lindenfors, P. (2005). Neocortex evolution in primates: The "social brain" is for females. *Biological Letters*, 1:407–10.

Lodi-Smith, J. & B. Roberts (2007). Social investment and personality: A meta-analytic analysis of the relationship of personality traits to investment in work, family, religion, and volunteerism. *Personality and Social Psychology Review*, 11:68–86.

Loehlin, J. (2000). Group differences in intelligence. In R. Sternberg (ed.). *Handbook of Intelligence*, pp. 176–93. Cambridge: Cambridge University Press.

Lopez-Rangel, E. & M. Lewis (2006). Loud and clear evidence for gene silencing by epigenetic mechanisms in autism spectrum and related neurodevelopmental disorders. *Clinical Genetics*, 69:21–5.

Lotrich, F., B. Pollock & R. Ferrell (2003). Serotonin transporter promoter polymorphism in African Americans: Allele frequencies and implications for treatment. *American Journal of Pharmacogenomics*, 3:145–7.

Lubinski, D. (2004). Introduction to the special section on cognitive abilities: 100 years after Spearman's (1904) "'General intelligence,' objectively determined and measured." *Journal of Personality and Social Psychology, 86,* 96–111

Lurigio, A.J. (2001). Effective services for parolees with mental illnesses. *Crime and Delinquency*, 47:446–61.

Lykken, D. (1995). *The Antisocial Personalities*. Hillsdale, NJ: Lawrence Erlbaum.

Lynam, D. (1996). Early identification of chronic offenders: Who is the fledgling psychopath? *Psychological Bulletin*, 120:209–34.

McBurnett, K., B. Lahey, P. Rathouz & R. Loeber (2000). Low salivary cortisol and persistent aggression in boys referred for disruptive behavior. *Archives of General Psychiatry*, 57:38–43.

McCrae, T. & A. Terracciano (2005). Universal features of personality traits from the observer's perspective: Data from 50 cultures. *Journal of Personality and Social Psychology*, 88:547–561.

McDermott, P., A. Alterman, J. Cacciola, M. Rutherford, J. Newman, & E. Mulholland (2000). Generality of Psychopathy Checklist Revised factors over prisoners and substance-dependent patients. *Journal of Consulting and Clinical Psychology*, 68:181–6.

——, D. Tingley, J. Cowden, G. Frazzetto & D. Johnson (2009). Monoamine oxidase A gene (MAOA) predicts behavioral aggression following provocation. *Proceedings of the National Academy of Sciences*, 106(7):2,118–23.

McDermott, R. (2004). The feeling of rationality: The meaning of neuroscientific advances for political science. *Perspectives on Politics*, 2:691–706.

McDonald, A., H. Thermenos, D. Barch & L. Seidman (2009). Imaging genetic liability to schizophrenia: Systematic review of fMRI studies of patients nonpsychotic relatives. *Schizophrenia Bulletin*, 35:1,142–62.

MacDonald, K. & T. MacDonald (2010). The peptide that binds: A systematic review of oxytocin and its prosocial effects in humans. *Harvard Review of Psychiatry*, 18:1–21.

McGowan, P., A. Sasaki, C. D'Alessio, S. Dymov, B. Labonté, M. Szyf, G. Turecki & M. Meaney (2009). Epigenetic regulation of the glucocorticoid receptor in human brain associates with childhood abuse *Nature Neuroscience*, 12:342–8.

McGregor, I., P. Callaghan & G. Hunt (2008). From ultrasocial to antisocial: A role for oxytocin in the acute reinforcing effects and long-term adverse consequences of drug use? *British Journal of Pharmacology*, 154:358–68.

McGue, M. (1999). The behavioral genetics of alcoholism. *Current Directions in Psychological Science*, 8:109–15.

McKeon, R. (ed) (1947). *Introduction to Aristotle*. New York: The Modern Library.

Mackintosh, N. (2000). Evolutionary psychology meets g. *Nature*, 420:378–9.

Madras, B. (2006). A "biochemical roadmap" of drug addiction. *On the Brain: Harvard Mahoney Neuroscience Newsletter*, 12(2):1–5.

Maniglio, R. (2009). Severe mental illness and criminal victimization: A systematic review. *Acta Psychiatrica Scandinavica*, 119:180–91.

Manning, J. (2007). The androgen receptor gene: A major modifier of speed of neuronal transmission and intelligence? *Medical Hypotheses* 68: 802–805.

Manning, M. & H. Hoyme (2007). Fetal alcohol syndrome disorders: A practical clinical approach to diagnosis. *Neuroscience and Biobehavioral Review*, 31:230–38.

Mannuzza, S., R. Klein & J. Moulton (2007). Lifetime criminality among boys with ADHD: A prospective follow-up study into adulthood using official arrest records. *Psychiatry Research*, 160:237–46.

Manzano, O., S. Cervenka, A. Karabanov, L. Farde & F. Ullén (2009). Thinking outside a less intact box: Thalamic dopamine D2 receptor densities are negatively related to psychometric creativity in healthy individuals. *PLoS One*, 5:e10670.

Martin, S. (2001). The links between alcohol, crime and the criminal justice system: Explanations, evidence and interventions. *The American Journal on Addictions*, 10:136–58.

Marzuk, P.M. (1996). Violence, crime, and mental illness: How strong a link? *Archives of General Psychiatry*, 53(6):481–6.

Massey, D. (2004). Segregation and stratification: A biosocial perspective. *Du Bois Review*, 1:7–25.

Matarazzo, J. (1976). *Wechsler's measurement and appraisal of adult intelligence*. Baltimore: Williams and Wilkins.

—— (1992). Psychological testing and assessment in the 21st century. *American Psychologist*, 47:1,007–18.

Maughan, B. (2005). Developmental trajectory modeling: A view from developmental psychopathology. *The Annals of the American Academy of Political and Social Science*, 602:118–30.

—— & A. Pickles (1990). Adopted and illegitimate children growing up. In L. Robins & M. Rutter (eds.). *Straight and Devious Pathways from Childhood to Adulthood*, pp. 36–61. Cambridge: Cambridge University Press.

——, R. Rowe, J. Messer, R. Goodman & H. Meltzer (2004). Conduct disorder and oppositional defiant disorder in a national sample: Developmental epidemiology. *Journal of Child Psychology and Psychiatry*, 43:609–21.

May, P. & P. Gossage (2008). *Estimating the prevalence of fetal alcohol syndrome: A summary*. National Institute of Alcohol Abuse and Alcoholism, National Institute of Health, <http://pubs.niaaa.nih.gov/publications/arh25-3/159-167. htm>.

Mayes, L., M. Bornstein, K. Chawarska, O. Haynes & R. Granger (1995). Informational processing and developmental assessment in 3-month-old infants exposed prenatally to cocaine. *Pediatrics*, 95:539–45.

Mazur, A. (2005). *Biosociology of dominance and deference*. Lanham, MD: Rowman & Littlefield.

—— & A. Booth (1998). Testosterone and dominance in men. *Behavioral and Brain Sciences*, 21:353–97.

Mead, M. (1935). *Sex and temperament in three primitive societies*. New York: Morrow.

—— (1949). *Male and female: A study of the sexes in a changing world*. New York: Morrow.

Meadows, R. & J. Kuehnel (2005) *Evil minds: Understanding and responding to violent predators*. Upper Saddle River, NJ: Prentice-Hall.

Mealey, L. (1995). The sociobiology of sociopathy: An integrated evolutionary model. *Behavioral and Brain Sciences*, 18:523–59.

—— (2000) *Sex differences: Developmental and evolutionary strategies.* London: Academic Press.

Meaney, F. & L. Miller (2003). A comparison of fetal alcohol syndrome surveillance network and birth defects surveillance methodology in determining prevalence rates of fetal alcohol syndrome. *Birth Defects Research*, 67:819–21.

Meaney, M. (2010). Epigenetics and the biological definition of gene x environment interaction. *Child Development*, 81:41–79.

Mednick, S., R. Machon & N. Huttunen (1988). Adult schizophrenia following prenatal exposure to an influenza epidemic. *Archives of General Psychiatry*, 45:189–92.

Mehta, P. & J. Beer (2009). Neural mechanisms of the testosterone–aggression relation: The role of the oribitofrontal cortex. *Journal of Cognitive Neuroscience*, 22:2,357–68.

Mekel-Bobrov, N., S. Gilbert, P. Evans, E. Vallender, J. Anderson, R. Hudson, S. Tishkoff & B. Lahn (2005). Ongoing adaptive evolution of *ASPM*, a brain size determinant in *Homo sapiens*. *Science*, 309:1,720–22

Menard, S., S. Mihalic & D. Huizinga (2001). Drugs and crime revisited. *Justice Quarterly*, 18:269–99.

Meyer, U. & J. Feldon (2009). Prenatal exposure to infection: A primary mechanism for abnormal dopaminergic development in schizophrenia. *Psychopharmacology*, 206:587–602.

Meyer-Lindenberg, J. Buckholtz, B. Kolachana, A. Hariri, L. Pezawas, G. Blasi, A. Wabnitz, R. Honea, B. Verchinski, J. Gallicott, M. Egan, V. Mattay & D. Weinberger (2006). Neural mechanisms of genetic risk for impulsivity in violence in humans. *Proceedings of the National Academy of Sciences*, 103:6,269–74.

Mill, J., A. Caspi, B. Williams, I. Craig, A. Taylor, M. Polo-Tomas, C. Berridge, R. Poulton & T. Moffitt (2006). Genetic polymorphisms in the dopamine system predict heterogeneity in intelligence and adult prognosis among children with attention-deficit hyperactivity disorder: Evidence from two birth cohorts. *Archives of General Psychiatry*, 63:462–9.

Miller, J. (1998). Up it up: Gender and the accomplishment of street robbery. *Criminology*, 36:37–65.

—— & D. Lynham (2001). Structural models of personality and their relation to antisocial behavior: A meta-analytic review. *Criminology*, 39:765–98.

Miller, L. (1987). Neuropsychology of the aggressive psychopath: An integrative review. *Aggressive Behavior*, 13:119–40.

Miller, T., D. Levey, M. Cohen & K. Cox (2006). Costs of alcohol and drug-related crime. *Prevention Science*, 7:333–42.

Miller-Butterworth, C., J. Kaplan, J. Shaffer, B. Devlin, S. Manuck & R. Ferrell (2008). Sequence variation in the primate dopamine transporter gene and its relationship to social dominance. *Molecular Biology and Evolution*, 25:18–28

Millon, T., E. Simonsen & M. Birket-Smith (2002). *Psychopathy: Antisocial, criminal and violent behavior*. New York: Guilford Press.

Mitchell, J. & R. Nelson-Gray (2006). Attention-deficit/hyperactivity disorder symptoms in adults: Relationship to Gray's behavioral approach system. *Personality and Individual Differences*, 40:749–60.

Mitchell, K. (2007). The genetics of brain wiring: From molecule to mind. *PLoS Biology*, 4:690–92.

Mithen, S. & L. Parsons (2008). The brain as a cultural artifact. *Cambridge Archeological Journal*, 18:415–22.

Moffitt, T. (1993). Adolescent-limited and life-course-persistent antisocial behavior: A developmental taxonomy. *Psychological Review*, 100:674–701.

—— (2005). The new look of behavioral genetics in developmental psychopathology: Gene–environment interplay in antisocial behavior. *Psychological Bulletin*, 131:533–54.

—— & the E-Risk Study Team (2002). Teen-aged mothers in contemporary Britain. *Journal of Child Psychology and Psychiatry*, 43:1–16.

—— & A. Walsh (2003) The adolescence-limited/life-course persistent theory of antisocial behavior: What have we learned? In A. Walsh & L. Ellis (eds.). *Biosocial criminology: Challenging environmentalism's supremacy*, pp. 125–44. Hauppauge, NY: Nova Science.

——, D. Lynam & P. Silva (1994). Neuropsychological tests predicting persistent male delinquency. *Criminology*, 32:277–300.

——, A. Caspi, M. Rutter & P. Silva (2001). *Sex differences in antisocial behaviour: Conduct disorder, delinquency and violence in the Dunedin longitudinal study*. Cambridge: Cambridge University Press.

Moll, J., F. Krueger, R. Zahn, M. Pardini, R. de Oliveira-Souza & J. Grafman (2006). Human fronto-mesolimbic networks guide decisions about charitable donation. *Proceedings of the National Academy of Sciences of the United States of America*, 103:15,623–8.

Monk, C., R. Klein, E. Telzer, E. Schroth, S. Mannuzza, J. Moulton, M. Guardino, C. Masten, E. McClure-Tone, S. Fromm, R. Blair, D. Pine & M. Ernst (2008). Amygdala and nucleus accumbens activation to emotional facial expressions in children and adolescents at risk for major depression *American Journal of Psychiatry*, 165:90–98.

Montagu, A. (1981). *Growing young*. New York: McGraw-Hill.

Moore, C. & M. Rose (1995). Adaptive and nonadaptive explanations of sociopathy. *Behavior and Brain Sciences*, 18:566–7.

Moore, K. & S. Miller (2008). Living the high life. The role of drug taking in young people's lives. In H. Wilson (ed.). *Drugs, society, and behavior*, pp. 5–8. Dubuque, IA. McGraw-Hill.

Mori, S. & J. Zhang (2006). Principles of diffusion tensor imaging and its application to neuroscience research. *Neuron*, 51:527–39.

Morse, R. & D. Flavin (1992). The definition of alcoholism. The Joint Committee of the National Council on Alcoholism and Drug Dependence and the American Society of Addiction Medicine to Study the Definition and Criteria for the Diagnosis of Alcoholism. *JAMA: The Journal of the American Medical Association*, 268:1,012–14.

Moussas, G., C. Christodoulou & A. Douzenis (2009). A short review on the aetiology and pathophysiology of alcoholism. *Annals of General Psychiatry*, 8:1–4.

Muller, J. (2010). Psychopathy: An approach to neuroscientific research in forensic psychiatry. *Behavioral Science and the Law*, 28:129–47.

Muller, N. & N. Schwarz (2006). Schizophrenia as an inflammation-mediated dysbalance of glutamatergic neurotransmission. *Neurotoxicity Research*, 10:131–48.

—— & S. Dursun (2010). Schizophrenia genes, epigenetics and psychoneuro-immunology therapeutics: All make sense now? *Journal of Psychopharmacology*, doi: 10.1177/0269881110364268.

Munafo, M.R., S.M. Brown & A.R. Hariri (2008). Serotonin transporter (5HTTLPR) genotype and amygdala activation: A meta-analysis. *Biological Psychiatry*, 63:852–7.

———, C. Durrant, G. Lewsi & J. Flint (2009). Gene x environment interactions at the serotonin transporter locus. *Biological Psychiatry*, 65:211.

Murphy, J. (1976) Psychiatric labeling in cross-cultural perspective. *Science*, 191:1,019–28.

Murray, C. (2002). IQ and income inequality in a sample of sibling pairs from advantaged family backgrounds. *The American Economic Review*, 92:339–43.

Murray, J., M. Liotti, H. Mayberg, Y. Pu, F. Zamarripa & Y. Liu (2006). Children's brain activations while viewing televised violence revealed by fMRI. *Media Psychology*, 8:25–37.

Nagin, D. & K. Land (1993). Age, criminal careers, and population heterogeneity: Specification and estimation of a nonparametric, mixed poisson model. *Criminology*, 31:327–62.

Nair, H. & L. Young (2006). Vasopressin and pair-bond formation: Genes to brain to behavior. *Physiology*, 21:146–52.

Narvaez, D. & J. Vaydich (2008). Moral development and behaviour under the spotlight of the neurobiological sciences. *Journal of Moral Education*, 37:289–312.

Needleman, H. (2004). Lead poisoning. *Annual Review of Medicine*, 55:209–22.

Neisser, U., G. Boodoo, T. Bouchard, A. Boykin, N. Brody, S. Ceci, D. Halpern, J. Loehlin, R. Perloff, R. Sternberg & S. Urbina (1995). *Intelligence: Knowns and unknowns. Report of a task force established by the board of scientific affairs of the American Psychological Association.* Washington, DC: American Psychological Association.

Nelson, C. (2007). A neurobiological perspective on early human deprivation. *Child Development Perspectives*, 1:13–18.

Nelson, K. & J. White (2002). Androgen receptor CAG repeats and prostate cancer. *American Journal of Epidemiology*, 155:883–90

Nestler, E., M. Barrot & D. Self (2001). ΔFosB: A sustained molecular switch for addiction. *Proceedings of the National Academy of Sciences*, 98:11,042–6.

Nettle, D. (2003). Intelligence and class mobility in the British population. *British Journal of Psychology*, 94:551–61.

——— & H. Clegg (2005). Schizotypy, creativity and mating success in humans. *Proceedings of the Royal Society: Biology*, 3,349:1–5.

Nettler, G. (1984). *Explaining crime* (3rd ed.). New York: McGraw-Hill.

Neubauer, A. & A. Fink (2009). Intelligence and neural efficiency. *Neuroscience and Biobehavioral Reviews*, 33:1,004–23.

Nicholson, S. (2002). On the genealogy of norms: A case for the role of emotion in cultural evolution. *Philosophy of Science*, 69:234–55.

Niehoff, D. (2003). A vicious circle: The neurobiological foundations of violent behavior. *Modern Psychoanalysis*, 28:235–45.

Nielsen, F. (2006). Achievement and ascription in educational attainment: Genetic and environmental influences on adolescent schooling. *Social Forces*, 85:193–216.

Noble, M., M. Mayer-Proschel & R. Miller (2005). The oligodendrocyte. In M. Rao & M. Jacobson (eds.). *Developmental neurobiology*, pp. 151–96. New York: Kluwer/Plenum.

Nolan, J.L.J. (2002). Drug treatment courts and the disease paradigm. *Substance Use & Misuse*, 37(12):1,723–50.

O'Brien, C.P. (2003). Research advances in understanding and treatment of addiction. *The American Journal on Addictions*, 12(2):536–47.

O'Leary, C. (2004). Fetal alcohol syndrome: Diagnosis, epidemiology, and developmental outcomes. *Journal of Paediatrics and Child Health*, 40:2–7.

O'Leary, M., B. Loney & L. Eckel (2007). Gender differences in the association between psychopathic personality traits and cortisol response to induced stress. *Psychoneuroendocrinology*, 32:183–91.

Oh, G. & A. Petronis (2008). Environmental studies of schizophrenia through the prism of epigenetics. *Schizophrenia Bulletin*, 34:1,122–9.

Ohnishi, T., R. Hashimoto, T. Mori, K. Nemoto, Y. Moriguchi, H. Iida, H. Noguchi, T. Nakabayashi, H. Hori, M. Ohmori, R. Tsukue, K. Anami, N. Hirabayashi, S. Harada, K. Arima, O. Saitoh & H. Kunugi (2006). The association between the val[158]met polymorphism of the catechol-O-methyl transferase gene and morphological abnormalities of the brain in chronic schizophrenia. *Brain*, 129:399–410.

Ortiz, J. & A. Raine (2004). Heart rate level and antisocial behavior in children and adolescents: A meta-analysis. *Journal of the American Academy of Child and Adolescent Psychiatry*, 43:154–62.

Osgood, D. & J. Chambers (2003). Community correlates of rural youth violence. *Juvenile Justice Bulletin*, May. Washington, DC: US Department of Justice.

Osofsky, J. (1995). The effects of exposure to violence on young children. *American Psychologist*, 50:782–8.

Padilla, F. (1992) *The gang as an American enterprise*. New Brunswick, NJ: Rutgers University Press.

Palmer, C. & C. Tilley (1995) Sexual access to females as a motivation for joining gangs: An evolutionary approach. *The Journal of Sex Research*, 32:213–17.

Panksepp, J. (1998). Attention deficit hyperactivity disorders, psychostimulants, and intolerance of childhood playfulness: A tragedy in the making. *Current Directions in Psychological Science*, 7:91–8.

Parsons, L. & D. Osherson (2001). New evidence for distinct right and left brain systems for deductive versus probabilistic reasoning. *Cerebral Cortex*, 11:954–65.

Patel, N., N. Vyas, B. Puri, S. Nijran & A. Al-Nahhas (2010). Positron emission tomography in schizophrenia: A new perspective. *Journal of Nuclear Medicine*, 51:511–20.

Patrick, C. (2006). Back to the future: Cleckley as a guide to the next generation of psychopathy research. In: C. Patrick (ed.). *Handbook of psychopathy*, pp. 605–17. New York: Guilford Press.

Patterson, O. (1998). *Rituals of blood: Consequences of slavery in two American centuries*. Washington, DC: Civitas Counterpoint.

Paus, T. (2010). Population neuroscience: Why and how. *Human Brain Mapping*, 31:891–903.

——, M. Keshavan & J. Giedd (2008). Why do so many psychiatric disorders emerge during adolescence? *Nature Reviews: Neuroscience*, 9:947–57.

Penn, A. (2001). Early brain wiring: Activity-dependent processes. *Schizophrenia Bulletin*, 27:337–48.

Perrin, J., P. Herve, G. Leonard, M. Perron, G. Pike, A. Pitiot, L. Richer, S. Veillette, Z. Pausova & T. Paus (2008). Growth of white matter in the adolescent brain: role of testosterone and androgen receptor. *The Journal of Neuroscience*, 28:9,519–24.

Perry, B. (2002). Childhood experience and the expression of genetic potential: What childhood neglect tells us about nature and nurture. *Brain and Mind*, 3:79–100.

—— & R. Pollard (1998). Homeostasis, stress, trauma, and adaptation: A neurodevelopmental view of childhood trauma. *Child and Adolescent Psychiatric Clinics of America*, 7:33–51.

Phelps, E. (2006). Emotion and cognition: Insights from studies of the human amygdala. *Annual Review of Psychology*, 57:27–53.

Piper, G. & S. Schnepf (2008). Gender differences in charitable giving in Great Britain. *Voluntas*, 19:103–24.

Pitchford, I. (2001). The origins of violence: Is psychopathy and adaptation? *Human Nature Review*, 1:28–38.

Plavcan, J. & C. van Schaik (1997). Intrasexual competition and body weight dimorphism in anthropoid primates. *American Journal of Physical Anthropology*, 103:37–68.

Plomin, R., L. Hill, I. Craig, P. McGuffin, S. Purcell, P. Sham, D. Lubinski, L. Thompson, P. Fisher, D. Turic & M. Owen (2001). A genome-wide scan of 1842 DNA markers for allelic associations with general cognitive ability: A five-stage design using DNA pooling and extreme selected groups. *Behavior Genetics*, 31:497–509.

Posthuma, D., E. de Geus & D. Boomsma (2003). Genetic contributions to anatomical, behavioral, and neurophysiological indices of cognition. In R. Plomin, J. Defries, I. Craig & P. McGuffin (eds.). *Behavioral genetics in the postgenomic era*, pp. 141–61. Washington, DC: American Psychological Association.

Posthumus, J., K. Böcker, M. Raaijmakers, H. Van Engeland & W. Matthys (2009). Heart rate and skin conductance in four-year-old children with aggressive behavior. *Biological Psychology*, 82:164–8.

Powell, K. (2006). How does the teenage brain work? *Nature*, 442:865–7.

Powledge, T.M. (2009). Epigenetics and development. *BioScience*, 59:736–41.

Pratt, T., F. Cullen, K. Blevins & L. Unnever (2002), The relationship of attention deficit hyperactivity disorder to crime and delinquency: A meta-analysis, *International Journal of Police Science and Management*, 4:344–60.

Prayer, D., G. Kasprian, E. Krampl, B. Ulm, L. Witzani, L. Prayer & P. Brugger (2006). MRI of normal fetal brain development. *European Journal of Radiology*, 57:199–216.

Prescott, C. (2002). Sex differences in the genetic risk for alcoholism. *Alcohol Research & Health*, 26:264–74.

Price, B. & N. Sokoloff (1995). Theories and facts about women offenders. In B. Price & N. Sokoloff (eds.). *The criminal justice system and women: Offenders, victims, and workers*, pp. 1–10. New York: McGraw-Hill.

Pridemore, W. (2004). Weekend effects on binge drinking and homicide: The social connection between alcohol and violence in Russia. *Addiction*, 99:1,034–41.

Quartz, S. & T. Sejnowski (1997). The neural basis of cognitive development: A constructivist manifesto. *Behavioral and Brain Sciences*, 20:537–96.

Quay, H. (1997). Inhibition and attention deficit hyperactivity disorder. *Journal of Abnormal Child Psychology*, 25:7–13.

Quinn, J. & Z. Sneed (2008). Drugs and crime: An empirically based interdisciplinary model. *Journal of Teaching in the Addictions*, 70:16–28.

Quinsey, V. (2002). Evolutionary theory and criminal behavior. *Legal and Criminological Psychology*, 7:1–14.

Qvarnstrom, A., J. Brommer & L. Gustafsson (2006). Testing the genetics underlying the co-evolution of mate choice and ornament in the wild. *Nature*, 44:84–6.

Raine, A. (2008). From genes to brain to antisocial behavior. *Current Direction in Psychological Science*, 17:323–8.

Rajender, S., G. Pandu, J. Sharma, K. Ghandi, L. Singh & K. Thangaraj (2008). Reduced CAG repeats length in androgen receptor gene is associated with violent criminal behavior. *International Journal of Legal Medicine*, 122:367–72.

Rasanen, P., H. Hakko, M. Isohanni, S. Hodkins, M. Jarvalin & J. Tiihonen (1999). Maternal smoking during pregnancy and risk of criminal behavior among adult male offspring in the Northern Finland 1966 birth cohort. *American Journal of Psychiatry*, 156:857–62.

Renthal, W. & E. Nestler (2009). Chromatin regulation in drug addiction and depression. *Dialogues in Clinical Neuroscience*, 11:257–68.

Restak, R. (2001). *The secret life of the brain*. New York: Dana Press and Joseph Henry Press.

Retz, W. & M. Rosler (2009). The relation of ADHD and violent aggression: What can we learn from epidemiological and genetic studies? *International journal of Law and Psychiatry*, 32:235–43.

Reyna, V. & F. Farley (2006). Risk and rationality in adolescent decision making: Implications for theory, practice, and public policy. *Psychological Science in the Public Interest*, 7:1–44.

Rhee, S. & I. Waldman (2002). Genetic and environmental influences on antisocial behavior A meta-analysis of twin and adoption studies. *Psychological Bulletin*, 128:490–529.

Richter-Levin, G. (2004). The amygdala, the hippocampus, and emotional modulation of memory. *The Neuroscientist*, 10:31–9.

Ridley, M. (2003). *Nature via nurture: Genes, experience and what makes us human.* New York: HarperCollins.

Robinson, M. (2004). *Why crime? An integrated systems theory of antisocial behavior.* Upper Saddle River, NJ: Prentice-Hall.

—— (2005). *Justice blind: Ideals and realities of American criminal justice.* Upper Saddle River, NJ: Prentice-Hall.

Robinson, T. & K. Berridge (2003). Addiction. *Annual Review of Psychology*, 54:25–53.

—— (2008). The incentive sensitization theory of addiction: some current issues. *Philosophical Transactions. Biological Sciences*, 363:3137–3146.

Rodkin, P., T. Farmer, R. Pearl & R. Van Acker (2000). Heterogeneity of popular boys: Antisocial and prosocial configurations. *Developmental Psychology*, 36:14–24.

Romer, D. (2010). Adolescent risk taking, impulsivity, and brain development: Implications for prevention. *Developmental Psychobiology*, 52:263–76.

Romine, C. & C. Reynolds (2005). A model of the development of frontal lobe functioning: Findings from a meta-analysis. *Applied Neuropsychology*, 12:190–201.

Roscoe, P. (2003). Margaret Mead, Reo Fortune, and Mountain Apapesh warfare. *American Anthropologist*, 105:581–91.

Rose, S. (2001). Moving on from old dichotomies: Beyond nature-nurture towards a lifeline perspective. *British Journal of Psychiatry*, 178:3–7.

Rösler, M., W. Retz, P. Retz, G. Hengesch, M. Schneider & T. Supprian (2004). Prevalence of attention deficit-hyperactivity disorder and comorbid disorders in young male prison inmates, *European Archives of Psychiatry: Clinical Neuroscience*, 254:365–71.

Rowe, D. (1992). Three shocks to socialization research. *Behavioral and Brain Sciences*, 14:401–2.

—— (1997). Are parents to blame? A look at the antisocial personalities. *Psychological Inquiry*, 8:251–60.

—— (2002). *Biology and crime.* Los Angeles, CA: Roxbury.

—— & D. Farrington (1997). The familial transmission of criminal convictions. *Criminology*, 35:177–201.

——, K. Jacobson & E. van den Oord (1999). Genetic and environmental influences on vocabulary IQ: Parents education level as moderator. *Child Development*, 70:1,151–62.

Rushton, J. & G. Whitney (2002). Cross-national variation in violent crime rates: Race, r-K theory, and income. *Population and Environment*, 23:501–11.

Rutten, B. & J. Mill (2009). Epigenetic mediation of environmental influences in major psychotic disorders. *Schizophrenia Bulletin*, 35:1,045–56.

Sampson, R. (1999). Techniques of research neutralization. *Theoretical Criminology*, 3:438–50.

——— & W.J. Wilson (2000). Toward a theory of race, crime, and urban inequality. In S. Cooper (ed.). *Criminology*, pp. 149–60. Madison, WI: Coursewise.

——— & J. Laub (2005). A life-course view of the development of crime. *American Academy of Political & Social Sciences*, 602:12–45.

Sanderson, S. (2001). *The evolution of human sociality: A Darwinian conflict perspective*. Lanham, MD: Rowman & Littlefield.

Sapolsky, R. (1997). *The trouble with testosterone and other essays on the biology of the human predicament*. New York: Scribner.

Sasi, R. (2010). Attention-deficit hyperactivity disorder and gender. *Archives of Women's Mental Health*, 13:29–31.

Sax, L. (2006). Six degrees of separation: What teachers need to know about the emerging science of sex differences. *Educational Horizons*, 84:190–212.

Scarpa, A. & A. Raine (2003). The psychophysiology of antisocial behavior: Interactions with environmental experiences. In A. Walsh & L. Ellis (eds.). *Biosocial criminology: Challenging environmentalism's supremacy*, pp. 209–26. Hauppauge, NY: Nova Science.

Schilling, C., A. Walsh & I. Yun (2011). ADHD and criminality: A review of the genetic, neurobiological, evolutionary and treatment literature. *Journal of Criminal Justice*. 39:3–11.

Schmalleger, F. (2004). *Criminology today* (3rd ed.). Upper Saddle River, NJ: Prentice-Hall.

Schmidt, F. & K. Hunter (2004). General mental ability in the world of work: Occupational attainment and job performance. *Journal of Personality and Social Psychology*, 86:162–73.

Schmitt, D., A. Realo, M. Voracek & J. Allik (2008). Why can't a man be more like a woman? Sex differences in big five personality traits across 55 cultures. *Journal of Personality and Social Psychology*, 94:168–82.

Schon, R. & M. Silven (2007). Natural parenting: Back to basics in infant care. *Evolutionary Psychology*, 5:102–83.

Schug, R. & A. Raine (2009). Comparative meta-analysis of neuropsychological functioning in antisocial schizophrenic persons. *Clinical Psychology Review*, 29:230–42.

Schulte-Rüther, M., H. Markowitsch, G. Fink & M. Piefke (2007). Mirror neuron and theory of mind mechanisms involved in face-to-face interactions: A functional magnetic resonance imaging approach to empathy. *Journal of Cognitive Neuroscience*, 19:1,354–72.

Schutter, D., A. De Weijer, J. Meuwese, B. Morgan & J. van Honk (2008). Interrelations between motivational stance, cortical excitability, and the frontal electroencephalogram asymmetry of emotion: A transcranial magnetic stimulation study. *Human Brain Mapping*, 29:574–80.

Schwekendick, D. (2009). Height and weight differences between North and South Korea. *Journal of Biosocial Science*, 41:446–54.

Seligman, D. (1992*). A question of intelligence: The IQ debate in America*. New York: Birch Lane Press.

Sergeant, J., H. Geurts, S. Huijbregts, A. Scheres & J. Ooserlan (2003). The top and bottom of ADHD: A neuropsychological perspective. *Neuroscience and Biobehavioral Reviews*, 27:583–92.

Shavit, Y. & A. Rattner (1988). Age, crime, and the early lifecourse. *American Journal of Sociology*, 93:1,457–70.

Shaw, C. & H. McKay (1972). *Juvenile delinquency and urban areas*. Chicago, IL: University of Chicago Press.

Shaw, P., K. Eckstrand, W. Sharp, J. Blumenthal, J. Lerch, D. Greenstein, L. Clasen, A. Evans, J. Giedd & J. Rapoport (2007). Attention-deficit/hyperactivity disorder is characterized by a delay in cortical maturation. *Proceedings of the National Academy of Sciences of the United States of America*, 104:19,649–54.

Shedler, J. & J. Block (1990). Adolescent drug use and psychological health. *American Psychologist*, 45, 612–30.

Shi, S., T. Cheng, L. Jan & Y. Jan (2004). The immunoglobin family member dendrite arborization and synapse maturation 1 (Dasm1) controls excitatory synapse maturation. *Proceedings of the National Academy of Sciences*, 101:13,246–351.

Shirtcliff, E., M. Vitacco, A. Graf, A. Gosttisha, J. Merz & C. ZahnWaxler (2009). Neurobiology of empathy and callousness: Implications for the development of antisocial behavior. *Behavioral Sciences and the Law*, 27:137–71.

Silfver, M. & H. Klaus (2007). Empathy, guilt, and gender: A comparison of two measures of guilt. *Scandinavian Journal of Psychology*, 48:239–46.

———, K. Helkama, J. Lonnqvist & M. Verkasalo (2008). The relation between value priorities and proneness to guilt, shame, and empathy. *Motivation and Emotion*, 32:69–80.

Silverman, I., J. Choi & M. Peters (2007). The hunter-gatherer theory of sex differences in spatial abilities: Data from 40 countries. *Archives of Sexual Behavior*, 36:261–8.

Sisk, C. & J. Zehr (2005). Pubertal hormones organize the adolescent brain and behavior. *Frontiers in Neuroendocrinology*, 26:163–74.

Skilling, T., V. Quinsey & W. Craig (2001). Evidence of a taxon underlying serious antisocial behavior in boys. *Criminal Justice and Behavior*, 28:450–70.

Smetana, J., N. Campione-Barr & A. Metzger (2006). Adolescent development in interpersonal and societal contexts. *Annual Review of Psychology*, 57:255–84.

Soderstrom, H., K. Blennow, A.-K. Sjodin & A. Forsman (2003). New evidence for an association between the CSF HVA:5-HIAA ratio and psychopathic traits. *Journal of Neurology, Neurosurgery and Psychiatry*, 74:918–21.

Sodhi, M. & E. Sanders-Bush (2004). Serotonin and brain development. *International Review of Neurobiology*, 59:111–74.

Sokol, R., V. Delaney-Black & B. Nordstrom (2003). Fetal alcohol spectrum disorder. *Journal of the American Medical Association*, 290:2,996–9.

Solomon, R. (1980). The opponent-process theory of acquired motivation: The costs of pleasure and the benefits of pain. *American Psychologist*, 35:691–712.

Somerville, L., R. Jones & B. Casey (2010). A time of change: Behavioral and neural correlates of adolescent sensitivity to appetitive and aversive environmental cues. *Brain and Cognition*, 72:124–33.

Sowell, E., P. Thompson & A. Toga (2004). Mapping changes in the human cortex throughout the span of life. *Neuroscientist*, 10:372–92

Spear, L. (2000). Neurobehavioral changes in adolescence. *Current Directions in Psychological Science*, 9:111–14.

Spencer, T., J. Biederman, T. Wilens & S. Farone (2002). Overview of the neurobiology of attention-deficit/hyperactivity disorder. *Journal of Clinical Psychiatry*, 63:3–9.

Stålenheim, E., E. Erikson, L. von Knorring & L. Wide (1998). Testosterone as a biological marker in psychopathy and alcoholism. *Psychiatry research*, 77:79–88.

Stampp, K. (1956). *The peculiar institution: Slavery in the antebellum South*. New York: Vintage.

Steimer, T. (2002). The biology of fear- and anxiety-related behaviors. *Dialogues in Clinical Neurosciences*, 4:231–49.

Steinberg, L. (2005). Cognitive and affective development in adolescence. *Trends in Cognitive Sciences*, 9:69–74.

—— (2007). Risk taking in adolescence: New perspectives from brain and behavioral research. *Current Directions in Psychological Science*, 16:55–9.

Stewart, D., A. Cohen & A. Copeland (2010). Cigarette smoking across the schizotypy spectrum. *Psychiatry Research*, 179:113–15.

Stohr, M., A. Walsh & C. Hemmens (2009). *Corrections: A text/reader.* Thousand Oaks, CA: Sage Publications.

Stoltenberg, S. & P. Nag (2007). Applying control system modeling to understanding how genetic variation influences serotonin functioning and behavior. In J. Lassau (ed.). *Neural synapse research trends*, pp. 1–39. New York: Nova Science.

Stouthamer-Loeber, M. & E. Wei (1998). The precursors of young fatherhood and its effect on delinquency of teenage males. *Journal of Adolescent Health Research*, 22:56–65.

Sullivan, P., K. Kendler & M. Neale (2003). Schizophrenia as a complex trait: evidence from a meta-analysis of twin studies. *Archives of General Psychiatry*, 60:1,187–92.

Sundet, J., D. Barlaug & T. Torjussen (2004). The end of the Flynn effect? A study of secular trends in mean intelligence test scores of Norwegian conscripts during half a century. *Intelligence*, 32:349–62.

Tancredi, L. (2005). *Hardwired behavior: What neuroscience reveals about morality*. Cambridge: Cambridge University Press.

—— (2009). Imaging and genetics: Future applications in the emergency room. *Primary Psychiatry*, 16:54–9.

Taylor, S. (2006). Tend and Befriend: Biobehavioral bases of affiliation under stress. *Current Directions in Psychological Science*, 15:273–7.

——, L. Klien, B. Lewis, T. Gruenwald, R. Gurung & J. Updegraff (2000). Biobehavioral responses to stress in females: Tend-and-befriend, not fight-or-flight. *Psychological Review*, 107:411–29.

Teasdale, T. & D. Owen (2007). Secular declines in cognitive test scores: A reversal of the Flynn effect. *Intelligence*, 36:121–6.

Terburg, D., B. Morgan & J. van Honk (2009). The testosterone–cortisol ratio: A hormonal marker for proneness to social aggression. *International Journal of Law and Psychiatry*, 32:216–23.

Terranova, A., A. Morris & P. Boxer (2008). Fear reactivity and effortful control in overt and relational bullying: A six-month longitudinal study. *Aggressive Behavior*, 34:104–15.

Thaker, G., H. Adami & J. Gold (2001). Functional deterioration in individuals with schizophrenia spectrum personality symptoms. *Journal of personality disorders*, 15:229–34.

Thapar, A., K. Langley, T. Fowler, F. Rice, D. Turic, N. Whittinger, J. Aggleton, M. Van den Bree, M. Owen & M. O'Donovan (2005). Catechol O-methyltransferase gene variant and birth weight predict early-onset antisocial behavior in children with attention-deficit/hyperactivity disorder. *Archives of General Psychiatry*, 62:1,275–8.

Thornberry, T., E. Wei, M. Stouthamer-Loeber & J. Van Dyke (2000). Teenage fatherhood and delinquent behavior. *Juvenile Justice Bulletin*. Washington, DC: Office of Justice and Delinquency Prevention.

——, D. Huizinga & R. Loeber (2004). The causes and correlates studies: Findings and policy implication. *Juvenile Justice*, 9:3–19.

Tibbetts, S. & C. Hemmens (2010). *Theoretical criminology*. Thousand Oaks, CA: Sage.

Tinbergen, N. (1963). On aims and methods in ethology. *Zeitschrift für Tierpsychologie*, 20:410–33.

Toga, A., P. Thompson & E. Sowell (2006). Mapping brain maturation. *Trends in Neuroscience*, 29:148–59.

Toplak, M., L. Connors, J. Shuster, B. Knezevic & S. Parks (2008). Review of cognitive, cognitive-behavioral, and neural-based interventions for Attention-Deficit/Hyperactivity Disorder (ADHD). *Clinical Psychology Review*, 28:801–23.

Tracy, P., M. Wolfgang, & R. Figlio (1990) *Delinquency careers in two birth cohorts*. New York: Plenum.

Tremblay, R. (2008). Understanding development and prevention of physical aggression: Towards experimental epigenetic studies. *Philosophical Transactions of the Royal Society B: Biological Sciences*, 363:2,613–22.

Tripp, G. & J. Wickens (2009). Neurobiology of ADHD. *Neuropharmacology*, 57:579–89.

Trommsdorff, G. (2002). An eco-cultural and interpersonal relations approach to development over the life span. *Online Readings in Psychology and Culture*, Unit 12, Chapter 1. International Association for Cross-Cultural Psychology.

Tsai, H., F. Zhang, A. Adamantidis, G. Stuber, A. Bonci, L. de Lecea & K. Deisseroth (2009). Phasic firing in dopaminergic neurons is sufficient for behavioral conditioning. *Science*, 24:1,080–84.

Tsankova, N., W. Renthal, A. Kumar & E.J. Nestler (2007). Epigenetic regulation in psychiatric disorders. *Nature Reviews: Neuroscience*, 8:355–67.

Tuninger, E., S. Levander, R. Bernce & G. Johansson (2001). Criminality and aggression among psychotic in-patients: Frequency and clinical correlates. *Acta Psychiatrica Scandinavica*, 103:294–300.

Turkheimer, E., A. Haley, M. Waldron, B. D'Onofrio & I. Gottesman (2003). Socioeconomic status modifies heritability of IQ in young children. *Psychological Science*, 14:623–8.

Twardosz, S. & J. Lutzker (2010). Child maltreatment and the developing brain: A review of neuroscience perspectives. *Aggression and Violent Behavior*, 15:59–68.

Unnever, J., F. Cullen & T. Pratt (2003). Parental management, ADHD, and delinquent involvement: Reassessing Gottfredson and Hirschi's general theory. *Justice Quarterly*, 20:471–500.

Valera, E., S. Faraone, K. Murray & L. Seidman (2007). Meta-analysis of structural imaging findings in attention-deficit/hyperactivity disorder. *Biological Psychiatry*, 61:1,361–9.

Van As, A., G. Fieggen & P. Tobias (2007). Severe abuse of infants: An evolutionary price for human development? *South African Journal of Children's Health*, 1:54–7.

Van Bokhoven, I., S. van Goozen, H. Engeland, B. Schaal, L. Arseneault, J. Seguin, J. Assaad, D. Nagin, F. Vitaro & R. Tremblay (2006). Salivary testosterone and aggression, delinquency, and social dominance, in a population-based longitudinal study of adolescent males. *Hormones and Behavior*, 50:118–25.

Van Goozen, S., G. Fairchild, H. Snoek & G. Harold (2007). The evidence for a neurobiological model of childhood antisocial behavior. *Psychological Bulletin*, 133:149–82.

Van Honk, J., E. Hermans, A. D'Alfonso, D. Schutter, L. Van Doornen & E. De Haan (2002). A left-prefrontal lateralized, sympathetic mechanism directs attention towards social threat in humans: Evidence from repetitive transcranial magnetic stimulation. *Neuroscience Letters*, 319:99–102.

——, J. Peper & D. Schutter (2005). Testosterone reduces unconscious fear but not consciously experienced anxiety: Implications for the disorders of fear and anxiety. *Biological Psychiatry*, 58:218–25.

——, E. Harmon-Jones, B. Morgan & D. Schutter (2010). Socially explosive minds: The triple imbalance hypothesis of reactive aggression. *Journal of Personality*, 78:67–94.

Van Loo, K.M.J. & G.J.M. Martens (2007). Genetic and environmental factors in complex neurodevelopmental disorders. *Current Genomics*, 8(7):429–44.

Van Voorhees, E. & A. Scarpa (2004). The effects of child maltreatment on the hypothalamic–pituitary–adrenal axis. *Trauma, Violence, and Abuse*, 5:333–52.

Vandermassen, G. (2004). Sexual selection: A tale of male bias and feminist denial. *The European Journal of Women's Studies*, 11:9–26.

Vaughn, M., M. DeLisi, K. Beaver & J. Wright (2009). DAT1 and 5HTT are associated with pathological criminal behavior in a nationally representative sample of youth. *Criminal Justice and Behavior*, 36:1,113–24.

Verona, E. & J. Vitale (2006). Psychopathy in women: Assessment, manifestations, and etiology. In C. Patrick (ed.). *Handbook of psychopathy*, pp. 415–36. New York: Guilford Press.

Vervoort, L., L. Wolters, S. Hogendoorn, E. Haan, F. Boer & P. Prins (2010). Sensitivity of Gray's Behavioral Inhibition System in clinically anxious and non-anxious children and adolescents. *Personality and Individual Differences*, 48:629–33.

Viding, W., J. Blair, T. Moffitt & R. Plomin (2005). Evidence for substantial genetic risk for psychopathy in 7-year-olds. *Journal of Child Psychology and Psychiatry*, 46:592–7.

Vila, B. (1997). Human nature and crime control: Improving the feasibility of nurturant strategies. *Politics and the Life Sciences*, 16:3–21.

Vocci, F.J. & N.M. Appel (2007). Approaches to the development of medications for the treatment of methamphetamine dependence. *Addictions*, 102(1):96–106.

Vold, G., T. Bernard & J. Snipes (1998). *Theoretical criminology*. New York: Oxford University Press.

Wagner, S., Ö. Baskaya, N. Anicker, N. Dahmen, K. Lieb & A. Tadić (2009). The catechol o-methyltransferase (COMT) val[158]met polymorphism modulates the association of serious life events (SLE) and impulsive aggression in female patients with borderline personality disorder (BPD). *Acta Psychiatrica Scandinavica*, doi: 10.1111/j.1600-0447.2009.01501.x.

Wakschlag, L., K. Pickett, E. Cook, N. Benowitz & B. Leventhal (2002). Maternal smoking during pregnancy and severe antisocial behavior in offspring: A review. *American Journal of Public Health*, 92:966–74.

Walderhaug, E., A. Magnusson, A. Neumeister, J. Lappalainen, H. Lunde, H. Refsum & N. Landrø (2007). Interactive effects of sex and 5-HTTLPR on mood and impulsivity during tryptophan depletion in healthy people. *Biological Psychiatry*, 62:593–9.

Waldman, I. & S. Rhee, S.Y. (2007). Genetic and environmental influences on psychopathy and antisocial behavior. In C.J. Patrick (ed.), *Handbook of Psychopathy* (pp. 229–250). New York: The Guilford Press.

Walker, E. (2002). Adolescent neurodevelopment and psychopathology. *Current Directions in Psychological Science*. 11:24–8.

Wallis, D., H. Russell & M. Muenke (2008). Review: Genetics of attention deficit/hyperactivity disorder. *Journal of Pediatric Psychology*, 33(8):6–12.

Walsh, A. (1979). The relation of blood pressure levels to the assimilation of immigrants and intolerance of ambiguity. *The Journal of Social Psychology*, 107:257–265.

—— (1995). Parental attachment, drug use, and facultative sexual strategies. *Social Biology*, 42:95–107.

—— (1998). Religion and hypertension: Testing alternative explanations among immigrants. *Behavioral Medicine*, 24:122–30.

—— (2002). *Biosocial criminology: Introduction and integration*. Cincinnati, OH: Anderson.

—— (2003a). Intelligence and antisocial behavior. In A. Walsh & L. Ellis (eds.). *Biosocial criminology: Challenging environmentalism's supremacy*, pp. 105– 24. Huntington, NY: Nova Science.

—— (2003b). The sex ratio: A biosocial explanation for racial variation in crime rates. In A. Walsh & L. Ellis (eds.). *Biosocial criminology: Challenging environmentalism's supremacy*, pp. 61–82. Huntington, NY: Nova Science.

—— (2006). Evolutionary psychology and criminal behavior. In J. Barkow (ed.). *Missing the revolution: Darwinism for social scientists*, pp. 225–68. Oxford: Oxford University Press.

—— (2009a). *Biology and criminology: The biosocial synthesis*. New York: Routledge.

—— (2009b). *Race and crime: A biosocial analysis*. New York: Nova Science.

—— & H.-H. Wu (2008). Differentiating antisocial personality disorder, psychopathy, and sociopathy: Evolutionary, genetic, neurological, and sociological considerations. *Criminal Justice Studies*, 21:135–52.

Wand, G. (2008). The influence of stress on the transition from drug use to addiction. *Alcohol Research & Health*, 31(2):119–36.

Wang, Y., H.R. Krishnan, A. Ghezzi, J.C.P. Yin & N.S. Atkinson (2007). Drug-induced epigenetic changes produce drug tolerance. *PLoS Biology*, 5(10):2,342–53.

Warneken, F. & M. Tomasello (2009). The roots of human altruism. *British Journal of Psychology*, 100:455–71.

Warr, M. (2002). *Companions in crime: The social aspects of criminal conduct*. New York: Cambridge University Press.

Warren, J., S. South, M. Burnette, A. Rogers, R. Friend, R. Bale & I. Van Patten (2005). Understanding the risk factors for violence and criminality in women: The concurrent validity of the PCL-R and the HCR-20. *International Journal of Law and Psychiatry*, 28:269–89.

Waschbusch, D., W. Pelham Jr., J. Jennings, A. Greiner, R. Tarter & H. Moss (2002). Reactive aggression in boys with disruptive behavior disorders: Behavior, physiology, and affect. *Journal of Abnormal Child Psychology*, 30:641–56.

Watters, E. (2006). DNA is not destiny. *Discover: Science, Technology and the Future*. November.

Weaver, I., N. Cervoni, F. Champagne, A. D'Alessio, S. Sharma, J. Seckl, S. Dymov, M. Szyf & M. Meaney (2004). Epigenetic programming by maternal behavior, *Nature Neuroscience*, 7:847–54.

Weber, S., U. Habel, K. Amunts & F. Schneider (2008) Structural brain abnormalities in psychopaths: A review. *Behavioral Science and the Law*, 26:7–28.

Wechsler, D. (1958). *The measurement and appraisal of adult intelligence.* Baltimore, MD: Williams & Wilkins.

Weinberger, D., B. Elvevag & J. Giedd (2005) *The Adolescent Brain: A Work in Progress.* Washington, DC: The National Campaign to Prevent Teen Pregnancy.

Weinhold, B. (2006). Epigenetics: The science of change. *Environmental Health Perspectives*, 114:161–7.

Wells, B. (1980). *Personality and heredity.* London: Longman.

Welte, J., G. Barnes, H. Hoffman, W. Wieczorek & L. Zhang (2005). Substance involvement and the trajectory of criminal offending in young males. *American Journal of Drug and Alcohol Abuse*, 31:667–84.

West, D. & D. Farrington (1977). *The delinquent way of life.* New York: Crane Russak.

——, S. Claes & D. Deboutte (2009). Differences in hypothalamic–pituitary–adrenal axis functioning among children with ADHD predominantly inattentive and combined types. *European Child and Adolescent Psychiatry*, 18:543–53.

White, A. (2004). *Substance use and the adolescent brain: An overview with the focus on alcohol.* Durham, NC: Duke University Medical Center.

Whitwell, J. (2009). Straight gyrus morphology in first-episode schizophrenia-spectrum patients. *The Journal of Neuroscience*, 29:9,661–4.

Widom, C. & L. Brzustowicz (2006). MAOA and the "cycle of violence": Childhood abuse and neglect—MAOA genotype and the risk for violent and antisocial behavior. *Biological Psychiatry*, 60:684–9.

Wiebe, R. (2004). Psychopathy and sexual coercion: A Darwinian analysis. *Counseling and Clinical Psychology Journal*, 1:23–41.

Williams, J. & E. Taylor (2006). The evolution of hyperactivity, impulsivity and cognitive diversity. *Journal of the Royal Society Interface*, 3:399–413.

Williams, K. & D. Paulhus (2004). Factor structure of the Self-Report Psychopathy Scale (SRP-II) in non-forensic samples. *Personality and Individual Differences*, 37:765–78.

Williams, L., M. Barton, A. Kemp, B. Liddell, A. Peduto, E. Gordon & R. Bryant (2005). Distinct amygdala–autonomic arousal profiles in response to fear signals in healthy males and females. *Neuroimage*, 28:618–26.

——, J. Gatt, S. Kuan, C. Dobson-Stone, D. Palmer, R. Paul, L. Song, P. Costa, P. Schofield & E. Gordon (2009). A polymorphism of the *MAOA* gene is associated with emotional brain markers and personality traits on an antisocial index. *Neuropsychopharmacology*, 34:1,797–809.

Willoughby, M. (2003). Developmental course of ADHD symptomology during the transition from childhood to adolescence: A review with recommendations. *Journal of Child Psychology and Psychiatry*, 43:609–21.

Wilson, J. & R. Herrnstein (1985). *Crime and human nature.* New York: Simon & Schuster.

Wilson, M. & M. Daly (1997). Life expectancy, economic inequality, homicide and reproductive timing in Chicago neighborhoods. *British Medical Journal,* 314:1,271–4.

Wilson, W.J. (1987). *The Truly Disadvantaged.* Chicago, IL: University of Chicago Press.

Winterer, G. & D.R. Weinberger (2003). Cortical signal-to-noise ratio: Insight into the pathophysiology and genetics of schizophrenia. *Clinical Neuroscience Research,* 3:55–66.

Wismer Fries, A., T. Ziegler, J. Kurian, S. Jacoris & S. Pollak (2005). Early experience in humans is associated with changes in neuropeptides critical for regulating social behavior. *Proceedings of the National Academy of Sciences,* 102:17,237–40

Witt, L., L. Burke, M. Barrick & M. Mount (2002). The interactive effects of conscientiousness and agreeableness on job performance. *Journal of Applied Psychology,* 87:164–9.

Wolfgang, M. & F. Ferracutti (1967). *The subculture of violence: Towards an integrated theory in criminology.* London: Tavistock.

——, R. Figlio & T. Sellin (1972). *Delinquency in a birth cohort.* Chicago, IL: University of Chicago Press.

Wong, C., A. Caspi, B. Williams, I. Craig, R. Houts, A. Ambler, T. Moffitt & J. Mill (2010). A longitudinal study of epigenetic variation in twins. *Epigenetics,* 5:1–11.

Wood, W. & A. Eagly (2002). A cross-cultural analysis of the behavior of women and men: Implications for the origins of sex difference. *Psychological Bulletin,* 128:699–727.

Wrangham, R. & D. Peterson (1996). *Demonic males: Apes and the origins of human violence.* Boston, MA: Houghton Mifflin.

Wright, J. & D. Boisvert (2009). What biosocial criminology offers criminology. *Criminal Justice and Behavior,* 36:1,228–40.

——, K. Dietrich, M. Ris, R. Hornung, S. Wessel & B. Lanphear (2008). Association of prenatal and childhood blood lead concentrations with criminal arrests in early childhood. *PLoS Medicine,* 5:732–40.

——, D. Boisvert, K. Dietrich & M. Ris (2009). The ghost in the machine and criminal behavior: Criminology for the 21st century. In A. Walsh & K. Beaver (eds.). *Biosocial criminology: New directions in theory and research,* pp. 73–89. New York: Routledge.

Wright, R.A. & J. Miller (1998). Taboo until today? The coverage of biological arguments in criminology textbooks, 1961 to 1970 and 1987 to 1996. *Journal of Criminal Justice,* 26:1–19.

Yacubian, J., T. Sommer, K. Schroeder, J. Gläscher, R. Kalisch, B. Leuenberger, D.F. Braus & C. Büchel (2007). Gene–gene interaction associated with neural reward sensitivity, *Proceedings of the National Academy of Sciences*, 104:8,125–30.

Yamasue, H., O. Abe, M. Suga, H. Yamada, M. Rogers, A. Shigeki, N. Kato & K. Kasai (2008). Sex-linked neuroanatomical basis of human altruistic cooperativeness. *Cerebral Cortex*, 18:2,331–40.

Yang, J., L. Baskin & M. DiSandro (2010). Gender identity in disorders of sex development: Review article. *Urology*, 75:153–9.

Young, S., G. Gudjonsson, J. Wells, P. Asherson, D. Theobald, B. Oliver, C. Scott & A. Mooney (2009). Attention deficit hyperactivity disorder and critical incidents in a Scottish prison population. *Personality and Individual Differences*, 46:265–9.

Zechel, J., J. Gamboa, A. Peterson, M. Puchowicz, W. Selman & D. Lust (2005). Neuronal migration is transiently delayed by prenatal exposure to intermittent hypoxia. *Birth Defects Research*, 74:287–99.

Zuckerman, M. (2007). *Sensation seeking and risky behavior*. Washington, DC: American Psychological Association.

Index